THE BLUE WALL OF SILENCE

The Blue Wall of Silence

The Morris Tribunal and Police Accountability in Ireland

VICKY CONWAY

Queen's University Belfast

Foreword by Dermot Walsh

IRISH ACADEMIC PRESS
DUBLIN • PORTLAND, OR

First published in 2010 by Irish Academic Press

2 Brookside,	920 NE 58th Avenue, Suite 300
Dundrum Road,	Portland, Oregon,
Dublin 14,	97213-3786
Ireland	USA

www.iap.ie

British Library Cataloguing in Publication Data
An entry can be found on request

ISBN 978 0 7165 3030 5 (cloth)
ISBN 978 0 7165 3031 2 (paper)

Library of Congress Cataloging-in-Publication Data
An entry can be found on request

Printed in Great Britain by the MPG Books Group, Bodmin and King's Lynn

Contents

Acknowledgements

Over the last decade the Irish public has been made aware of the activities of Gardai in Donegal through the work of the families involved, politicians, journalists and Justice Morris. What has emerged has shocked many and led to significant reforms in the policing of Ireland. This book is an attempt to document the events of the last number of years, particularly how citizens of this State were treated by members of the police force and how the government responded. It is important that society acknowledge these failings. We must not forget the experiences of the citizens of Donegal who endured so much but still fought for justice and the Barron family who still have questions unanswered as to what happened their husband, father, grandfather that night. A number of those at the heart of that campaign including Frank McBrearty Jnr and some of the politicians involved took time to speak with me, for which I am very grateful.

The origins of this book stem from part of my PhD thesis, completed at Queen's University Belfast. I was lucky to have Prof Phil Scraton and Dr Graham Ellison as supervisors. They challenged my thinking on issues of policing at every turn and inspired me to pursue this research. Prof Scott Poynting and Prof Shadd Maruna, as examiners of that thesis, encouraged me through their comments and feedback to develop that work further. I am grateful to my now colleagues at Queen's University Belfast for providing space to complete this work and their encouragement at the tough points. I am also grateful to my former colleagues at the University of Limerick for their support and discussions on this work. In particular I would like to thank Prof Dermot Walsh for his generous foreword to this work. Further thanks are owed to Dr Edel Hughes and the Masters students of 2008/09 for their discussion and feedback on the ideas in this book. A big thank you to Dr Michael Mulqueen for reading sections of this work and discussing it enthusiastically over many coffees.

The publishers of this work, Irish Academic Press, have made the process far easier than I imagined. In particular I would like to thank Lisa Hyde for supporting this project from the beginning and her guidance throughout. Had it not been for her, I would probably still be writing and tinkering. I am grateful to Aonghus Meaney for his editing skills.

I am indebted to my parents, Rory and Jean, for their support and belief in me. They have always encouraged me to learn and question. Thanks to my siblings, Dermot, Susan, Bryan and Craig for their support and the endless laughter. Myrt, thanks for always believing that I could do this and Grandpa who made me want to know more. Dr Louise Mallinder and Dr Anna Eriksson know far more about Irish policing than either wanted to but their friendship and support have been fantastic over the last few years. Finally, an enormous thank you to my partner Darren. I can't begin to thank you properly for all your assistance with this; reading and commenting on the full draft, late night reads of redrafted chapters, reassuring me whenever it all felt it was getting too tough and distracting me when that was needed. Your contribution has been enormous, though I concede that any mistakes or inaccuracies are mine.

Vicky Conway
January 2010

This book is dedicated to Chara, Rory, Alex, Cian and Julie

Foreword

Since the early 1920s extensive police power and security authority have been concentrated in the hands of a single, national, hierarchical organisation under the direct control of central government. In a constitutional democracy based on respect for human rights this arrangement has potential to prevent the police functioning as a powerful unaccountable entity with their own narrow institutional, political and social agendas. It can also operate as a constraint on police corruption and abuse. Equally, however, it renders the police vulnerable to being used by dominant interests as a vehicle for protecting their privilege through the suppression of minority views and lifestyles and for the short-circuiting of due process standards in the prevention and detection of crime. Where such goals have the express or tacit support of the government and a silent majority throughout the country, the arrangement can provide a cover for police corruption and abuse to proliferate.

The history of policing in the State is littered with examples of government parties flexing their muscles to exert control over the Garda Síochána whenever that was deemed necessary to pursue or protect their own political or institutional interests. On some occasions this has taken the form of direct executive action, while in others the government has seen fit to negotiate a compromise. Prominent examples of the former include the sackings of Commissioners O'Duffy in 1933 and Garvey in 1978, the executive appointment of a body of active supporters of the government directly to the armed Special Branch in 1933 and the imposition of the Garda Reserve against the wishes of the rank and file in 2006. Examples of compromise include the resolution of the 'Kildare mutiny' in 1922 even before the force had been fully established, and the settlement of rank and file grievances over pay and conditions in the 1960s and in 1998.

Instances of the government exerting control to address corrupt and abusive policing practices have been more tentative by comparison, at least up until the twenty first century. In 1937, for example, FitzGerald

J., when giving judgment in the High Court in a civil action by the parents of a youth who had been shot dead by Gardaí, felt compelled to say of the Special Branch detective members of the force who had fired the shots that: "These 'S' men are not real Civic Guards. They are an excrescence upon that reputable body". Nevertheless, the government of the day took no remedial action. When Garda interrogation practices provoked serious public concern in the 1970s, the government's belated response was limited to a complaints system and police custody regulations that ranked among the least intrusive in the Western world. It took another ten years before regulations were introduced on the electronic recording of Garda interrogations, and about another ten years after that before the regulations could be said to be fully operational throughout the State. Meanwhile, the Garda was the subject of a whole series of credible abuse allegations spanning almost every aspect of the policing function and organisation. Not only did the government refuse to acknowledge the compelling case for reform throughout this period, but it even launched a major programme of expansion in police powers and resources in the mid-1990s.

The first decade of the twenty first century has witnessed the opportunity for a major sea change in this cosy relationship between government and police. The establishment of the Morris Tribunal of Inquiry, despite limitations in its terms of reference, offered the potential for the first major investigation and evaluation of policies, organisation and practices across key aspects of policing in the history of the State. Mr Justice Morris did not disappoint. With profound patience, resilience, determination, frankness and balance, he exposed with a meticulous and razor-like efficiency an incredible litany of corruption, abuse and negligence at several levels of the Garda organisation. In its voluminous reports, published between 2004 and 2008, the Tribunal set out in consummate detail the nature and extent of this abuse. Applying basic standards of human rights and due process, and drawing on best practice in other jurisdictions, it offered a substantial catalogue of recommendations which, at the very least, would make a vital contribution to the fundamental reform that was long overdue across all aspects of policing in the State. It should also be noted that these coincided with far reaching reform recommendations on other aspects of police and government emanating from sources such as the report of the Barr Tribunal of Inquiry on the fatal shooting of John Carty, the Ionann human rights audit on the Garda Síochána and the reports of the recently established Garda Inspectorate. Taken together, these offered an unprecedented opportunity to put policing structures, policies, strategies and practices in the State on a par with the highest human rights, due process and accountability standards. The key question now is whether that opportunity has been grasped.

In her outstanding book Vicky Conway assesses the impact of the Morris Tribunal on policing and police accountability in Ireland. Commendably, she manages to distil the essence of Morris' findings, analysis and recommendations into an accessible package that loses none of their importance and punch. Indeed, she contributes substantially to our understanding of their significance by weaving them seamlessly into the wider social, political and historical context of policing in Ireland, and by locating them within the broader international literature on the science of police governance and accountability. Her analysis reveals how Morris, guided throughout by the seminal values of police accountability in a legal and parliamentary democracy, delivered the results that the established institutional mechanisms had so patently failed to deliver. In a clinical and compelling manner she goes on to show how the media, the government, the political parties and the Garda have combined to frustrate the longer term accountability dividends that could and should have resulted. The Garda Síochána Act 2005 and associated measures have introduced some necessary reforms, but have not delivered sufficient means to overcome the embedded cultural problems underpinning indiscipline and the 'blue wall' so searingly exposed by Morris. More, much more, is needed. In particular, as Conway argues cogently, there is an urgent need for the State to adopt a proactive approach to police reform through the establishment of an independent Commission on policing along the lines of the Patten Commission in Northern Ireland:

> "There is a real need in Ireland to understand the true extent of police misconduct, mal-governance and the state of police morale. This can best be achieved by an independent commission on policing with a broad consultative mandate. A Commission will not eliminate all police misconduct, but it will provide knowledge of the current operation of policing in Ireland, as well as an understanding of what Irish society wants them to achieve and how best they can achieve it. It could further provide an opportunity to explore with the communities the limitations of policing, contributing to realistic goals for the Gardaí, and a realisation of the role of others in the policing function. From here, a cultural shift

in how Ireland (including the Gardaí) thinks about policing could begin and targeted reforms with a clear philosophical underpinning could be implemented."

The importance of Conway's book is not confined to the richness of its research and analysis or the profound insights on policing that underpin it. Policing in Ireland had been a relatively barren subject for academic research and publications up until Conor Brady's excellent book, *Guardians of the Peace*, which was first published in 1974. While a few notable publications have followed in its wake, Irish policing has still not been subjected to the levels of sustained academic research that characterises policing in many other Western style democracies. Conway's book makes a signal contribution to addressing that deficit. She is a leading member of a new generation of academics who are enthusiastically applying their critical faculties to this most vital of subjects. If this book is an indication of what is to come, then there will soon be an embarrassment of riches to choose from when compiling reading lists for third and forth level modules on Irish policing.

D. P. J. Walsh
January 2010

Chapter One

Introduction

That which separates the police from other members of society is the powers they are afforded. Rights to privacy, liberty, bodily integrity, property, all can be superseded by the need for the police to perform their functions – the prevention and investigation of crime – effectively. In order to enhance the rights of all, the police often need to constrain the rights of some.

To balance the interference with these rights, the police are required to answer for the use of their powers, to ensure they are being used in an effort to enhance the rights of the majority. This is particularly true in terms of the police power to use force. The police have the monopoly on the legitimate use of force in civil society,[1] as the protectors of public order and the 'strong arm' of the law. It is permissible and legal for a police officer to use reasonable force to achieve their duty, where the same action by an ordinary citizen would be illegal. This power is limited by obligations to the rights of citizens; particularly, the right to life and the right not to be subjected to torture and inhumane or degrading treatment. The use of force must be applied only when necessary, and in respect of these rights.[2] Accountability ensures the police their powers only when they should.

However, the power of the police stretches far beyond the specific powers which are legislated for, and in ways which are far more difficult to hold to account. Police have a great deal of power in society to make people do things they would not otherwise do, and thus to influence decision-making.[3] The police do not necessarily have to resort to legislative powers but can compel compliance through this power potential; the knowledge of the public that the police *could* exercise these powers is sufficient. This coercive power[4] can make the police powerful political forces in society and, equally, it can make people reticent to complain when rights are breached.

Compounding the extent of police powers is the level of discretion involved in policing decisions. In any situation the police have the discretion to decide whether or not to act, and if so, how, with numerous factors influencing this decision.[5] For one, there are resource limitations. Newburn and Jones note that while 'the opportunities for law enforcement are limitless' it is not possible for the police to enforce the law in each situation.[6] Nor would we want every legal infraction policed.

In police forces, discretion rests in the lower ranks[7] who make the on-the-spot decisions, without supervision, about whether to stop and search, arrest, use of force and so on.[8] Inaction cannot be accounted for and even when action is taken it can be hard to hold them accountable for it. Lundman explains that, in the extreme, 'Officers are therefore free to make discriminatory arrests and to accept money, goods or services for special favours or for ignoring illegal actions.'[9] Legally, officers are required to exercise this discretion lawfully and reasonably,[10] but concepts of reasonableness are informed by subjective values and inherent difficulties in determining 'reasonableness', thus limiting the controlling potential of legal requirements.[11]

The discretionary nature of police powers can enable police misconduct, and more seriously, police corruption, both of which can be classified in different ways.[12] Morton differentiates between officers who are 'bent for self' and 'bent for the job'.[13] 'Bent for self' covers those officers who engage in corrupt activities for personal benefit, including accepting bribes, protecting criminals, taking stolen items or prisoners' property, suppressing evidence and obtaining financial benefits from their occupation. It can be individual or institutionalised.[14] According to Sherman[15] it occurs for a number of reasons including the discretionary nature of the job, low managerial visibility, low public visibility, police culture, association with law breakers, opportunities, and lack of sufficient controls. Overriding may be a sense that they have the power to do so.[16]

'Bent for the job' describes officers who act corruptly to achieve the demands of the job. This 'noble cause' corruption serves no personal benefit.[17] It is driven by the belief that an individual has committed a crime and that the ends (conviction of the offender) justify the means, which can be 'the verbal or, as it was known, "gilding the lily" (inserting words to produce a confession), brutality or trickery to extract a confession, and planting evidence'.[18] The motivation may stem from external pressure to secure a conviction, or from belief in the guilt of the suspect but an inability to obtain the necessary evidence.

This distinction is paramount in understanding and combating corruption. If an officer is 'bent for the job' they are unlikely to believe that they are corrupt. They will invariably have the support of fellow officers who will not speak out against them – known as the blue wall of silence – because they sympathise with the pressures of the job. Combating such corruption centres on accepting the true capacities of the police and diffusing the pressure they are under, given necessary legal restrictions. The culture of the police, which can endorse such behaviour, also needs to be challenged, particularly where there may be an institutional basis for the motivations.[19]

A well-developed and efficiently functioning system of accountability enables the public to understand police actions, thereby enhancing levels of trust. Thus, accountability contributes to the legitimacy of the police by helping the public believe they are working towards the same set of shared beliefs, which Beetham sets as a central characteristic to the legitimate use of power.[20] The more legitimate the police are perceived, the more the public will co-operate with them, aiding police efficiency. Police legitimacy is precarious. In the UK it is tied up in the concept of 'policing by consent' whereby the police and their powers were accepted by the public as they were seen as 'citizens in uniform'.[21] This fractured through the 1970s and 1980s, with confrontational events such as miners' strikes and racial disturbances exposing, '... contradictions between different value systems, types of rule, and objectives leading to systematic ambiguity about the mission and about what counts as appropriate behaviour for a police officer. The specific reasons why the cracks began to show ... were all signs of disunity and fracture too deep to disguise.'[22] Although such cracks in the 'shared beliefs' nullify the police's legitimacy, they can be negated by an effective accountability system.

The Knapp Commission, investigating corruption in New York in the 1970s, referred to the 'code of silence' encountered in the course of its investigations.[23] Skolnick examined it further:

> Like criminal law itself, the 'Blue Code of Silence' is a normative injunction, but an unwritten one. Sometimes called a blue wall, curtain or cocoon of silence, it is embedded in police subculture. At its best, the feelings of loyalty and brotherhood sustaining the 'Code of Silence' may facilitate policing and protect police against genuine threats to safety and well-being. Yet the same code of loyalty

can, as a 'Code of Silence', sustain an oppositional criminal subculture protecting the interests of police who violate the criminal law.[24]

Police culture engrains solidarity and loyalty, leaving police officers universally unwilling to answer questions concerning the misconduct and
corruption of others, let alone report it.[25] Police cynicism contributes
to the code, as officers see their job as a fight for truth and justice and
do not feel it is justified to report their partner's misconduct, who
would take enormous and dangerous risks for them.[26] That said, Kleinig
contends that those who choose to shelter behind this wall

> ... cannot justify their silence by claiming they morally owe
> loyalty to their fellows. That they might sometimes do so shows the
> corrosive effect of a cynicism that reduces loyalty to a tribal value
> that insulates oneself and one's group against a hostile world.[27]

This is not a new phenomenon. The Wickersham Commission in
America in 1929 documented the 'blue curtain of secrecy'[28] and it has
been evidenced by numerous academics.[29] Westmarland documented
its continued existence as recently as 2005.[30] The blue wall of silence
can be exceptionally damaging. It can prevent misconduct from being
exposed at the time of occurrence through failed reporting and can stall
investigations if those tasked with that job are not given accurate
information. Even if investigators get beyond such problems, it can
delay and limit the extent of that investigation. It is damaging to the
victims of misconduct and those who encounter this wall in their efforts
to expose it. It indicates a belief on the part of the officers involved that
they will 'get away with' not answering questions. The Christopher
Commission, set up in Los Angeles following the beating of Rodney
King, documented the internal negativity caused by the code:

> Under the code it is impermissible to criticise other police. Such
> criticism is viewed as particularly reprehensible if it is made to
> outsiders. Any criticism which does occur is kept under the con-
> trol of those who have authority and influence within the Force.
> Any dissidents are able to be dealt with for a breach of the code,
> with approval of other police.[31]

The pervasive strength of this code for officers who may consider
speaking out is debilitating. More broadly, where revealed, it brings the
legitimacy of the police force into question, causing the public to

believe that the police cannot be trusted. It creates an 'us and them' mentality between the police and the public, with stark implications for the criminal justice system.

POLICING AND POLICE MISCONDUCT IN IRELAND

For 100 years pre-independence, Ireland was policed by the Royal Irish Constabulary (RIC),[32] a force which enjoyed a positive relationship with the public in peaceful times[33] but as the nationalist movement grew towards the end of the 1800s, became increasingly hated. Armed, it was viewed as the symbol of British oppression and was regularly attacked. In 1920–1 there were over 10,000 attacks and 355 officers killed.[34] This animosity had a profound impact when it came to establishing a police force in independent Ireland.

Negotiations on the Anglo-Irish Treaty in 1921 involved a decision to disband the RIC. Despite six months' notice, a Police Organising Committee was given just three weeks to organise a new force. This, in addition to the committee's perceived satisfaction with previous arrangements, led to the structure of the RIC being largely replicated. The Civic Guard, renamed An Garda Síochána when it merged with the Dublin Metropolitan Police in 1925, faced enormous challenges, emerging in the context of a Civil War which had left crime and disorder widespread in the country. There was neither time nor money for proper recruitment, training or facilities. Substantial portions of the public challenged their authority as an institution of the Free State, which was not accepted by all.[35] For reasons of loyalty, no members of the RIC were allowed to join, unless they had politically disaffected, with the result that only 2 per cent of the Civic Guard had policing experience.[36] It was only after a mutiny over the promotion of former RIC men that the force was disarmed,[37] the most symbolic move in distinguishing the Guards from their predecessors, which created a perception of independence during the Civil War. O'Halpin argues that this pivotal decision led to the Guards not being targeted by the IRA during the Civil War, allowing them to focus on 'ordinary' problems of crime and disorder.[38] The first commissioner, Michael Staines, declared: 'We will succeed not by force of arms, but on our moral authority as servants of the people.'[39]

Eoin O'Duffy, commissioner from 1922 to 1933, encouraged his men to espouse nationalist ideals, something which ingratiated them to the public. The men were pioneers who disrupted the poitin trade, spoke Irish, played national sports and were devout Catholics.[40] Their status was contested by the IRA, posing a policing challenge for members with minimal experience. Four officers were killed in 1923 and reports began to appear of abuse of prisoners in police stations.[41] For the next twenty years a common pattern emerged of IRA attacks on the Guards followed by reports of abuse by the police.[42] With the Civil War fresh in the minds of all, and a determination to stabilise the new state, successive governments assisted the Guards through legislation which strengthened police powers, as well as introducing military tribunals and the Special Criminal Court. These factors combined to give the Guards social capital as defenders of the fledgling Irish State. As the country experienced more settled times in the 1950s and 1960s, the Guards reinforced this status, assuming a dominant, unquestionable role in the community, alongside the parish priest.[43] In an Ireland which enshrined the place of the Catholic Church in its constitution, both were pillars of society who engaged in a policing function which kept crime levels low.

While developments such as membership of the European Union, population growth, changing economic circumstances and a number of scandals led to a significant decline in Irish peoples' faith in the Church through the 1970s–90s,[44] the experience for the Gardaí was entirely different. The emergence of the Northern Irish conflict placed them once again in the role of defending the State against subversives. For the first time in thirty years, Guards were being killed in the performance of their duties, with Garda Richard Fallon shot dead in 1972 having attended an armed bank robbery.[45] A new generation of officers felt this threat along with the other challenges of the conflict: explosions and deaths of civilians, riots, armed robberies, border duty and prison work.[46] On the one hand, these created substantive policing obstacles for the Gardaí, but, on the other hand copper-fastened the support of the public. So even when, in the late 1970s, allegations emerged of a 'heavy gang' operating within the force using brutality to secure confessions from suspected terrorists,[47] this did not appear to alter public perceptions. In February 1977 *The Irish Times* dedicated a week of front pages to exposing the gang and its violent tactics.[48] A study conducted on public confidence in the mid-1980s by Bohan and Yorke found that while 56 per cent of those surveyed believed the police abused suspects physically or mentally, and 40 per cent believed they lied in court, more than 62 per cent expressed satisfaction with the police and more than 70 per cent believed they did not get enough recognition for risking their lives.[49] In spite of mounting evidence of abuse of detainees, including an Amnesty International report,[50] the State provided further legislative support for the Guards by lengthening detention times (the 1976 Emergency Powers Act), introducing arrest without charge (1984 Criminal Justice Act) and re-establishing the Special Criminal Court (by government declaration in 1972). Farrell expressed surprise 'that such inroads on human and democratic rights could be made with so little protest'.[51] But it appears to have been accepted that the challenges of the conflict necessitated these inroads. Even when Nicky Kelly[52] and Peter Pringle[53] were wrongfully convicted, this did not dissuade opinion on the performance of the Gardaí. Hardiman and Whelan found, in 1994, that public confidence was at a rate of 85 per cent, 20 per cent above the European average.[54] This was just two years before the death of Richard Barron. The Garda Public Attitudes Surveys conducted over the last decade report similar, if not higher, levels of confidence.[55]

What is suggested is that the circumstances and challenges faced by the force have contributed to the Guards blindly receiving an exceptionally high level of public confidence. This is not to say, necessarily, that they did not deserve that level of confidence, and certainly the dedication of the force to unarmed policing throughout this period is both unusual and commendable. If the period prior to the death of Richard Barron is examined in greater detail, however, there are many incidents and events which could have had a more deleterious impact on public attitudes to the police, but did not. A review of the high-profile cases in this period confirms the existence of major shortcomings with regard to interrogations and the taking of confessions, use of force, both in public and in detention, deaths in custody and fabrication of evidence.

In 1984, a young woman, Joanne Hayes, and four family members provided confessions for killing and disposing of a baby, a crime which they had not committed. Widely known as the Kerry Babies case, these events led to the establishment of a tribunal under Justice Lynch to examine how a family could have given false but corroborating statements. Inglis notes that some of the officers involved were drawn from the same division as the 'heavy gang'.[56] The Tribunal declined to find why the family had given false confessions, rejecting the allegations of physical abuse of Ms Hayes and her family. McAleese argued the report of the Tribunal was not sufficiently critical of the Gardaí,[57] which is substantiated by Maguire's analysis that 'of Lynch's forty-three findings, at least twenty-five addressed the actions and statements of the Hayes family while only four addressed allegations of garda misconduct.'[58] Inglis contends the Tribunal was an exercise in vilifying Ms Hayes.[59]

The political attitudes underpinning the establishment of the Tribunal, embodied by the Minister for Justice's refusal to afford the Tribunal power to make recommendations, on account of the claim that Garda authorities could respond as they felt necessary and on this occasion it would not be appropriate for an independent body to make recommendations, is also worrying. Such an approach was indicative of a failure to appreciate the severity of the allegations involved, evidenced in the concluding comments of the debate:

> Since the foundation of the State the Garda Síochána have had a role vital to the maintenance of the institutions of democracy. The force have served this State outstandingly well and will, I am in no doubt at all, continue to do so in the future. Its members have done so frequently at great cost to themselves. Since 1970, 11 members have been murdered ... Many members place their own safety at risk day after day in the defence of the community ...
>
> Whatever the outcome of this inquiry may be – even if the result is unfavourable to one or more members – it should not cause us for one instant to forget what we owe to the force.[60]

That is not to say the case did not have an impact. It led to the disbandment of the Murder Squad and to the establishment of the Garda Síochána Complaints Board (GSCB),[61] but the following decades saw further allegations of Garda misconduct and abuse of power. It could be that the failure to respond critically in this instance engrained a belief that misconduct would not be sanctioned.

Interrogation methods adopted by the Gardaí have been highly problematic.[62] The prosecution of Damien Marsh in 1994 for murdering a tourist, on the basis of Garda evidence of a confession,[63] collapsed when the original confession could not be produced in court and two Guards contradicted each other in evidence. In April 1995, Vincent Connell had his conviction for murder quashed by the Court of Criminal Appeal due to oppressive interrogation methods.[64] Just as in the Marsh case, the interrogation methods came under scrutiny. Despite recommendations in the late 1970s for the recording of interview,[65] it was not until the late 1990s that this was introduced. Under the Electronic Recording of Interviews Regulations 1997, interviews must be recorded where a suspect is charged in relation to particular, serious offences.[66] This has been implemented in sufficient stations that all interviews can now be recorded,[67] though there is the problem that many suspects will have to travel long distances to have their interview taped, raising concerns as to the taking of the 'scenic route' to the station.[68] The 2006 European Committee for the Prevention of Torture (ECPT) report indicated that suspects not charged in relation to a 'serious offence' 'ran a greater risk of ill-treatment by Garda officers. This was particularly the case when the suspects were foreign and/or drug addicts.'[69] The treatment of vulnerable witnesses, which may include those suffering from drug addictions or with language difficulties, has arisen as a particular problem, as considered below.

Another high-profile case relating to interrogation methods concerned the murder of Veronica Guerin in 1996 while she was investigating the largest criminal gang in Ireland. The public outcry at her death was unprecedented, bringing exceptional pressure on the police to secure a conviction. Paul Ward was convicted of her murder in the Special Criminal Court[70] on the basis of 'supergrass' testimony. Confessional evidence had been rejected by the court due to oppressive interrogation methods.[71] His conviction was overturned by the Court of Criminal Appeal, which would not rely on the supergrass testimony, in 2002.[72]A statement by the Garda Commissioner is a useful example of how such cases, explicitly critical of Gardaí, are not internalised by the force:

> These things happen. The judges and the courts make their decision and we respect those decisions and go on and continue our policing operations ... At the end of the day we do our best in gathering the evidence. It's put before the courts and they make the decision and we respect their decision and carry on with our business after that.[73]

The Commissioner could suggest that An Garda Síochána had done its best, when this was clearly not the case. That same year, Garda Gerry McCabe was killed just outside Limerick city by members of the Provisional IRA. In the intensity of the aftermath, allegations of abuse of detainees in Limerick soon emerged.[74] Nonetheless, while both cases raised considerable concerns about Garda handling of serious investigations, that year the government passed legislation expanding the powers of An Garda Síochána.[75]

In March 1997 two women were murdered in Grangegorman, Dublin. That July, a homeless heroin addict, Dean Lyons, made a detailed and seemingly accurate confession[76] and was charged. Another man, Mark Nash, arrested for the murder of a couple in Roscommon, confessed to the Grangegorman murders in September.[77] Lyons was released in April 1998 having spent nine months in prison. The Garda Commissioner apologised to his family in March 2005, five years after Lyons died by overdose. Nash was not charged until October 2009.[78] A commission to investigate the case was set up in May 2005 and reported in September 2006, finding that there had been no abuse or ill-treatment, but that overly-leading questions may have been asked.[79]

Frank Shortt was convicted in 1995 of allowing drugs to be sold in his pub in Donegal and spent two years in prison. The Court of Appeal declared this a miscarriage of justice in 2005, finding that two members of An Garda Síochána fabricated evidence and perjured themselves at his trial. In 2007, the Supreme Court awarded €4.5 million in damages.[80] Describing this case as 'a stain of the darkest dye on the otherwise generally fine tradition of the institution of An Garda Síochána', Chief Justice Murray stressed that

> … this affair cannot be bracketed as a couple of bad apples in the proverbial barrel. The misconduct penetrated the system of law enforcement too deeply and persisted over too long a period to be discounted in such a fashion … The cavalier manner in which those two members set about concocting evidence and subsequently persisted in trying to cover up their misdeeds, not entirely out of sight of other Garda members, displayed a worrying confidence on their part that they could get away with it.[81]

The officers at the heart of this case were Garda McMahon and Superintendent Lennon, who were severely criticised by the Morris Tribunal, as detailed in Chapter 3. It was determined by the Court, in a judgement that was unusual in its criticism of An Garda Síochána, that 'the conduct of the Garda officers involved set at nought core constitutional rights of the plaintiff to due process and a fair trial.'[82]

In addition to the interrogation and investigation techniques used by Gardaí, ill-treatment has been prevalent in the policing of Ireland over the last two decades. The European Committee for the Prevention of Torture has found significant problems of ill-treatment of detainees in its visits.[83] A total of €34 million has been paid out in civil actions in the last ten years, much of this for assault.[84] A particularly contentious case is that of John Carthy, a 29-year-old with a depressive illness, who was killed by members of the Emergency Response Unit at Abbeylara, County Longford in April 2000 following a protracted siege in which he barricaded himself in the family home and fired thirty shots, some aimed towards Gardaí.[85] The internal inquiry exonerated the actions of An Garda Síochána. In contrast, the Barr Tribunal, which published its report into the events in July 2006, identified 'crucial failures' in the handling of the situation by Gardaí, a lack of experience of those in command and a lack of non-lethal weapons, such as stun-guns.[86] Overall, while identifying failures on the part of those members involved in the incident, the Barr Tribunal report was relatively sympathetic to those officers at the scene given the unusual circumstances. It declined to conclude whether the result would have differed had the officers acted more appropriately. A subsequent Garda Inspectorate review of barricade incidents evidenced seventy-three such cases between 2000 and 2006. Twelve of these involved a firearm, another fifteen involved another form of weapon.[87] Abbeylara was not a 'one-off', and a more forthright report from Justice Barr could have prompted a determined response from senior officials.[88]

Similar problems occurred when, in 2002, during the infamous May Day protests in Dublin, violence by Gardaí was filmed. This prompted forty-one complaints to the Complaints Board,[89] which appointed a special investigator, former Assistant Commissioner (AC) James McHugh. A file submitted to the DPP resulted in seven prosecutions but only one conviction.[90]

In May 2005 two men were shot dead by Gardaí as they tried to raid a post office in Lusk, County Dublin. Amnesty International and the Irish Council for Civil Liberties called for an inquiry to be established into the events.[91] This has not happened and no results of any internal inquiries have been made public.

On occasion, this use of force has resulted in deaths in custody. In April 1982 a man, Peter Matthews, died in Shercock Garda station, County Cavan.[92] With a history of heart trouble, he was arrested in relation to obtaining of a small amount of money by false pretences and died in custody. The Minister for Justice later stated that the heart attack which killed him 'was precipitated by shock due to injury and by stress'.[93] Two Gardaí were acquitted of criminal charges relating to the incident but were dismissed following an internal inquiry. Members of the Dáil unsuccessfully called for a sworn inquiry.[94] Mr Matthews' widow was subsequently awarded £90,000 in a settlement with the State.[95]

The Hartnett Inquiry, established in June 2005, examined the circumstances surrounding the death of 14-year-old Brian Rossiter in Clonmel Garda station, arrested in September 2002 on suspicion of public order offences. Rossiter was held overnight and was found in the cell in a coma the following day. He died three days later in hospital. It is claimed he suffered injuries while in custody. The Hartnett report found that, while unlawfully detained, he was not assaulted during the detention.[96] The inquiry found a failure to maintain the custody record accurately and that the investigation into his death was not properly conducted. His family settled an action against the State for €200,000.[97]

The families of two other young men are seeking the establishment of inquiries into their deaths. Terrence Wheelock died in September 2005, aged twenty, having been found hanging in Store Street Garda station, Dublin. Following an internal inquiry, the Director of Public Prosecutions (DPP) ruled there would be no prosecutions in the case. John Maloney had been arrested in May 2003 at Rathfarnham Garda station and was found unconscious on the street one hour after his release. He died eleven days later. Questions being asked by his family surrounding his release include why he did not sign the release papers, why he left personal items behind and why Gardaí denied that he had been in custody.

The above incidents, when taken together, provide evidence of serious misconduct within An Garda Síochána, including: use of oppressive questioning techniques; perjury; failure to disclose evidence; mistreatment of vulnerable witnesses; assault; excessive use of force; and failure to care for detainees. These are just the high-profile cases. In 2004, the Garda Síochána Complaints Board received over 530 admissible complaints.[98] Of these, thirty-one were deemed to involve minor breaches of discipline whereas twenty-seven involved serious breaches of discipline, a 50 per cent increase on the previous year. What is also evident is the minimal effort made to hold these officers to account.

POLICE ACCOUNTABILITY IN IRELAND

At the time of Richard Barron's death in 1996, the accountability mechanisms included citizen complaints, legal avenues of criminal and civil proceedings and democratic accountability, all of which were being severely criticised.[99] The internal disciplinary codes had dominated from the creation of the force until 1986. They provided for internal investigations, determined on the basis of the disciplinary code which was updated on a number of occasions since the force's creation. Members who had retired or resigned could not be investigated by way of the internal mechanism. Walsh has criticised the fact that this was used to avoid discipline.[100]

The Complaints Board, created in 1986, dealt with complaints from the public. Complaints were still investigated by members of the force but the board could supervise investigations, judged on the basis of the disciplinary code. The Board received a report from the investigator and determined whether to revert the case to the Commissioner, send it to the DPP or set up a tribunal comprised of members of the board and a representative of the Commissioner. This tribunal could determine the disciplinary action to be taken, if necessary. The Board suffered heavily from a lack of independence and resources, on occasion suspending operations and pointing out its inability to perform its statutory functions. Walsh further points to the low rate of complaint substantiation and the high rate of inadmissibility.[101] As shall be seen in later chapters, an entire module of the Morris Tribunal was dedicated to the Board's response to complaints arising from Donegal.

Beyond citizen complaints, criminal or civil proceedings could be initiated against a Guard. Criminal proceedings are notoriously difficult to pursue against members, due to legal intention requirements, investigation by other members of the force and the use of Gardaí as witnesses, bringing the blue wall of silence into play. The procedures used are more favourable when a Guard is being investigated;[102] they understand them well and will have the support of the Garda associations.[103] Further, Conor Brady of the Garda Síochána Ombudsman Commission (GSOC), which replaced the Complaints Board in 2007, has commented on the difficulties of convincing juries to convict Gardaí.[104]

Civil actions, on the other hand, require an applicant who can afford to engage in the process. At the same time, the lower standard of proof compared to criminal actions gives a greater chance of success.

The problem that the individual Guard may not be able to afford to pay damages is overcome by the concept of vicarious liability, whereby the State, as employer, can be held responsible for their actions.[105] As stated previously, €34 million has been paid in damages since 1997.

The other potential source of accountability is through some democratic process. In the UK this is achieved through Police Boards and Authorities, which combine local representatives, politicians and police, have powers over budget and contribute to policing plans.[106] In Ireland it is achieved through the Oireachtas. This involves the Minister for Justice answering all questions on policing in Ireland, for which he relies on answers from the Commissioner. Walsh's study of the operation of democratic accountability through the Dáil was highly critical of its ability to provide meaningful accountability.[107] The limitations of the Minister's information, combined with the determination of most politicians to prove their support and dedication to the force, serves to limit the Dáil's potential to hold the force to account. In this context, Connolly argues that 'the Minister's role could be interpreted as being designed to protect the Garda against the full rigours of democratic accountability.'[108] Supporting Connolly's thesis, one Minister stated:

> While people in this House and people in the media may have freedom to criticise, the Government of the day should not criticise the Garda Síochána ... it is obscene that the Government and the Minister responsible should be the first to lead the charge in the criticism of the Garda Síochána.[109]

This relationship between the Gardaí and the people it polices is supported by all parties. An Garda Síochána takes great pride in a history of policing by consent. Reciprocity is reflected in the annual Garda Public Attitudes Survey, the most recent of which reports that over 81 per cent of the public have high confidence in the force.[110] This relationship plays a key role in accountability. At any moment of challenge for the Gardaí, be it problem criminal elements, under-resourcing, or the behaviour of some officers giving rise to concerns, the strong relationship between the police and the public is recalled, reminding us of how well they have served us in the past, facing up to serious danger for our protection. For instance, in November 2006, following the publication of further Morris Tribunal reports, as well as the Dean Lyons and Abbeylara inquiries,[111] arguably a time of crisis of legitimacy for the force, the Minister for Justice stated: 'I and members of the public still retain full confidence in the Garda Síochána as an organisation. Its members are in the front line in the fight against crime and deserve our full support.'[112] Equally, following a collapsed murder trial due to the failure of Gardaí to reveal inconsistencies in witness statements,[113] Justice Barr determined that senior officers 'consciously and deliberately resorted to a policy ... to deprive the accused of his constitutional right'.[114] The Minister for Justice, Mr O'Donoghue, told the Dáil that an internal investigation found 'no action was warranted in respect of any of the members of An Garda Síochána involved'.[115] It is difficult to reconcile the statements of the judge with a finding that no disciplinary action was warranted.

At the time of Richard Barron's death in October 1996, the formal mechanisms for accountability in An Garda Síochána were demonstrably weak, a matter compounded by a societal and political denial of the realities of misconduct within the force. One further option for accountability which prevails in Ireland is the establishment of a tribunal of inquiry, the chosen method for the events under consideration in this book. This is an exceptional mechanism, acquiring substantial public attention, attracting large financial costs, but lacking the sanctioning effects of other methods. It arises, as an option, when all other accountability mechanisms have failed.

It is in that context that the establishment, the work of and the response to the Morris Tribunal will be examined. The purpose of this book is to determine what this period tells us about policing and police accountability in Ireland, but also to assess the contribution which the Tribunal has made to those issues. Chapter 2 centres on the emergence of allegations about corrupt activity in Donegal and the parliamentary process of deciding to establish a tribunal. The government did not take the decision to establish the Tribunal until 2002, despite the Minister's confirmation that irregularities were brought to the attention of the department in 1997. Throughout this book it will be argued that social, political and media responses are just as central to the state and development of police accountability as the police and the accountability mechanisms themselves. The delay on the part of the government in taking action, until it had become a highly politicised issue due to the work of a number of TDs in opposition parties, is fundamentally linked to the operation of accountability. An analysis of this period will reveal the contributions of each of these actors, positive or negative, to the efforts to uncover what had occurred in Donegal. It will also provide an understanding of the pervading attitudes when the Tribunal was set up.

Chapter 3 considers the reports themselves, outlining what Justice Morris determined to have occurred in Donegal and his recommendations. The scale of the misconduct (at times corruption and abuse) established is not the only noteworthy aspect of these reports. Justice Morris' candour in producing these reports and his willingness to criticise the force are equally important as they represent a significant moment in Irish policing. Not only does he make findings of specific abuse but he extrapolates from these conclusions about the state of discipline and accountability in the force as a whole, and the presence of a blue wall of silence.

As Chapter 4 will explore the media presentations of the reports, which through highlighting certain aspects and even through their linguistic phraseology, have prevented the absorption of Justice Morris' more overarching findings. The power of the media, particularly where public attendance at the Tribunal was low, to dictate the focus of discussions and discourses will be explored. That chapter will argue that through some discernable themes which the media emphasised, they enabled a fractured understanding of the findings and recommendations, which allowed the Irish public to accept that wrongs had occurred but also to deny a need for ongoing concerns for its police force. It will also consider the official police statements in the wake of the reports, and analyse what they reveal about the mindset of the force at this key moment.

It is against the backdrop of highly critical findings understood through the refracting light of the media that the government and the Gardaí themselves set about reforming the force. Chapter 5 concerns itself with the reforms implemented in the years following the Tribunal, as well as the political discourses out of which they emerged. The purpose of this chapter is to question the extent to which the Morris reports fed into these discourses and what imprints it left on reforms. In questioning this, the aim is to understand how those charged with responding to the Tribunal completed the task. To what extent did Morris influence their work and to what extent can it be said that the problems which the Tribunal found to exist in An Garda Síochána have been addressed? Further, how have these reforms been presented to the public and how have they impacted on their perceptions?

The concluding chapter will draw together this work to analyse the impact of the Tribunal and the state of both police accountability and public confidence in the police in its wake. In particular, it will question the usefulness of a tribunal in a scenario such as this and evaluate whether the fundamental problem of the blue wall of silence, which was so debilitating, has been overcome. Conclusions will be drawn on accountability and reform in police organisations, and on the lessons that can be learned from the Irish response to a policing scandal.

NOTES

1. Other agencies such as the army and prisons services may use force outside of civil society. The concept of the monopoly of violence was presented by M. Weber, *Economy and Society: An Outline of Interpretive Society* (Berkeley, CA: University of California Press, 1958).
2. Herbert describes that 'the police represent both the majesty and tyranny of state authority'; S. Herbert, 'Tangled Up in Blue: Conflicting Paths to Police Legitimacy', *Theoretical Criminology*, 10, 4 (2006), p.481.
3. L. Lukes, *Power: A Radical View* (London: Macmillan, 1974), p.43.
4. See Herbert, 'Tangled up in Blue' p.481 for a discussion of the police coercive power.
5. L. Lustgarten, *The Governance of the Police* (London: Sweet & Maxwell, 1986), p.10; M. Brogden, T. Jefferson and S. Walklate, *Introducing Policework* (London: Unwin Hyman, 1988), p.94.
6. T. Newburn and T. Jones, *Police Accountability*, in W. Salsbury, J. Mott and T. Newburn, *Themes in Contemporary Policing* (London: Police Studies Institute, 1996) p.120.
7. L. Johnston, 'Controlling Policework: Problems of Organisation Reform in Large Public Bureaucracies', *Work, Employment and Society*, 2, 1 (1988), pp 51–70.
8. P. Scraton, *The State of the Police: Is Law and Order Out of Control?* (London: Pluto Press, 1985), p.42.
9. R. Lundman, *Controlling Police and Policing: An Introduction* (London: Holt, Reinhart & Winston, 1980), p.169.
10. In the UK the Police and Criminal Evidence Act 1984 (PACE) requires police to have reasonable suspicion before conducting a stop and search.
11. See generally D. Smith and J. Gray, *Police and People in London* (London: Policy Studies Institute, 1995); R. Kinsey, J. Lea and J. Young, 'Discretion and Accountability: Proposals for a New Police Authority', in R. Kinsey, J. Lea, and J. Young (eds), *Losing the Fight Against Crime* (London: Basil Blackwell, 1986), p.161.
12. An alternative typology is presented by J.B. Roebuck and T. Barker, 'A Typology of Police Corruption', *Social Problems*, 21, 3 (1974), pp.423–38 and by T. Sayed and D. Bruce, 'Police Corruption: Towards a Working Definition', *African Security Review*, 7, 2 (1998). Morton's analysis has been adopted as it provides a grounding in the reasons why officers chose to engage in this activity, as opposed to simply outlining the various forms it can take.
13. J. Morton, *Bent Coppers* (London: Warner Books, 1993), p.207.
14. Ibid., p.212; T. Newburn, *Understanding and Preventing Police Corruption: Lessons from the Literature*, Police Research Series Paper (PRSP) 110 (London: HMSO, 1999), p.vi; J. Kleinig, *The Ethics of Policing* (Cambridge: Cambridge University Press, 1996), p.67.
15. L. Sherman, *Police Corruption: A Sociological Perspective* (New York: Anchor Press, 1974), p.108.
16. M. Punch, *Conduct Unbecoming: The Social Construction of Police Deviance and Control* (London: Tavistock, 1995), p.9.
17. C. Klockars, 'The Dirty Harry Problem', in T. Newburn, *Policing: Key Readings* (Devon: Willan, 2005), p.581; M. Punch, 'Police Corruption and its Prevention', *European Journal of Criminal Policy and Research*, 8, 3 (2000), pp.301–24, at p.305.
18. Morton, *Bent Coppers*, p.251.
19. J. Chan, 'Governing Police Practice: The Limits of the New Accountability', *British Journal of Criminology*, 50, 2 (1999), p.251.
20. D. Beetham, *The Legitimation of Power* (London: Macmillan, 1991), p.64.
21. As Lord Lee stated in the 1929 *Royal Commission on Police Activities and Procedures:* 'The police of this country have never been recognized either in law or by tradition as a force distinct from the general body of citizens ... a police officer ... is only a person paid to perform,

as a matter of duty, acts which, if he were so minded, he might have done voluntarily' (cited in Scraton, *The State of the Police*, p.8).

22. D. Smith, *New Challenges to Police Legitimacy*, Centre for Law and Society Annual Lecture, University of Edinburgh (2006), p.9.
23. W. Knapp, *The Commission to Investigate Allegations of Police Corruption* (New York: Braziller, 1972).
24. J. Skolnick, 'Corruption and the Blue Code of Silence', *Police Practice and Research*, 3, 1 (2002), p.7.
25. Reiner, *The Politics of the Police*, p.138.
26. L. Westmarland, 'Police Ethics and Integrity: Breaking the Blue Code of Silence', *Policing and Society*, 15, 2 (2005), p.145; L. Sherman, 'Police Corruption Control: Environmental Context versus Organizational Policy', in D.H. Bayley (ed.), *Police and Society* (Beverly Hills, CA: Sage, 1977).
27. Kleinig, *The Ethics of Policing*, p.76, see also E. McGrath 'Professional Ethics and Policing', in M.L. Dantzker (ed.), *Contemporary Policing: Personnel, Issues and Trends* (Oxford: Butterworth-Heinemann, 1997), p.145.
28. Sherman, 'Police Corruption Control', p. 121.
29. G. Chin and C. Wells, 'The "Blue Wall of Silence" as Evidence of Bias and Motive to Lie: A New Approach to Police Perjury', *University of Pittsburgh Law Review*, 59, 2 (1998), p.237; J. van Maanen, 'Kinsmen in Response: Occupational Perspectives of Patrolmen', in P. Manning and J. Van Maanen (eds), *Policing: A View from the Street* (Santa Monica: Goodyear Publishing, 1978); J. Kleinig, 'The Blue Wall of Silence: An Ethical Analysis', Occasional Paper XIII, Centre for Research in Crime and Justice, New York University, School of Law, 2000.
30. Westmarland, 'Police Ethics and Integrity'.
31. W. Christopher, *Report of the Independent Commission on the Los Angeles Police Department* (Los Angeles, 1991), p.1, cited in Skolnick, 'Corruption and the Blue Code of Silence', p.9.
32. See G. Allen, *The Garda Síochána: Policing Independent Ireland 1922–82* (Dublin: Gill & Macmillan, 1999); C. Brady, *Guardians of the Peace* (Dublin: Prendeville Publishing, 2000); S. Breathnach, *The Irish Police: From Earliest Times to Present Day* (Dublin: Anvil Press, 1974); L. McNiffe, *A History of An Garda Síochána* (Dublin: Wolfhound Press, 1997).
33. W.J. Lowe, 'The War Against the RIC 1919–1921', *Éire: Ireland*, 37, 3 (2002), p.79.
34. Ibid., p.89.
35. The Treaty was passed in the Dáil by a vote of 64 to 57.
36. Brady, *Guardians of the Peace*, p.122.
37. Allen, *An Garda Síochána*, p.31.
38. E. O'Halpin, *Defending Ireland: The Irish State and Its Enemies Since 1922* (Oxford: Oxford University Press, 1999), p.41.
39. Cited in D. Walsh, *The Irish Police: A Legal and Constitutional Perspective* (Dublin: Round Hall, 1998), p.10.
40. This had become a serious problem throughout the country during the Civil War and was destroying communities. Allen, *An Garda Síochána*, p.62.
41. Brady, *Guardians of the Peace*, p.115.
42. See Allen, *An Garda Síochána*, p.69; Breathnach, *The Irish Police*, p.165.
43. T. Inglis, *Moral Monopoly: The Rise and Fall of the Catholic Church in Modern Ireland* (Dublin: University College Dublin Press, 1998), p.177.
44. Ibid; H. Tovey and P. Share, *A Sociology of Ireland* (Dublin: Gill & Macmillan, 2000).
45. In 1972 Garda Fallon became the first Guard killed in the line of duty in more than thirty years when he intercepted an armed robbery being carried out by paramilitary men. L. Walsh, *The Final Beat: Gardaí Killed in the Line of Duty* (Dublin: Gill & Macmillan, 2001), p.1.
46. A. Mulcahy, 'The Impact of the Northern Ireland Troubles on Criminal Justice in the Irish Republic', in P. O'Mahony (ed.), *Criminal Justice in Ireland* (Dublin: Institute of Public Administration, 2000), p.275; T.C. Salmon, 'The Case of Ireland', in J. Roach and J. Thomaneck (eds), *Police and Public Order in Europe* (London: Croom Helm, 1985), p.73.
47. S. Kilcommins, I. O'Donnell, E. O'Sullivan and B. Vaughan, *Crime, Punishment and the Search for Order in Ireland* (Dublin: Institute of Public Administration, 2004), p.208.
48. 'Gardaí using North-style brutality in interrogation techniques' (14 February 1977), 'Beaten by

six Guards' (14 February 1977), 'Heavy gang used new act to intensify pressure on suspects' (15 February 1977), 'Claustrophobia victim says Gardaí shut him in locker' (16 February, 1977). In one case reported, the suspect ended a six-hour interrogation by jumping out the window in a suicide attempt (*Irish Times*, 14 February 1977).

49. Bohan and D. Yorke, 'Law Enforcement Marketing: Perceptions of a Police Force', *Irish Marketing Review*, vol. 2 (1987), pp.72–86.
50. Amnesty International report 1978, cited in L. McFarlane, *Human Rights: Realities and Possibilities* (New York: St Martin's Press, 1990).
51. M. Farrell, 'Anti-Terrorism and Ireland: The Experience of the Irish Republic', in T. Bunyan (ed.), *Statewatching the New Europe* (London: Statewatch, 1993), p.128.
52. *People v. Kelly* [1983] IR 1 and P. McGarry, *When Justice Slept: The True Story of Nicky Kelly and the Sallins Mail Train Robbery* (Dublin: Liffey Press, 2006).
53. *DPP v. Pringle* (1995), Unreported, Court of Criminal Appeal, 16 May 1995.
54. N. Hardiman and C.T. Whelan, 'Politics and Democratic Values', in C.T. Whelan, *Values and Social Change in Ireland* (Dublin: Gill & Macmillan, 1994), p.100.
55. Garda Research Unit, *Garda Public Attitudes Survey 2002* (2002); K. O'Dwyer, P. Kennedy and W. Ryan, *Garda Public Attitudes Survey 2005* (2005); P. Kennedy and C. Browne, *Garda Public Attitudes Survey 2006* (2006); P. Kennedy and C. Browne, *Garda Public Attitudes Survey 2007* (2007); C. Browne, *Garda Public Attitudes Survey 2008* (2008).
56. T. Inglis, *Truth, Power and Lies: Irish Society and the Case of the Kerry Babies* (Dublin: University College Dublin Press, 2003), p.191.
57. M. McAleese, 'Police and People', *Dublin University Law Journal* (1987), p.45.
58. M. Maguire, 'The Changing Face of Catholic Ireland: Conservatism and Liberalism in the Ann Lovett and Kerry Babies Scandals [Part 2 of 3]', *Feminist Studies*, 27, 2 (2001), p.335.
59. Inglis, *Truth, Power and Lies*, p.221.
60. 29 January 1985, Michael Noonan, Dáil Éireann, vol. 355, col. 861.
61. Garda Síochána (Complaints) Act 1986.
62. See J. White, 'The Confessional State – Police Interrogation in the Irish Republic: Part I', *Irish Criminal Law Journal*, 10, 1 (2000), p.17; Part II, *Irish Criminal Law Journal*, 10, 2 (2000), p.2.
63. P. O'Mahony, 'The Ethics of Police Interrogation and the Garda Síochána', *Irish Criminal Law Journal* (1996), p.51.
64. *People v. O'Connell* [1995] 1 IR 244.
65. B. Ó Briain, *Report of the Committee to Recommend Certain Safeguards for Persons in Custody and for Members of An Garda Síochána* (Dublin: The Stationery Office, 1978).
66. Namely, under s.4 of the Criminal Justice Act 1984, s.30 of the Offences Against the State Act 1939, and s.2 of the Criminal Justice (Drug Trafficking) Act 1996.
67. The government response to the 2006 ECPT report indicated that 98 per cent of interviews were now recorded.
68. L. Bridges and M. McConville, 'Keeping Faith with their Own Convictions: The Royal Commission on Criminal Justice', *Modern Law Review*, 57, 1 (1994), p.7.
69. European Committee for the Prevention of Torture, *Report to the Government of Ireland on the Visit to Ireland 2–13 October 2006* (Strasbourg, 2007), p.14.
70. The Special Criminal Court was reserved, prior to this case, for the trying of terrorist offences and this case marked the extension to gang crime.
71. *DPP v. Ward*, Unreported Judgement, Special Criminal Court, 27 November 1998.
72. *DPP v. Ward*, Court of Criminal Appeal, 22 March 2002.
73. Commissioner Byrne, *Irish Examiner*, 23 February 2002.
74. Irish Council of Civil Liberties report, 30 September 1997.
75. For a discussion of the legislative response to these deaths see C. Hamilton, *The Presumption of Innocence and the Irish Criminal Law* (Dublin: Institute of Public Administration, 2007), pp.100–54.
76. G. Kerrigan and P. Brennan, *This Great Little Nation: The A–Z of Irish Scandals and Controversies* (Dublin: Gill & Macmillan, 1999), p.198.
77. E. Ó Cuiv, Dáil Éireann, 30 May 2001, vol. 537, col. 709.
78. *Western People*, 9 March 2005.
79. G. Birmingham, *Report of the Commission of Investigation (Dean Lyons Case)* (Dublin: Stationery Office, 2006), p.7.

80. *Shortt v. Commissioner of An Garda Síochána and Ors* [2007] IESC 9.
81. *Shortt v. An Garda Commissioner* [2007] IESC 9.
82. Ibid.
83. European Committee for the Prevention of Torture, *Report to the Irish Government on the Visit to Ireland*, 1993, 1998, 2003, 2007.
84. McDowell, M., Minister for Justice, Dáil Éireann, 27 November 2002, vol. 558, col. 509; 23 June 2005 vol. 605, col. 172; 27 April 2006, vol. 618, col. 1056; 4 April 2007, vol. 635, col. 752.
85. J. Barr, *The Tribunal of Inquiry into the Facts and Circumstances Surrounding the Fatal Shooting of John Carthy at Abbeylara, Co. Longford on 20 April 2000* (Dublin: The Stationery Office, 2006).
86. Ibid.
87. Garda Inspectorate, *Review of Practices and Procedures for Barricade Incidents* (Dublin, 2007), p.7.
88. The only change introduced as a response to this killing has been the introduction of TASER guns for the Emergency Response Unit, Dept of Justice, 3 April 2007.
89. *GSCB Annual Report 2002* (Dublin, 2002), p.11.
90. Ibid.
91. Irish Council for Civil Liberties, 27 May 2005.
92. McAleese, *Police and People*, p.48.
93. Dáil Éireann, 24 October 1989, vol. 392, col. 190.
94. Dáil Éireann, 23 October 1984.
95. McAleese, *Police and People*, p.50.
96. H. Hartnett, *Inquiry Pursuant to the Dublin Police Act 1924 as Amended by the Police Force Amalgamation Act 1925* (Dublin, 2008), pp.2/3.
97. 'Father of Schoolboy Welcomes End to Legal Battle after State Settlement', *Irish Times*, 20 December 2008.
98. Some 660 further complaints were deemed inadmissible, *GSCB Annual Report 2004*, p.21.
99. Walsh, *The Irish Police,* p.260; European Committee for the Prevention of Torture, *Report to the Irish Government on Visit to Ireland* (Strasbourg, 1993).
100. Walsh, *The Irish Police*, p.249.
101. Ibid., p.271.
102. Ibid., p.347.
103. Walsh, *The Irish Police*, p.347 and G. Smith, 'Rethinking Police Complaints', *British Journal of Criminology*, 44, 1 (2004), pp.15–33 on the same process in the UK.
104. '... the difficulty of getting convictions from a jury is clear ... Juries are very reluctant. You saw it in the May Day protests, people were seen on television doing unspeakable things, and they were acquitted by a jury' (Conor Brady, *Irish Independent*, 20 May 2007).
105. B. McMahon and W. Binchy, *Irish Law of Torts*, 3rd edition (Dublin: Butterworths, 2000), p.1,095.
106. For a review, see M. Kempa, 'Tracing the Diffusion of Police Governance Models from the British Isles and Back Again: Some Directions for Democratic Reform in Troubled Times', *Police Research and Practice*, 8, 2 (2007), p.107.
107. Walsh, *The Irish Police*, p.367.
108. J. Connolly, 'Do We Need Patten Type Reforms in the South?', paper presented to the James Connolly Education Trust (2000), p.6.
109. M. Noonan, Minister for Justice, Dáil Éireann, 10 November 1987, vol. 375, col. 227.
110. Browne, *Garda Public Attitudes Survey 2008*.
111. Birmingham, *Report of Commission of Investigation (Dean Lyons Case)*; Barr, *Tribunal of Inquiry Into Shooting of John Carthy*.
112. Statement by Minister McDowell on accountability, 29 November 2006.
113. *DPP v. Flannery* (1996) Unreported Judgement of Central Criminal Court, 25 June 1996.
114. Ibid.
115. John O'Donoghue, Minister for Justice, Dáil Éireann, 20 March 2002, vol. 550, col. 1373.

Chapter Two

The Road to Morris

On 28 March 2002 the Irish government passed a motion through the Dáil establishing a tribunal to investigate allegations of corruption arising out of the death of Richard Barron in Raphoe, County Donegal, five years and five months previously. Public inquiries, or tribunals, are established in Ireland on occasions where it is believed a matter 'of urgent public importance' needs to be examined.[1] Hardiman and Scott define tribunals as 'investigatory bodies set up to examine policy failures, shortcomings in executive functioning, or suspicion of political malpractice'.[2] The Law Reform Commission (LRC) recognised the potential of tribunals to achieve six separate functions:

- To establish what happened, especially in circumstances where the facts are disputed, or the course and causation of events is not clear,
- To learn from what happened, and so helping to prevent their recurrence by distilling lessons, which can be used to change practice,
- To provide catharsis or therapeutic exposure, providing an opportunity for reconciliation and resolution, by bringing protagonists face to face with each other's perspectives and problems,
- To provide reassurance, by rebuilding public confidence after a major failure;
- To establish accountability, blame, and retribution – holding people and organisations to account, and sometimes indirectly contributing to assigning blame and to mechanisms for retribution,
- For political considerations – serving a wider political agenda for government either in demonstrating that 'something is being done' or in providing leverage for change.[3]

TRIBUNALS

The Tribunals of Inquiry (Evidence) Acts 1921–2004 govern the establishment and procedure of tribunals in Ireland. The power to create one
rests with the government, though such a decision must be approved by
both houses of the Oireachtas. Their appeal lies in a number of defining
characteristics. Primarily, tribunals are inquisitorial in nature, not
accusatorial, meaning that they make findings of fact, not law, and are
not involved in the administration of justice.[4] This form of inquiry shifts
the focus from questioning whether identified persons are responsible
for certain actions to examining what happened in a broader sense. So
while a criminal prosecution has the potential to determine that an
individual is not responsible, thereby not providing any answers, a tribunal focuses on providing these answers. The inquisitorial method permits
the chairperson to take an active role and interject with questions. As Leyland and Anthony state, 'Faced with an inarticulate and unrepresented
applicant, the panel must attempt to uncover truth by gentle inquiry.'[5]

The legislation provides powers similar to the High Court in terms of
compelling witnesses to attend, examining witnesses under oath and
compelling the production of documents.[6] Tribunals are permitted
under s.4 of the 1979 Act to make whatever orders necessary to perform their functions, mirroring the powers of a High Court judge.
Sanctions for failure to comply with an order of a tribunal attach.[7]
These substantive and enforcement powers are what set tribunals of
inquiry apart from any other form of investigation which the government may initiate, such as non-statutory inquiries. In many instances
these inquisitorial powers provide the only means of ascertaining the
facts of a complex or secretive event.[8]

Another key characteristic is that, by convention, tribunals are
chaired by members of the judiciary. The appeal of an independent
judicial figure, performing inquisitorial functions, creates a confidence
in tribunals, particularly given that the powers afforded to tribunals
could impact on the constitutional rights of citizens.[9] Scraton suggests
that: 'Inquiries are assumed to be less partisan, unfettered by theatrical,
procedural and material constraints of prosecution.'[10] That said, the
LRC pointed out that as this role is not a judicial one, the constitutional
provisions of judicial independence do not apply.[11]

From a practical point of view there are numerous factors which
curtail the effectiveness of tribunals. The result of their political nature

is that 'Official inquiries into circumstances which challenge the legitimacy and authority of state institutions are often undermined by partial investigation and restricted disclosure.'[12] They may be restricted by their terms of reference, the person conducting the inquiry, those assisting them, and the resources available. They can, as a result, fail to take the broader socio-political factors into account. Furthermore, the persons undertaking the inquiry can have preconceptions about what they will find.

But overriding these concerns is the belief that tribunals will, through using these powers and their independence, be able to determine the truth of a matter where a conflict of accounts of a particular incident arises. This assumes that there is an objective truth which can be discovered.[13] The legal system, and in particular courts, work on the premise of determining an objective truth, particularly in criminal cases, where a decision is made 'beyond all reasonable doubt'. There may be an objective truth to be discerned in relation to certain facts, but this usually relates to scientific matters.[14] On the other hand, as Inglis says, 'What is true is what people believe to be true. Truth is agreed after rational debate among reasonable people. Truth is relative.'[15]

So in a context of potentially different and multiple truths, in any given situation a tribunal will need to determine, rationally, what is the reasonable truth or give recognition to the multiplicity of truths. The report produced by a tribunal will be interpreted by many as 'the official truth', but caution should be exercised. Tribunals, which make findings on the balance of probabilities, are established by government, chaired by members of the judiciary, to investigate the activities of state institutions; they are effectively an exercise of state power regulating state power. For Burton and Carlen the product of such tribunals and inquiries, official discourse, 'functions via its attempts (successfully and unsuccessfully, and always unfinished) to repair the fractured image of the self-acclaimed essentially just characterisation of the state's repressive and ideological apparatuses'.[16] In the Kerry Babies case, the evidence of the police ill-treatment of suspects was played down and the inconsistencies in the statements of the Hayes family were highlighted, reaffirming the legitimacy and power of the police. The facts of a case can be manipulated in the discovery of truth. The truth as determined by a tribunal cannot, then, be said, inherently, to be objective.

The findings of tribunals do not result in sanctions, but this is not to say they do not apportion blame. Scraton comments on the importance for victims: 'While responsibility, culpability and acknowledgement are significant, they rarely take precedence over "knowing".'[17] Tribunals actively make findings as to whom, or what, caused what to happen. These findings, publicly reported on, can result in a trial by media of individuals who have been apportioned blame by the tribunal. That tribunals cannot result in sanction may be true in the legal sense, but the punishment endured through the public reporting may be equally damaging to the individual concerned. And because it was a tribunal, and not a trial scenario, there was not the preoccupation with the rights of the accused. Questions arise as to what happens to victims who disagree with the truth as determined by the tribunal, as has been the case in so many instances.

In spite of these limitations, the combination of independence and inquisitorial powers has given tribunals an important role in Irish political life.[18] In 1990's Ireland the establishment of tribunals had become an almost annual event. The Beef Tribunal under Justice Hamilton was set up in 1994. Two years later came the Finlay Tribunal concerning the Blood Transfusion Service Board (BTSB) and the infection of women with Hepatitis C. In 1997 the McCracken, Moriarty and Flood Tribunals into the Dunnes payments, payments to politicians and planning matters respectively were all created. The century closed with the creation of the Lindsay Tribunal into the infection of haemophiliacs with HIV and Hepatitis C in 1999. This is in addition to numerous non-statutory inquiries, parliamentary inquiries, companies' inquiries and air, sea and rail inquiries. Corcoran and White conclude that tribunals are now 'something of a fixture in the national consciousness', with galleries filled with members of the public on a daily basis and 'tribunal exchanges ... re-enacted on national radio by professional actors'.[19]

Perhaps in this light the setting up of the Morris Tribunal in relation to events in Donegal seems like the natural response to the allegations as they emerged. It would, nonetheless, be a mistake to normalise or trivialise this decision of government. The establishment of a tribunal requires an investment of significant time and resources on the part of the government. In March 2002, the month that the Morris Tribunal was established, it was reported that ongoing tribunals had cost over €43 million to date.[20] Additionally, the government must commit to respond to the findings and implement recommendations. It also involves an admission that the parliamentary system of accountability has failed. As noted by MacCarthaigh, 'Almost all of the allegations of maladministration and improper conduct among public representatives, as later revealed by the tribunals, originated in the Dáil during Question Time and debates ... Indeed a recurring theme of recent tribunals of inquiry has been that parliamentary procedures such as Question Time and adjournment debates have failed in their role of overseeing the executive.'[21] This impact has not gone unnoticed. Brady, for instance, has commented that so frequent have they become that 'an aspect of rule by government is now being replaced by rule by tribunal.'[22]

In this context it might therefore be expected that, politically speaking, any government would be reticent to pursue this approach. Legislatively, as we have seen, they are to be reserved for matters of 'urgent public importance'. Clarification of what constitutes such a matter has been provided by the Irish Supreme Court, in the case of *Redmond v. Flood*, where Hamilton CJ articulated that tribunals may be 'necessary to preserve the purity and integrity of public life'.[23] In *Haughey No. 2* the Supreme Court ruled that the use of a tribunal should be 'confined to matters of vital public importance concerning which there is something in the nature of a nation-wide crisis of confidence'.[24] The Court in that case adopted the position of the Salmon report of the Royal Commission on Public Inquiries in the UK,

> ... it is essential that on the very rare occasions when crises of public confidence occur, the evil, if it exists, shall be exposed so that it may be rooted out; or if it does not exist, the public shall be satisfied that in reality there is no substance in the prevalent rumours and suspicions by which they have been disturbed.[25]

That Royal Commission was of the opinion that only a tribunal of inquiry with the inquisitorial powers legislatively provided could achieve this end. This not only suggests that the substance of allegations needs to be known due to public disquiet, but that this needs to be known to prevent (further) damage to some aspect of public life. Corcoran and White are critical that this is too broad a definition,[26] but it is difficult to imagine concrete indicators of social disquiet. Analysis of previous instances does not easily provide an accurate formula of measurement. MacCarthaigh's review of the six major tribunals established in the 1990s shows that in each case it took a combination of media reporting, lobbying by interested/affected groups and parliamentary debate for the issue in question to come to light.[27] In some instances legal action from private citizens had been initiated.[28] There is, therefore, no certainty as to what combination of events or stimuli will invoke this response.

It could be questioned why there have been so many tribunals in Ireland in the last two decades: was there more behaviour meriting examination? Did the standards of behaviour which cause public disquiet lessen? Or was it, in fact, due an increased sense among the Irish public of their rights and entitlement to question those in authority? Factors such as globalisation, membership of the EU, the decline of the influence of the Church (which brought an enhanced sense of rights) and the economic boom may well suggest accuracy in this concept of entitlement.[29] It is these societal changes which may explain the recourse to tribunals, rather than any normalisation of this avenue or, indeed, increased occurrence of activities meriting such examination.[30]

This chapter will explore the establishment of the Morris Tribunal. In contrast to many of the tribunals which have occurred in Ireland, the Morris Tribunal does not directly concern the activities of politicians but instead members of An Garda Síochána. This is an important distinction, especially given the status which the Irish police have traditionally held in Irish society. Since 1990 national trust in politicians has rarely been recorded at higher than 50 per cent,[31] whereas for An Garda Síochána trust has, according to official statistics, rarely dipped below 80 per cent.[32] The establishment of a tribunal to investigate their activities therefore becomes more unusual, and the repercussions in terms of the information which might be revealed, and the changes which may have to be implemented, become more striking. The Lynch Tribunal into the Kerry Babies case[33] stands as one of the exceptions, but, as noted previously, that tribunal was specifically not afforded the power to make recommendations. Other instances expose the government's unwillingness to question the police force, such as the public controversy regarding the 'heavy gang' in 1978, when the government did not order an investigation into the claims.[34] The government similarly took no action in respect of such calls following the killing of two raiders in Lusk, County Dublin in 2005.[35] In the case of Donegal, Mr Barron had died in 1996 and, despite the Department of Justice being informed of concerns in 1997 and allegations being expressed in the media from early 1999, the government did not act decisively until 2002.

This chapter will therefore examine the context of establishing the Morris Tribunal from the position that establishing a tribunal is a significant step, especially one concerning actions of An Garda Síochána. Media and political debates will be considered in order to assess how the situation came to be considered a matter of 'urgent public importance' by the government.

BARRON'S DEATH AND POLITICAL ATTENTION

Mr Barron died shortly after his arrival at hospital, having been found injured on a roadside just outside the town of Raphoe, County Donegal, early in the morning of 14 October 1996. 'Man (55) Killed in Hit and Run' was the headline in the *Irish Times* the following day.[36] As would be detailed in the findings of the Tribunal, serious derelictions of duty (failure to attend the scene promptly, failure to preserve the scene, failure to request an autopsy by the State pathologist among others) occurred in the immediate aftermath[37] and soon the police had decided that Mr Barron had been murdered, without evidence to support this conclusion. Eight individuals were detained in connection with the death in December, two of whom were held overnight, including Frank McBrearty Jnr, who made a false confession to murder.[38] Seventeen months later, in May 1998, a file was sent to the DPP regarding three people and at this point it was reported that 'investigating officers are now satisfied that Mr Barron was not struck by a car, but was violently assaulted.'[39] An autopsy in 2001 would confirm that he was killed by hit-and-run, not murder.

The first concerns regarding the investigation by Gardaí into this death were expressed by Garda Headquarters to the Minister for Justice, Nora Owen, on 27 February 1997; this would not be publicly revealed until November 2001.[40] Media attention in the case was sparked in early 1999 by a request from Supt Lennon, the officer in charge of the investigation from February 1997, to be transferred from the Letterkenny district. Brady of the *Irish Independent* reported on 16 April that an internal inquiry had been established to investigate allegations of harassment stemming from the killing, or murder as it was then believed to be, of Richie Barron.[41] He also reported that allegations had been made by a 'local woman' to the investigation team about the planting of hoax bombs, which Lennon was later found to be central to. The Gardaí involved were reported to be 'strenuously' denying the allegations. Deputy Jim Higgins of Fine Gael asked the first question on the matter in Dáil Éireann on 5 May 1999 in response to which the Minister for

Justice confirmed the nature of the allegations and that Assistant Commissioner Carty had been appointed to investigate them.[42]

In the coming months the media attention grew, particularly after the Supreme Court expressed concern at 160 summonses being pursued against Frank McBrearty for breaches of licensing laws. Mr McBrearty claimed his family had been harassed by the local Gardaí ever since his son had become a key suspect in the 'murder' case.[43] Deputy Higgins questioned the Minister for Justice throughout 1999 and a number of other deputies began to voice concerns on the matter.[44] In December 1999 an action was taken by a private investigator, Mr Flynn, who had been employed by the McBrearty family to investigate the death of Mr Barron.[45] Flynn alleged he had been assaulted by members of the Barron family during his investigation. These allegations had been investigated by Supt Lennon, who informed Flynn that no charges would be pressed in relation to the incident. Flynn requested an 'unbiased' officer be appointed to investigate the allegations.

By 2000 many of the details that would later come to light through the Tribunal were making their way into the public domain through the national media and Dáil debates. Brophy in the *Irish Examiner* reported in March that half a dozen civil actions were pending before the courts at this point.[46] It was then that Fine Gael spokesperson on Justice, Jim Higgins, appearing in the Dáil with the McBrearty family, who were still being prosecuted for breaches of licensing laws, first called for the establishment of a tribunal 'to have this matter fully investigated to establish the full facts and to ensure we do not have a repeat of the nightmare to which these people have been subjected'.[47] He also questioned the failure to transfer or suspend the officers under investigation in the internal inquiry. The Minister for Justice, John O'Donoghue's (hereinafter the Minister) response was to stress the need to wait for the outcome of ongoing inquiries before considering whether a tribunal was appropriate; he failed to comment on the disciplining of officers. The first arrest and suspension of an officer came just weeks later, though he was released from custody without charge.[48] Later that month, the prosecution of 160 summonses against Frank McBrearty was adjourned after prosecuting counsel informed the judge that the DPP's office now had, as a result of the ongoing Carty investigation, information of relevance to Mr McBrearty's defence.[49]

By June 2000 Deputy Howlin of the Labour party was in a position to present to the Dáil *prima facie* evidence of activities which would

later be confirmed by the Tribunal, including: the withdrawal of summons against the McBreartys; the campaign of harassment that family
was subjected to; the framing of individuals for the murder; and
details concerning the arms and explosives which had been hidden by
Gardaí.[50] Despite Howlin's angry calls for the publication of the Carty
report, the Minister refused to commit to do so. That same day, charges
against the McBreartys were dropped by the DPP, at the last minute,
after forty days of hearings.[51] The McBreartys' solicitor noted it was
striking how vigorously the charges had been pursued, and then
dropped: 'Had it not been for the tenacity and financial resources of Mr
McBrearty, it could have simply gone through the courts.'[52] Indeed, this
is true of many of the events which came under scrutiny in the coming
years. After the decision of the DPP, Mr McBrearty lodged further complaints with the Complaints Board and initiated civil actions against the
Gardaí. These proceedings all contributed to a building of pressure on
the government to act. Senior Garda sources were now being quoted as
believing in the necessity of an inquiry.[53]

This was not the end of the prosecutions against Mr McBrearty, and
the very next day he was back in court in relation to another series
of charges for breaches of licensing laws. In this instance, the judge
adjourned the hearing to seek clarification from the DPP, who had not
expressed his intention with regard to these other proceedings in his
direction the previous day.[54] Allen in the *Irish Independent* reported
that the reason for the dropping of the charges related to documents
which indicated a campaign of harassment by Gardaí against Mr
McBrearty and his family; these would have to have been released under
the rules of disclosure had the case continued.[55] The information came
to light from a Garda who alleged ostracisation and intimidation after
speaking to the Carty inquiry about this matter. The dropping of the
charges added to media speculation as to the findings of the Carty
inquiry and what had occurred in Donegal over the previous decade,
with attention moving beyond the death of Mr Barron and the explosives finds to, as Murphy wrote '... the possible existence of wrongful
convictions or miscarriages of justice in Donegal, assaults and intimidation of civilians by officers and the use of Garda informers who
allegedly made false allegations'.[56]

Allegations also began to appear in the British media at this point.
On 25 June 2000 the *Sunday Times* detailed what was suspected in a
2,050 word piece.[57] In July the media began reporting on allegations

from other families who claimed wrongful arrest, harassment and intimidation.[58] Nor were concerns limited to Donegal. On 11 July 2000 a murder trial in Limerick was adjourned until the completion of the McBrearty investigations due to concerns that investigating Gardaí in that case had been implicated in the Donegal investigations.[59] Just one day prior the Minister had stated that he was not opposed to an inquiry: 'I will do whatever is necessary to get to the truth of the matter. I am the Minister for Justice and I must ensure that justice will be done.'[60] That these allegations could be impacting on murder trials around the country warranted decisive action from a Minister with a stated commitment to justice, particularly given his concern that a tribunal would prejudice ongoing cases: the delay was affecting ongoing criminal trials.[61]

Details of the findings of the Carty inquiry began to appear in the media that summer, with Cusack of the *Irish Times* reporting that a Garda who had already been arrested in connection to events in Donegal had met with a senior police officer and secretly recorded their conversation, in which he threatened to release information if prosecuted.[62] The senior officer allegedly made a proposal to his subordinate. Gardaí also allegedly fabricated documents to secure bogus expense claims for witness appearances in court.[63] Garda Tina Fowley, who alleged a campaign of harassment having made statements to the Carty inquiry, announced her intention to take action against the State in relation to her treatment and was met by the attorney general (AG).[64] At this point, the *Irish Examiner* ran a headline, 'Public inquiry expected into alleged Garda corruption',[65] indicating the media belief that an inquiry was now both necessary and imminent.

The Garda Commissioner received the Carty report at the end of July 2000[66] and announced that a chief superintendent, two superintendents and two Gardaí would be transferred. In doing so, the Commissioner stated this was necessary to ensure public confidence in the force but 'emphasised there was no indication of any wrongdoing on their part'.[67] Opposition called again for the publication of the report and the establishment of a tribunal. The government was not forthcoming. At the end of August it emerged that the telephones of the McBreartys and their lawyers had been tapped by Gardaí.[68] The Law Society and the Bar Council expressed concerns on this issue to the Commissioner and the Minister for Justice. *Magill* magazine reported that Gardaí had delivered papers concerning the McBrearty case to a barrister whom solicitors had mentioned in a phone call but had never contacted.[69] At this point Deputy Howlin revealed that when he refused to name the source of related allegations which had been made to him, senior Gardaí threatened to search his phone records for the information.[70]

Leaks continued to emerge into the autumn, with the *Irish Independent* writing that the Commissioner had deferred the transfer of officers and suspended disciplinary investigations and that the publication had received documentation on the initial Garda inquiry into the Barron investigation (that which pre-dated the Carty inquiry) which cast doubt on whether there had in fact been a murder.[71] The impact of months of speculation was now a matter of media discussion, with Doyle and Andrews writing that 'After six months in which the force has been exposed to an unprecedented level of scrutiny and criticism, a combination of public disaffection and political impatience with its performance across a wide range of areas is threatening the relative autonomy it has enjoyed up to now.'[72]

Events in Donegal were now being linked to policing more generally. Doyle and Andrews' article expressed grave concern at the decline in people reporting crimes to the Gardaí, stating that in that year a third of assault cases, half of all robberies involving violence and 40 per cent of vandalism incidents were not being reported to the force.[73] The implication was that the rumours of what had occurred in Donegal were having a deleterious impact on public confidence in the police.

In October 2000 the Minister confirmed, having been questioned further on the matter by Deputies Howlin and Shatter, that six civil actions had been initiated, criminal proceedings were being considered by the DPP, the Commissioner was considering disciplinary action and the Garda Síochána Complaints Board was also dealing with complaints lodged.[74] The Carty investigation, which the Minister credited with having taken over a thousand statements, had focused on three main issues: the investigation into the death of Richie Barron; the allegations of a campaign of harassment by the McBrearty family; the allegations of hoax bomb finds on both sides of the border. He revealed that two further investigations were ongoing: one by Assistant Commissioner Murphy into information which Deputies Howlin and Higgins had passed to the Minister concerning the investigations and, more vaguely, that a chief superintendent had been appointed to investigate a matter raised by a member of the Gardaí in relation to the original investigation.[75]

Yet again, a call for the Carty report to be published was dismissed by the Minister as 'wholly inappropriate'.[76]

At this point, although every available avenue of accountability was being pursued, little action was being taken in terms of the officers at the centre of the inquiry. It appeared that very serious breaches of discipline had occurred on a large scale in Donegal, at times culminating in criminal activity. Given that criticisms of the accountability mechanisms in place were abounding,[77] it should have been evident that an independent investigation was required if the truth of what occurred was to be known. The facts emerging constituted a matter of 'urgent public importance', particularly given that the McBreartys were alleging that even at this point they continued to be subject to harassment by Gardaí in Donegal.[78]

Frank Shortt had been convicted in 1995 after Gardaí in Donegal raided his licensed premises and found controlled drugs. His conviction and three-year sentence were overturned in the Court of Criminal Appeal in November 2000.[79] During the hearing reference was made to the allegations against Gardaí in Donegal, indicating a connection between the cases and adding to existing concerns. Supt Lennon was, for instance, largely implicated in the judgment.[80]

Cusack of the *Irish Times* and Brophy of the *Irish Examiner* both reported in January 2001 that the government was planning on establishing an inquiry under a senior legal or judicial figure.[81] The DPP had stated that charges would not be brought against officers involved in the Barron investigation. He had not yet made a decision in relation to those alleged to be involved in the hoax bomb finds, the locations of which were now being reported in the media.[82] Opposition parties continued with vigorous calls for publication of the Carty report and for the establishment of a tribunal. The government was cited by Cusack in the *Irish Times* as having concerns about the cost and time attaching to a tribunal.[83] It was locally reported that Frank McBrearty was considering bringing private criminal proceedings against certain Gardaí.[84] It was also reported by Mara, in January, that a new prime suspect had emerged in the Barron investigation, and it was again suggested that he had been murdered,[85] despite the lack of a state autopsy.[86]

Pushed further by the opposition, the Minister stated in early February 2001 that he was awaiting reports from two further inquiries before making a decision on whether to hold an inquiry.[87] These inquiries, however, related to Deputies Howlin and Higgins' information about claims against senior Gardaí and Garda Fowley's allegations of harassment. They did not go to the heart of the allegations and it was unnecessary to delay the establishment of an inquiry on the basis of these. The DPP announced, at the end of February, that charges were to be pressed against a civilian, but no Gardaí, after examination of the Carty inquiry: charges against two Gardaí may follow.[88] A month later Bernard Conlon was charged in Sligo with knowingly making a false statement to Gardaí, but no Gardaí faced prosecution.[89]

The Minister announced in May 2001 that he had consulted the Attorney General on whether to establish a tribunal of inquiry.[90] Questioned on the need to restore confidence in the Gardaí in light of the allegations, he stated in the Dáil: '... the question is how we best achieve this in an open and transparent way that will achieve the desired results without interfering with potential civil and criminal proceedings.'[91] For the next year this would be the sticking point in relation to establishing the Tribunal – whether it could be done without interfering with ongoing civil and criminal proceedings. This argument from the government, supposedly based on the advice of the Attorney General (who would become the next Minister for Justice), would eventually be side-stepped through further legislation. Additionally, the concerns of the opposition began to alter somewhat at this stage, as expressed by Deputy Shatter:

> There is a widespread perception that no serious attempt is being made to come to terms with the serious allegations which have been made but that he [the Minister for Justice], his Department and those involved in this matter are engaged in covering up what occurred. Does he accept that there has been an utter failure by senior members of the Garda to confront the seriousness of the issue which has implications for the public credibility of the Garda?[92]

Dismissed by the Minister as 'ill-tempered, outrageous and unfounded', this statement would come to represent a central debate over the terms of reference.

In June 2001, almost a year after the Carty inquiry submitted its report to the Commissioner, it was reported by Brady that four officers were facing disciplinary proceedings.[93] This action, however, stemmed from a separate investigation conducted by Chief Supt McAndrew and related to discreditable conduct. It was also reported that two other officers were facing disciplinary action on the basis of a different investigation conducted by Chief Supt Smith. Brady, writing for the *Irish Independent*, reported that 'The disciplinary action relates to incidents not under consideration by the DPP, to avoid anybody facing the risk of double jeopardy through criminal and disciplinary proceedings.'[94] There is, however, no legal bar on pursuing both legal and disciplinary proceedings against a Garda, indeed it would be expected. There had, at this point, been no disciplinary action taken on foot of the Carty report.

The Garda investigation into the death of Mr Barron had continued and in July, four and a half years after his death, an exhumation order was granted in respect of Mr Barron, to allow for an official autopsy to determine the cause of death.[95] Mr Barron's family attended and it was reported locally that they had previously threatened to initiate High Court proceedings in relation to the failure to hold an inquest into his death.[96] The family had been informed, when the exhumation was conducted, that the results would be available within two weeks but they were not released until November; Gardaí had received the report in October.[97] In the meantime the final charges against Frank McBrearty were finally dropped on 4 September 2001.[98] The results of the autopsy showed that Mr Barron had in fact died in a hit-and-run accident and not due to murder. Until this point, the family of Richie Barron had believed that their husband and father had been murdered. Following what was described by some in the media as 'a major embarrassment', Deputy Higgins called on the Minister for Justice to resign, given his belief that the Minister was 'personally indicted for this shambles and disgrace'.[99] It was announced the following day that the Gardaí were planning to interview a number of local people in relation to the hit-and-run, some of whom were believed to be living in England.[100]

Two days after this report emerged, Deputies Shatter and Howlin again called for the establishment of a tribunal.[101] During this Dáil debate it emerged that the Department of Justice, which has the vested authority to authorise exhumations under the Coroners Act 1962, had been initially approached in October 1997 by Garda authorities seeking the exhumation of Richie Barron. Within a week, however, the same Garda requested this application be placed on hold. No action was taken until the request was made by the coroner for the district in July 2001. Shatter queried whether the Minister and his office had followed up on why the application was withdrawn in 1997. The Minister's response was that this had occurred 'prior to any report by Assistant Commissioner Carty. It was before any of the major controversy in relation to this matter arose.' However, the Minister had previously clarified to the House that concerns about the handling of the investigation had first been conveyed to the Department in February 1997 and that, although there had been a change of government in June 1997, there should have been concerns within the Department at the withdrawal of this request.

In relation to the request for a tribunal, the Minister reiterated the concerns expressed by the Attorney General while proceedings continued elsewhere and stated his intention to '... ask an eminent legal person to examine all the relevant papers and the progress on these investigations generally with a view to my receiving expert independent advice as to whether there are measures that might now be taken to bring matters to finality sooner rather than later'.[102] This proposal was not well received by opposition members. Referring to the length of time already dedicated to previous and ongoing investigations, Deputy Shatter stated: 'Another investigation of papers behind closed doors will be wholly inadequate in addressing the real concerns about policing, which is a fundamental branch of the administration of the State.'[103] It certainly appears difficult to reconcile the need to consult an eminent legal expert when the Minister had already consulted the Attorney General, the chief legal advisor to the government, on how to proceed. The editorial in the *Irish Times* the following day described the move as '... a limp response, to a most serious situation. It has the hallmarks of political window-dressing, aimed at creating the impression of action while buying time before a general election ... This is a smokescreen.'[104] Murray writing for the *Sunday Business Post* stated that it 'smacks of politicians reaching for an easy solution'.[105]

A week later Shatter and Howlin proposed legislation in the Dáil for the establishment of a tribunal to investigate the allegations of Garda ill-discipline and corruption in the Donegal district: '... the public interest in a full, public and impartial ventilation and determination of the facts, and a consideration of the issues of public policy arising therefrom, outweighs in importance the customary need to ensure pending or anticipated criminal proceedings are not put at unnecessary risk of frustration.'[106] This proposal was signed by all opposition party and independent TDs and was described by Deputy Howlin as 'one of the most important and significant motions to come before the House'.[107] In proposing the motion, Deputy Shatter outlined in detail many of the allegations which had been made, describing them as 'a festering sore on the integrity of the Gardaí'.[108] Shatter informed the House that the McBrearty family had confirmed their willingness to suspend civil actions should a tribunal be appointed, in response to the Minister's concerns regarding ongoing actions.

The Minister tabled an amendment of the motion in support of his move to appoint Shane Murphy SC to investigate the matter, arguing that the opposition's proposal was in breach of due process and that a prior investigation of this type could assist in a speedier resolution, even if a tribunal was subsequently established. Deputy Howlin countered that the appointment of Shane Murphy would achieve little as only a tribunal with all its powers of investigation could 'get to the bottom of this murky affair'.[109] Expressing concern as to what another investigation without the powers of a tribunal could achieve, Deputy Higgins claimed:

> What we are dealing with here is a deliberate miscarriage of justice. What we are dealing with here is a calculated decision taken within the Garda by senior gardaí to finger and frame the McBrearty family. Five years later the Carty inquiry or any of the other inquiries and investigations have failed to establish the facts ... All they have done is fuel frustration, confusion, doubt and cynicism.[110]

A total of eighteen members of the House contributed to the bitter debate, which was somewhat overshadowed by allegations made by Deputy Gildea, one of the two pivotal independent TDs, against a former Minister for Justice, which required the temporary suspension of the house.[111] The motion was defeated by just one vote (seventy-three to seventy-two), one of the tightest votes in the history of the Dáil and the closest faced by that government. Instead, the Dáil expressed its support for the Minister's decision to appoint Shane Murphy to investigate the matter, which, five years on, was the first action to be taken by the government on the matter.

This debate prompted the first consideration of the allegations by 'Prime Time', a leading current affairs programme on the national station, RTÉ.[112] The media fallout continued with the *Sunday Tribune* running the headline 'Sinister, Ruthless, Malicious'[113] and calling for 'a Garda force we can believe in'.[114] Murray in the *Sunday Business Post* wrote 'Garda corruption a national blight'.[115] Vincent Browne of the *Irish Times* dedicated his weekly column to quoting the allegations made by Deputy Higgins in the Dáil that week.[116] That leading Irish broadsheets, traditionally supportive of the force, were using such critical language is indicative of the seriousness of the situation.

The very same week McBrearty was back in court seeking an injunction to restrain the Garda Commissioner from circulating a document which required Gardaí in the Letterkenny division to report on the activities of Frank McBrearty, his family and his contacts.[117] An interim injunction was granted by the High Court. The fact that Garda misconduct continued was being ignored by the Minister who, just three days previously in the Dáil, expressed his determination 'to establish the truth of what *happened* in Donegal'[118] (emphasis added). Two weeks later, the first and only Garda to be prosecuted in relation to all of these events, Sergeant John White, was remanded on charges of possession of a firearm.[119] The Garda Commissioner was quoted at this time as saying 'things have been made out to be far worse than reality',[120] a position which was easy to maintain given the government's inaction.

Murphy SC's review took six weeks and the submission at the end of January 2002 concluded that the only viable action was to establish a tribunal.[121] In a complete about-face, the government announced, in February, that a tribunal was to be established and that Justice Morris, formerly of the High Court, was to chair.[122] The government was still faced, however, with its long-standing concern that establishing a tribunal at this point could prejudice ongoing criminal and civil actions. Its argument as to why it was, in March, in the final weeks of the government's life, appropriate to establish the Tribunal when it was not in November was that 'neither the criminal nor civil proceedings advanced very quickly and there was real concern … over the length of time it was taking to bring the various inquiries and proceedings to finality.'[123] To this end it first introduced the Tribunals of Inquiry (Evidence) (Amendment) Bill 2002 to enable the Tribunal to begin while other proceedings were ongoing. The haste to ensure that the legislation, necessary for the establishment of the Tribunal could be passed prior to the dissolution of the Dáil meant this amendment to the Tribunals of Inquiry legislation being passed through all five stages of enactment in one day.

The legislation permits a tribunal to exclude the public from certain proceedings, where it believes this is in the public interest or where it might prejudice criminal proceedings.[124] The Act also provides for an application to the court to prevent publication of any part of a report of a tribunal where to do so might prejudice criminal proceedings.[125] The opposition criticism of the Bill centred around the implications of these provisions on the basic notion of a *public* tribunal of inquiry. Numerous investigations had already been completed on the activities in Donegal, the reports of which had not been published. As Deputy Shatter noted, part of the purpose of tribunals is that there is a need to ensure 'the glare of publicity is available to ensure people are accountable for the evidence they give and that their evidence, if it can be challenged for truthfulness, is appropriately challenged.'[126] A substantial part of the problem was the delay in responding to the allegations.[127] Had the Minister moved more quickly to establish a tribunal, it would have occurred before any criminal or civil proceedings had been initiated, thereby avoiding the issue entirely. The delays had already had a corrosive effect on the force, with one editorial stating that the allegations 'have dripped like acid onto the reputation of An Garda Síochána'.[128]

There were also concerns about the standard required before a court could order part of a report to not be published: 'might', rather than 'would', prejudice criminal proceedings was deemed by the opposition to be a low threshold.[129] It was reiterated by the opposition that this legislation was unnecessary for the purpose of establishing the Morris Tribunal,[130] particularly given that only one criminal trial was pending and the McBrearty family had offered to suspend civil proceedings. Indeed the Bill addressed only criminal, not civil, proceedings. Serious concerns were expressed that the Bill would prompt numerous constitutional challenges similar to those witnessed regularly in relation to other tribunals.[131] The government nonetheless proceeded with enacting the legislation with alarming haste, just forty-eight hours after its publication. Following the announcement of the tribunal, the Barron family, who had largely remained silent as allegations were made, spoke out, calling for a focus on the murder of Richie Barron. Five and half years on his brother expressed his concern for Mr Barron's children:

> How can they get on with their lives, they are reminded of this every day. They know their father was murdered, worse than that they know who did it and they want justice … All week we heard about tribunals and investigations but never a word about a woman who lost her husband or children who lost their father at the hands of cold-blooded killers.[132]

THE TERMS OF REFERENCE

The terms of reference were presented to both the Dáil and Seanad at the end of March 2002, a week after the Bill was passed.[133] This was a contentious issue. Previous tribunals had shown that well-developed terms of reference were essential to ensure that the tribunal produced results which would satisfy the public disquiet. There had already been much debate as to what the terms should be for this tribunal,[134] and the opposition had presented terms as part of their motion the previous November. Subsequent to these debates, many members of the house had their attention drawn to further allegations unrelated to those which had previously been subject to investigation by the various inquiries. Deputy Reynolds, on one occasion, called for the terms to be broad enough to investigate concerns beyond those relating to the McBrearty family and what had occurred in Donegal.[135] In the end what was presented to parliament drew largely on Shane Murphy's recommendations, though neither this nor the Carty report had yet been published.

The terms as put to the House by the Minister were to establish a Tribunal, to inquire urgently into the following definite matters of urgent public importance:

   (a) The making of extortion and hoax telephone calls to the home of Michael and Charlotte Peoples on 9th November, 1996 and the subsequent Garda investigation into that complaint,

   (b) Investigations in relation to the death of Mr Richie Barron of Raphoe, County. Donegal on 14th October, 1996 with particular reference to the arrest and treatment of persons in custody in connection with that investigation, the progress, management and effectiveness of the Garda investigation with particular reference to the management of informants,

   (c) Allegations of harassment of the McBrearty family of Raphoe, County Donegal and of relatives, associates and agents of that family by members of the Garda Síochána subsequent to the death of Mr Barron including the issue and prosecution of summonses relating to offences alleged to have occurred between 28th October, 1996 and 28th September, 1998,

   (d) The circumstances surrounding the arrest and detention of Mark McConnell on 1st October, 1998 and Michael Peoples on 6th May, 1999,

   (e) Complaints that some Gardaí in County Donegal may have

been involved in hoax explosives and bomb-making equipment finds (in particular discoveries on 11th September, 1993, 19th November, 1993, 11th January, 1994, 14th March, 1994, 4th June, 1994, 13th June, 1994 and 18th July, 1994) and a review of the management and investigation of these issues,

(f) The circumstances surrounding the arrest and detention of Frank McBrearty Jnr on 4th February, 1997 and his subsequent prosecution in the Circuit Criminal Court in relation to an alleged assault in December, 1996 on Edward Moss with particular reference to the Garda investigation and the management of both the investigation and the role of the Gardaí in the subsequent prosecution,

(g) Allegations relating to the Garda investigation of an arson attack on property situated on the site of the telecommunications mast at Ardara, County Donegal in October/November 1996,

(h) Allegations contained in documents received by Deputy Jim Higgins on 25th June, 2000 and in information received by Deputy Brendan Howlin on 25th June, 2000 that two senior members of An Garda Síochána may have acted with impropriety,

(i) The circumstances surrounding the arrest and detention of seven persons at Burnfoot, County Donegal on 23rd May, 1998 and the investigation relating thereto,

(j) The effectiveness of the Garda Síochána Complaints inquiry process vis-à-vis the complaints made by Frank McBrearty Snr and his family between 1997 and 2001.[136]

The Tribunal was also instructed to

- report to the Minister with findings and recommendations when completed,
- report to the Minister within four months of establishment,
- and after the first ten days of oral hearings report on
  - o the parties being represented before the tribunal, its progress,
  - o the likely duration expected at those points,
  - o and any other matters it feels appropriate to inform the Minister.

The terms stated that the Tribunal should be conducted economically, as quickly as possible and within fourteen days of receipt of the report the Minister should lay it before the houses of the Oireachtas or apply to the High Court for direction on publication if necessary.

Shatter immediately called for an extension of the terms of reference to include two further issues: the Frank Shortt case, which had the previous week been declared a miscarriage of justice and involved the activities of many of the same Gardaí, and the way in which the Minister, the Department and the Garda authorities fulfilled their obligations with respect to the allegations covered by the terms of reference.[137] The latter referred to the frequently expressed concerns regarding the exhumation order and the extent to which the Gardaí had been keeping the Minister informed of the allegations and investigations. There were related concerns about how the Gardaí had internally handled the allegations as they emerged. It was unheard of that terms of reference for a tribunal did not encompass the parent Minister and Department. The Minister, however, dismissed this as a 'proposal directing the Tribunal to look for fire where there is no smoke simply because the Opposition is desperate to gain political advantage'.[138] Dismissing these issues as a political tactic ignores the details outlined in the preceding discussion. Other criticisms involved a failure to consult not just with opposition parties but also with the McBrearty families, as the central victims of the behaviour under consideration.[139] Deputy Higgins raised another case involving the Gallagher family who claimed to be subject to a campaign of harassment by the same Gardaí.[140] He also called for the terms to include the claims of phone tapping which had previously arisen. Similar concerns were raised in the Seanad.

Although the terms of reference were approved in both Houses, this did not translate into general satisfaction with what had been passed. In April 2002 the McBreartys and five other families deeply connected to the work of the Tribunal announced that they would not be co-operating with the Tribunal on the basis of the lack of information provided to them by the government, the failure to issue a state apology and the substantial costs involved in the Tribunal.[141] In May, McBrearty announced that he would be taking a challenge to the European Court of Human Rights in relation to the terms of reference.[142] A further attempt to have the costs for the McBrearty family included came later that year when, in November, Joe Costello of the Labour party introduced a motion in the Dáil to achieve both this and the extension of the terms to have the actions of the Minister, Department and Garda authorities included.[143] Precedent for both actions had previously been set by the Lindsay Tribunal where the Ministry of Health was specifically included in the terms of reference and the Irish Haemophilia Society was provided with 75 per cent of its legal costs in advance of any decision being made by the Tribunal on costs.[144]

Following the opening statements of the Tribunal and a formal application by the McBrearty family, Justice Morris stated that he did not intend to seek an extension of the terms of references as he viewed this as an attempt to reverse a decision of the people of Ireland. Describing the matter as 'one of the most serious issues ever to have been considered by the Dáil',[145] Costello accused the Minister of trying to avoid political responsibility for the response to the allegations. Deputy Higgins described how the 'extraordinary omission' had been 'deliberately and shamefacedly forced through'[146] the Dáil and challenged the new Minister to take this opportunity to rectify the situation. The new incumbent to the ministerial office, Michael McDowell, who, in his previous position as Attorney General had advised against establishment of the Tribunal, amended the motion, suggesting the matter could be kept under review, keeping open the possibility of amending the terms of reference in the future.[147] This never happened. The Minister argued that the broad nature of the existing terms, which permitted the Chair to make findings and recommendations 'as it sees fit in relation to these matters', did allow for an examination of the actions of the Minister, the Department and the Garda authorities, if it indeed saw fit. However, inclusion within the clearly defined terms of reference might have had a declaratory effect of expressing concerns in relation to the activities of these persons and bodies.

In relation to the matter of costs for the McBrearty family, the opposition stressed that the family had already invested a great deal of money in legal actions, both defending themselves against criminal actions and in initiating civil actions. Central as they were to the investigation of the Tribunal, the family would require legal representation for a substantial portion of the inquiry. Deputy Costello argued that to not award costs at this point would be to impose further injustices on the McBrearty family.[148] Deputy O'Sullivan equally expressed concern for this to be done 'in the interests of justice, the public at large and our confidence that this is a full, transparent and complete tribunal'.[149] The Minister argued to the contrary, adding that there were sound reasons to allow a tribunal to determine the issue of costs at the end of its business, as they were generally awarded to parties who had co-operated with a tribunal. Despite the existence of precedent on the matter, he argued that 'it would undermine the work of the Tribunal.' This position runs against the norm that parties directly involved in a tribunal are entitled to legal representation. The McBreartys' position was an unusual one and, if forced to pay for legal costs in advance there was a strong possibility, obvious at this point, that they would not be able to afford representation. This would place them at a disadvantage before the Tribunal as compared to many of the other parties: the Gardaí against whom the allegations were made were being represented at the expense of the Garda Representative Association (GRA). As Deputy Rabbitte questioned, 'How can he expect the average citizen to be pitted against the State, whether it be the Garda, the Government, the Minister or the Attorney General?'[150] Distinguishing this request from the provision of costs to the Irish Haemophilia Society before the Lindsay Tribunal, the Minister noted that the charity in that instance had informed the government that it may have to wind up due to the legal liabilities involved. This ignored the limited personal funds available to the McBreartys and the money which they had already spent in relation to other actions. These points were not addressed by the Minister, who expressed the view that he could not favour one party over another by making such a decision. Both motions were defeated.

COMMENT

Central to this discussion is the question of when the government considered that events could be considered a matter of 'urgent public importance', to the extent that a tribunal was warranted to maintain the 'purity and integrity of public life'. The announcement by the Minister for Justice in May 2001 that he had consulted the Attorney General about whether it was feasible to have a tribunal appears to indicate some acceptance on his part that the matter was of the requisite importance. Nothing would in fact change between then and March 2002, when the Minister finally laid the necessary motion before the Dáil. Realistically however, an analysis of the events indicates that a tribunal was warranted much earlier than this. It could be argued that it should have been considered a 'definite matter of urgent public importance' in late 1999, by which time the Carty Inquiry had heard the allegations of hoax bomb finds, Supt Lennon had requested a transfer, questions were being asked in the Dáil, and the Supreme Court had expressed concern regarding the prosecutions against Mr McBrearty. Most certainly it had reached this standard by the summer of 2000, when the Carty reports had been submitted, media speculation concerning all aspects of the investigation abounded both in Ireland and the UK, the DPP had dropped 160 charges against the McBreartys yet Mr McBrearty Jnr continued to be brought before the courts on separate counts, Deputies Higgins and Howlin had made additional allegations relating to these events, the Commissioner had announced that five officers were to be transferred, a murder trial in Limerick had been indefinitely adjourned pending the outcome of the investigations and phone tapping claims had been made. No criminal actions had as yet been initiated, meaning there were no existing impediments to a tribunal. The continuing refusal of the Minister to take this action between the summer of 2000 and the spring of 2002 represents a serious failure and one which exacerbated the suffering experienced by the Barrons, the McBreartys and the other families involved, particularly given a number of events such as the exhumation of Mr Barron, the submission of that report, the overturning of Frank Shortt's conviction, and the opposition's motion, which culminated in the closest vote in the history of that government. This was a significant constitutional moment which suggested that the issue ran beyond Garda accountability to the point of constituting a substantial political event.

The response was unusually slow as compared to the other tribunals of the time. The McCracken Tribunal, which would later become the Moriarty Tribunal, was established within a year of the payments under question being made.[151] The Beef Tribunal was created in May 1991 to deal with events which had occurred between 1987 and 1990. While the decision was mostly prompted by the airing of a documentary on the allegations by ITV (the motion came before the house just eleven days later), there had been over ninety questions asked in the Dáil in the preceding two years on the issue. For a policing comparator, the Lynch Tribunal, which investigated the Kerry Babies case, began work just eight months after the false confession was made by Joanne Hayes and her family. Most strikingly, the government took the action to establish a tribunal just two months after it was first raised in the Dáil.[152] Perhaps the creation of the Morris Tribunal bears more in common with the establishment of the BTSB/Finlay Tribunal, the process of which MacCarthaigh outlines: '… in the years before the establishment of the tribunal, and as details of the scandal emerged, successive governments were able to use the narrow doctrine of ministerial responsibility to insulate themselves and the BTSB from parliamentary scrutiny ... it was only when investigation of the matter became politically imperative that the government decided to act.'[153] Indeed it was maintained by numerous politicians and commentators that the decision to establish the Morris Tribunal had more to do with the impending general election of May 2002 than any desire to explore fully the ongoing events in Donegal. Drapier, in the *Irish Times*, described the effect of the opposition's motion thus: 'The result was that indefinable shift that takes place in the life of a parliament when the Opposition suddenly looks capable of replacing the Government, as distinct from merely defeating the Government on a headcount on the night.'[154]

It is also striking that the Taoiseach, Bertie Ahern, was not in attendance for the debate on the opposition's motion. Under the operation of the pairing system, where a government TD is absent on official business a member of the opposition is not allowed to vote. On this occasion the Taoiseach missed the vote to attend the opening of a pub, which raises a number of questions as to what, for instance, is considered 'official business', and the importance the government attached to the allegations concerning Donegal.

The about turn in the government position on the feasibility of a tribunal in March 2002 was equally striking. Suddenly the impossible was possible. Was this to do with the general election? Why was it then feasible to have a tribunal when it had not been before? Did the Murphy report say anything particularly different from the Carty report? This remains unknown, given the refusal to publish either report. Dixon has written in relation to the UK government decision to establish the Runciman Commission, following the Birmingham Six miscarriage of justice, that 'Establishing this Commission bought the government time and political distances, allowing them to insist that, while immediate action was inappropriate, their sincere commitment to putting things right was evident.'[155] The decision to establish the Tribunal may have been not just due to political pressure but also due to a desire to defer dealing with what was emerging in the Carty and Murphy reports to a future point.

The terms of reference, an issue which will be revisited, were clearly flawed. The exclusion of the response of the Minister for Justice, the Department of Justice and the Garda authorities is inexplicable other than to avoid criticism. Similarly, the exclusion of the Shortt case could only limit the extent of corruption exposed by the Tribunal. Had the government been seriously committed to clarifying the culmination of events, these issues would have been included for consideration. It was clear that the scale of the problem in Donegal was much broader than what the terms indicated. Moreover, given that many of the officers concerned had previously worked in other districts, and that this work was being called into question in the courts, concern for policing practices across the country was justified. The Tribunal would, however, proceed on the basis of the terms as put forth by government. This alone would consume the Tribunal for the next six years and would cost close to €80 million.

NOTES

1. Tribunals of Inquiry Act 1921, s.1(1).
2. N. Hardiman and C. Scott, 'Governance as Polity: An Institutional Approach to the Evolution of State Functions', *Public Administration* (2009).
3. Law Reform Commission, *Report on Public Inquiries Including Tribunals of Inquiry* (Dublin: LRC 73, 2005), p.20.
4. For a complete study of the legal status and powers of tribunals see G. Hogan and D.G. Morgan, *Administrative Law in Ireland*, 3rd edition (Dublin: Roundhall, 1998), Chapters 6 and 7. This was confirmed in the Irish Supreme Court in the cases of *Goodman International v. Hamilton* [1992] 2 IR 542 and *Boyhan v. Beef Tribunal* [1993] 1 IR 210.
5. M. Elliot et al., *Textbook on Administrative Law*, 3rd edition (Oxford: Oxford University Press, 2005), p.191.
6. Tribunals of Inquiry (Evidence) Act 1921, s.1.
7. See, for instance, the case of *Flood v. Lawlor* [2002] 2 IR 67 where it was held that criminal sanctions could apply for a failure to comply with an order for disclosure sufficiently.
8. The suitability of a tribunal will be considered in greater depth in the Conclusion.
9. Article 35.2 of the Irish constitution states that judges 'shall be independent in the exercise of their judicial functions and subject only to the Constitution and the law'. See J. Casey, *Constitutional Law in Ireland*, 2nd edition (London: Sweet & Maxwell, 1992), p.245.
10. P. Scraton, 'From Deceit to Disclosure: The Politics of Official Inquiries in the United Kingdom', in G. Gilligan and J. Pratt, *Crime, Truth and Justice* (Devon: Willan, 2004), p.47.
11. Law Reform Commission, *Report on Public Inquiries*, p.32.
12. Scraton, 'From Deceit to Disclosure', p.51.
13. See T. Inglis, *Truth, Power and Lies: Irish Society and the Case of the Kerry Babies* (Dublin: University College Dublin Press, 2003).
14. S. Leman-Langlois and C. Shearing, 'Repairing the Future: The South African Truth and Reconciliation Commission at Work', in Gilligan and Pratt, *Crime, Truth and Justice*, p.222.
15. T. Inglis, *Truth Power and Lies*, p.172.
16. F. Burton and P. Carlen, *Official Discourse: On Discourse Analysis, Government Publications, Ideology and the State* (London: Routledge, 1979), p.34.
17. Scraton, 'From Deceit to Disclosure', p.47.
18. For a full list, see Law Reform Commission, *Consultation Paper on Tribunals of Inquiry* (Dublin: LRC, 2002).
19. M. Corcoran and A. White, 'Irish Democracy and the Tribunals of Inquiry', in E. Slater and

M. Peillon, *Memories of the Past: A Sociological Chronology of Ireland* (Dublin: Institute of Public Administration, 2000), p.185.
20. A. Bushe, 'Trials and tribulations as tribunal bill tops EUR43m', *Sunday Mirror*, 31 March 2002.
21. M. MacCarthaigh, *Accountability in Irish Parliamentary Politics* (Dublin: Institute of Public Administration, 2005), p.187.
22. R. Brady, 'Reflections on Tribunals of Inquiry', *Bar Review* (1997), p.3.
23. [1999] 3 IR 79.
24. *Haughey & Ors v. Moriarty & Ors*, Unreported Supreme Court judgment, 28 July 1998.
25. Justice Salmon, *Royal Commission on Tribunals of Inquiry* (London: HMSO, 1966), para. 28.
26. Corcoran and White, 'Irish Democracy and Tribunals of Inquiry', p.187.
27. MacCarthaigh, *Accountability in Irish Parliamentary Politics*, p.197.
28. This occurred prior to both the McCracken Tribunal and the Flood Tribunal.
29. See generally on these issues C. Ó Gráda (ed.), *A Rocky Road: The Irish Economy Since the 1920s* (Manchester: Manchester University Press, 1997); T. Inglis, *Moral Monopoly: The Rise and Fall of the Catholic Church in Modern Ireland*, (Dublin: University College Dublin Press, 1998); H. Tovey and P. Share, *A Sociology of Ireland* (Dublin: Gill & Macmillan, 2000). For a full discussion of the impact of these changes, see P. Lyons, 'Ireland's Political Culture: Overlapping Consensus and Modus Vivendi', paper prepared for presentation at the International Political Science Association Conference, Fukuoka, Japan, 9–13 July 2006, available online at http://www.soc.cas.cz/articles/en/5/2946/Ireland-8217-s-Political-Culture-Overlapping-Consensus-and-Modus-Vivendi.html.
30. Corcoran and White differ in their understanding, contending that 'the tribunal is an ostensibly modern institution that embodies one of the preoccupations of modernity: the need to stand back and engage in a reflexive interrogation of the self;' 'Irish Democracy and the Tribunals of Inquiry', p.189.
31. MacCarthaigh, *Accountability in Irish Parliamentary Politics*, p.8.
32. Garda Research Unit, *Garda Public Attitudes Survey 2002*; Kennedy and Browne, *Garda Public Attitudes Survey 2006*; Kennedy and Browne, *Garda Public Attitudes Survey 2007*; Browne, *Garda Public Attitudes Survey 2008*.
33. K. Lynch, *Report of the Tribunal of Inquiry into the 'Kerry Babies Case'* (Dublin: Stationery Office, 1985).
34. In that instance despite a front-page campaign by the *Irish Times* exposing the allegations and a report by Amnesty International supporting the claims the government refused to investigate the claims.
35. 'Amnesty calls for inquiry into Lusk deaths', see http://www.rte.ie/news/2005/0526/dublin. html.
36. *Irish Independent*, 'Gardaí probe hit-and-run', Anon, 15 October 1996.
37. See further Chapter 3.
38. Anon, 'Two arrested over hit and run', *Irish Times*, 5 December 1996.
39. R. Balls, 'Murder now suspected in road death', *Irish Times*, 18 May 1998.
40. Minister for Justice, John O'Donoghue, Dáil Éireann, 20 November 2001, vol. 544, col. 599.
41. T. Brady, 'Hoax bomb among claims against Gardaí in probe', *Irish Independent*, 16 April 1999.
42. Dáil Éireann, 5 May 1999, vol. 504, col. 156.
43. Anon, 'Publican claims harassment by Gardaí after finding of body', *Irish Times*, 20 November 1999.
44. Higgins, 12 October 1999, vol. 509, col. 24; O'Shea, 12 October 1999, vol. 509, col. 153; Stagg, 23 November 1999, vol. 511, col. 579; Higgins, 16 December 1999, vol. 512, col. 1973.
45. Anon, 'Garda inquiry into assault claim challenged', *Irish Times*, 21 December 1999.
46. K. Brophy, 'Gardaí to be arrested in Donegal corruption scandal', *Irish Examiner*, 7 March 2000.
47. Higgins, Dáil Éireann, 7 March 2000, vol. 515, col. 1326.
48. K. Brophy, 'First Garda quizzed in probe into corruption', *Irish Examiner*, 23 March 2000.
49. Anon, 'Donegal harassment case against Gardaí adjourned', *Irish Times*, 29 March 2000.
50. Higgins, Dáil Éireann, 21 June 2000, vol. 521, col. 1278.
51. Anon, '2½ year case stopped by DPP', *Irish Times*, 22 June 2000.
52. Anon, 'I'm tough and I don't give in easy', *Irish Times*, 22 June 2000.

53. J. Cusack, 'Gardaí are taking allegations seriously', *Irish Times*, 8 April 2000.
54. Anon, 'McBrearty up in court again', *Irish Times*, 23 June 2000.
55. L. Allen, 'Garda alleges police led vendetta against publican', *Irish Independent*, 25 June 2000.
56. C. Murphy, 'Inquiry seeking to make sense of a web of claims', *Irish Times*, 22 June 2000.
57. M. Sheehan and J. Mooney, 'Fitted Up', *Sunday Times*, 25 June 2000.
58. C. Murphy, 'Inquiry on Donegal Gardaí widening', *Irish Times*, 8 July 2000.
59. Anon, 'Murder trial delay over Donegal case', *Irish Times*, 12 July 2000. The case did not proceed until November 2001. During the hearing the men continued to make allegations concerning the Garda handling of the investigation. They were convicted in 2002 and were unsuccessful in an appeal on these grounds in 2004, *DPP v. Raymond Casey and Anthony Casey* [2004] IECCA 49.
60. K. Hannon, 'Full inquiry into Garda corruption now likely', *Irish Examiner*, 10 July 2000.
61. Perhaps more so given that one officer who would be criticised by the tribunal, Joseph Shelley, had also been central to the Kerry Babies case and the death of John Carthy at Abbeylara in 2000. See C. McMorrow and J. Burke, 'Once, twice, three times a tribunal Garda', *Sunday Tribune*, 23 July 2006.
62. J. Cusack, 'Suspect Garda recorded conversation – report', *Irish Times*, 25 July 2000.
63. C. Cleary, 'Gardaí gave witness bogus expenses to appear in court', *Sunday Tribune*, 23 July 2000.
64. S. Smyth, 'Donegal scandal will damage the Garda Síochána', *Sunday Tribune*, 9 July 2000.
65. K. Brophy, *Irish Examiner*, 24 July 2000.
66. As an internal report it was not submitted to the Minister for Justice.
67. J. Cusack, 'Statement follows sixteen-month internal Garda inquiry', *Irish Times*, 27 July 2000.
68. C. Coulter and D. Coghlan, 'Law Society stands by claim lawyers' phones were tapped', *Irish Times*, 28 August 2000.
69. L. Allen and S. Mara, 'Clear and present danger', *Magill*, 29 August 2000.
70. K. Brophy, 'Gardaí threatened to search phone data: Howlin', *Irish Examiner*, 30 August 2000.
71. Anon, 'Transfer of Donegal inquiry Gardaí deferred', *Irish Independent*, 10 September 2000.
72. D. Doyle and R. Andrews, 'Forced to account', *Sunday Tribune*, 17 September 2000.
73. Ibid.
74. Minister for Justice O'Donoghue, Dáil Éireann, 5 October 2000, vol. 523, col. 1127.
75. Ibid. This would turn out to concern the allegations made by Garda Tina Fowley.
76. Ibid at col. 1129.
77. See generally, Walsh, *The Irish Police*. The Garda Síochána Complaints Board had itself called for the board to be replaced by an independent mechanism in its Annual Report for 2000.
78. Shatter, Dáil Éireann, 23 May 2001, vol. 536, col. 1414.
79. K. Brophy, 'Rough justice from the law of the land', *Irish Examiner*, 22 November 2000.
80. *The People (DPP) v. Shortt (No 2)* [2002] 2 IR 696.
81. K. Brophy, 'Gardaí face inquiry into corruption allegations', *Irish Examiner*, 2 January 2001; J. Cusack, 'Government considers inquiry plan on policing in Donegal', *Irish Times*, 24 January 2001.
82. T. Brady, 'DPP decision due on Garda corruption allegations', *Irish Independent*, 22 January 2001.
83. J. Cusack, 'Government considers inquiry plan on policing in Donegal', *Irish Times*, 24 January 2001.
84. Anon, 'McBrearty considers taking private criminal action against Gardaí', *Donegal News*, 26 January 2002.
85. S. Mara, 'New suspect revealed in Barron killing', *Sunday Tribune*, 28 January 2001.
86. An autopsy was conducted in the hospital but not by the State pathologist. Dr Barry was not a forensic pathologist and did not claim any expertise in the area. The norm would be for the State pathologist to conduct an autopsy where it is suspected that death was not by natural means (I/4.62).
87. Anon, 'No decision yet on whether to hold public inquiry into Donegal Gardaí', *Irish Times*, 8 February 2001.
88. C. Cleary, 'Civilian to be charged after probe of Garda misconduct', *Sunday Tribune*, 25 February 2001.

89. K. Brophy, 'Fine Gael fears corrupt Gardaí will walk free', *Irish Examiner*, 21 March 2001.
90. O'Donoghue, 23 May 2001, vol. 536 col. 1413.
91. Ibid.
92. Shatter, 23 May 2001, vol. 536, col. 1416.
93. T. Brady, 'Four Gardaí facing disciplinary action after inquiry', *Irish Independent*, 8 June 2001.
94. Ibid.
95. A. Guidera, 'Garda probe leads to exhumation', *Irish Independent*, 6 July 2001.
96. Anon, 'Dawn exhumation of Barron's body', *Donegal News*, 6 July 2001.
97. T. Judge, 'Gardaí receive Barron autopsy report', *Irish Times*, 12 October 2001.
98. Anon, 'Donegal publican refused leave to address court though State withdraws final case', *Irish Times*, 5 September 2001.
99. K. Donaghy, 'Pressure mounts for inquiry into "Garda corruption"', *Irish Independent*, 2 November 2001.
100. T. Judge, 'Barron case Gardaí to investigate locals over hit-and-run', *Irish Times*, 2 November 2001.
101. Shatter and Howlin, Dáil Éireann, 13 November 2001, vol. 543, col. 1299.
102. O'Donoghue, ibid, col. 1302.
103. Shatter, ibid, col. 1299.
104. Editorial, 'Investigating the Garda', *Irish Times*, 14 November 2001.
105. M. Murray, 'Garda corruption a national blight', *Sunday Business Post*, 2 December 2001.
106. 20 November 2001, vol. 544, col. 581.
107. Ibid., col. 592.
108. Shatter, 20 November 2001, vol. 544, col. 588.
109. Howlin, ibid., col. 595.
110. Higgins, 21 November 2001, vol. 544, col. 1015.
111. Gildea, 21 November 2001, vol. 544, col. 1005. These allegations later sparked a two-day boycott of the Dáil by the opposition: Editorial, 'Dangerous political games', *Irish Times*, 23 November 2001.
112. Aired on 27 November 2001.
113. L. Reid, H. McGee and C. Cleary, *Sunday Tribune*, 25 November 2001.
114. Ibid.
115. 2 December 2001.
116. V. Browne, 'Higgins' case against the Donegal Gardaí', *Irish Times*, 5 December 2001.
117. Anon, 'McBrearty tells court three senior Gardaí conspired against him', *Irish Times*, 23 November 2001.
118. O'Donoghue, 20 November 2001, vol. 544, col. 598.
119. Anon, 'Garda sergeant remanded on arms charge', *Irish Times*, 7 December 2001.
120. J. Guerin, 'More cases to follow on from Barron death probe', *Irish Independent*, 20 January 2002.
121. O'Donoghue, Dáil Éireann, 22 March 2002, vol. 551, col. 3.
122. F. Sheehan, 'Corruption claims spark new inquiry into Gardaí', *Irish Examiner*, 6 February 2002.
123. O'Donoghue, Dáil Éireann, 22 March 2002, vol. 551, col. 5.
124. S.2 Tribunals of Inquiry (Evidence) Act 2002.
125. S.3 2002 Act.
126. Shatter, Dáil Éireann, 22 March 2002, vol. 551, col. 15.
127. Shatter, ibid, alleged that in appointing Murphy to investigate, the Minister had expected that inquiry to take six months, by which time he would be out of office.
128. Editorial, 'Inquiring into the Garda', *Irish Times*, 13 February 2002.
129. Shatter, Dáil Éireann, 22 March 2002, vol. 551, col. 15.
130. Howlin, ibid., cols 19/20.
131. *McBrearty v. Morris* and another, unreported judgement of the High Court, 13 May 2003, *White v. Morris* [2007] IEHC 107.
132. J. Guerin, 'Family seek new Barron death probe', *Irish Independent*, 17 February 2002.
133. Dáil Éireann, 28 March 2002, vol. 551, col. 926.

134. There is no formal process for the writing of terms of reference though the Law Reform Commission *Report on Tribunals of Inquiry* outlines a nine-stage process which involves drafting by the sponsoring Department, review by the Attorney General, party whips, interest groups and the government before being presented to the House: p.35.
135. Reynolds, Dáil Éireann, 22 March 2002, vol. 551, col. 19.
136. O'Donoghue, Dáil Éireann, 28 March 2002, vol. 551, col. 927.
137. Shatter, Dáil Éireann, 28 March 2002, vol. 551, col. 933.
138. O'Donoghue, 28 March 2002, vol. 551, col. 942.
139. Howlin, ibid., col. 938.
140. Higgins, ibid., col. 940.
141. C. Cleary and H. McGee, 'Donegal Gardaí allegation families to opt out of inquiry', *Sunday Tribune*, 21 April 2002.
142. C. O'Brien, 'Government slammed over McBrearty probe', *Irish Examiner*, 6 May 2002. Though an application was made, no information can be found on how this progressed. It presumably was declared inadmissible at committee stage.
143. Costello, 26 November 2002, vol. 558, col. 85.
144. Costello, ibid., col. 87.
145. Ibid., col. 91.
146. Higgins, ibid., col. 93.
147. McDowell, ibid., col. 97.
148. Ibid., col. 86.
149. Ibid., col. 96.
150. Rabbitte, ibid., col. 104.
151. The payments had been made in 1996 and the tribunal was established in February 1997.
152. 16 October 1984, vol. 352, col. 2399.
153. MacCarthaigh, *Accountability in Irish Parliamentary Politics*, pp.211–12.
154. Drapier, 'Flaky week for coalition in face of united opposition', *Irish Times*, 24 November 2001.
155. D. Dixon, 'Police governance and official inquiry', in Gilligan and Pratt, *Crime, Truth and Justice*, p.126.

Chapter Three

The Findings

Justice Frederick Morris opened the Tribunal on 15 July 2002 and over the subsequent six years sat for 686 days of hearings. The eighth and final report was delivered in October 2008. At the opening hearing Justice Morris divided the terms of reference into modules,[1] breaking each down into component parts and outlining the issues it would seek to clarify and facts it would seek to establish. Expressing his condolences to the Barron family, he emphasised that it was not the function of the Tribunal to determine who caused the death of Mr Barron.[2] Counsel for the Tribunal[3] assisted Justice Morris in the preliminary investigation, which was reviewed in the opening statement of counsel to the Tribunal. This was over 500 pages in length and took ten days to deliver in November 2002. Hearings of the Tribunal then began and, between June 2004 and October 2008, eight reports were published totalling over 4,000 pages. What follows is a synopsis and analysis of the findings of those reports. The extent of misconduct outlined in the reports and what can be extrapolated regarding policing in Ireland more broadly will be considered at the end of the chapter. How these findings were responded to and how they influenced reforms to police accountability will be the subject of later chapters.

REPORT ONE: THE EXPLOSIVES FINDS[4]

The first report of the Tribunal, submitted to government in early July 2004 and published on the sixteenth of that month, dealt with the allegations that Gardaí were involved in the planting of explosives finds in Donegal. Sheenagh McMahon, the estranged wife of Garda Noel McMahon, came forward during the Carty inquiry and spoke of how she observed her husband storing what he claimed to be bomb-making equipment in their garage. She gave details of how he, with Inspector Lennon, had been manufacturing and planning hoax IRA bomb finds with local woman Adrienne McGlinchey.

In 1988 Adrienne McGlinchey befriended local Gardaí in Letterkenny who visited her family's restaurant during night shifts. Motivated by mischief, she passed on rumours she had heard relating to the IRA, giving Gardaí the impression that she had some association with the group. She was considered a 'useful, but low-grade informer'.[5] Three years later, she fell out with her family following an arrest in which she was questioned by Garda McMahon. She moved to Buncrana with Yvonne Devine, a young friend. Ms McGlinchey claimed that Garda McMahon sought her out to assist with inquiries concerning the movements of the Provisional IRA.[6] She was to pretend to be a member of the Provisional IRA and act as his informer. She claimed that he threatened her with arrests for past behaviour if she did not co-operate. To ensure her credibility among fellow officers Garda McMahon supplied her with bullets, tripods, rockets, balaclavas, angle grinders and so on,[7] or money and plans to build them. She was seen in possession of bullets by a Guard in December 1991. In August 1992, it was reported by Miss Devine that Adrienne had been kidnapped by members of the Provisional IRA. Within the policing district, she began to be considered McMahon's informer, which protected her from prosecution after arrests for an assortment of questionable behaviour.[8]

She alleged that Garda McMahon made her grind nitrate-based fertiliser in her flat. She claimed Inspector Lennon soon joined in the charade. She was connected by the Tribunal to six incidents involving the discovery of what appeared to be bomb-making equipment on both sides of the border over a ten-month period, all supposedly IRA bomb finds; September 1993 – Strabane, Northern Ireland; November 1993 – Ardchicken, near Donegal town; January 1994 – a roundabout at the border crossing at Bridgend; March 1994 – Ms McGlinchey's apartment; June 1994 – two finds at the McGlinchey family property; July 1994 – two farm outhouses at Rossnowlagh.[9] The officers involved were highly praised for each of the finds.[10]

Damningly, the Tribunal concluded in relation to the search of her apartment,

> … that the materials found by the search team … were materials which were … under the control of Detective Garda Noel McMahon and Detective Inspector Lennon for use as and when required by them for the purpose of planting them for later discovery in locations in Donegal … The Tribunal is satisfied beyond doubt

that these materials were intended for use in hoax finds of explosive materials orchestrated by Ms Adrienne McGlinchey, Detective Garda McMahon and Detective Inspector Lennon.[11]

On the Rossnowlagh find in particular, Justice Morris concluded: 'Detective Garda McMahon was involved in the preparation of materials and the movement of materials from the house and shed at Rossnowlagh. Detective Inspector Lennon was involved in organising this hoax with him.'[12] The misconduct did not end with these officers. The finds were not properly investigated or reported to headquarters. Garda procedure required detailed reports to be submitted to Garda headquarters on all finds; this was generally not done. Border Superintendent Denis Fitzpatrick was considered to be 'gravely at fault' for this.[13] Chief Superintendent Ginty was considered to be negligent in respect of these finds. The Tribunal identified further incidents in which Chief Superintendent Ginty failed to implement proper Garda procedure which, if followed, would have exposed the sham. The problem, therefore, was not a few rotten apples, but equally negligent oversight and management.

Ms McGlinchey's membership of the IRA should have been questioned earlier and, if done, this would likely have exposed the finds as hoax.[14] When some members of the Gardaí expressed concerns to Chief Superintendent Ginty, they were ignored. The failure to review her case involved a serious neglect of duty on the part of those officers involved. At one stage when a uniformed member suggested how she should be handled, Garda McMahon threatened him with a gun, an incident not recorded or reported by Superintendent Lennon, who was present at the time, despite being a breach of the disciplinary code.[15] This was categorised by Morris as abuse of a colleague, misuse of a firearm and a 'landmark' incident which underscored the relationship between Lennon and McMahon.[16] Despite their protestations to the contrary, the Tribunal held that McMahon and Lennon did not believe McGlinchey was an informer. Their evidence was considered 'bizarre', 'extraordinary', 'beyond credibility' and 'a tissue of lies': 'The story which Detective Garda McMahon and Superintendent Lennon have told the Tribunal has all the hallmarks of an invention cobbled together as a cover-up for their extraordinary activities.'[17]

The fault did not solely lie with those officers: 'The Tribunal has reluctantly been forced to come to the conclusion that there was corruption among a small number of individuals within the Donegal division but it has also been compelled to find that this situation could not have flourished and gone unchecked had the leadership of the Donegal division not behaved negligently and slothfully.'[18] Justice Morris criticised the promotion of officers who 'were unwilling or unable to give their vocation the energy and aptitude that it demands'.[19] Other officers were also criticised for failing 'to ask ordinary and obvious questions'.[20] Overall in relation to this module of the Tribunal, Justice Morris concluded:

> The scheme of deception could not have succeeded but for the negligent manner in which the Donegal division was being managed at the time. If even one event had been properly looked at by senior management, this hoax would have been uncovered. If Ms McGlinchey had even been prosecuted in respect of one of the criminal offences she committed from 1991 to 1994, she would have been stopped in her tracks. Detective Inspector Lennon and Detective Garda McMahon could operate in the confidence that their 'successes' would not be investigated.[21]

The scale and nature of misconduct, negligence and corruption found to be prevalent in the Donegal district is disturbing. The abuse of the security context in the planting of bomb finds to appear as IRA activities adds a particularly sinister element to the reports. It is clear that McMahon and Lennon believed that their activities would not be discovered, and in terms of internal oversight mechanisms they were correct. Their continued denial of involvement even at the Tribunal shows the depth of the blue wall in this division. That others attempted to question the handling of Adrienne McGlinchey and were threatened with a gun exposes not just bullying but a completely unacceptable attitude to policing.

The report produced an extensive list of recommendations which ran to nearly fifty pages. These related to a number of key issues including, among others: the role of Garda headquarters in investigations; reporting to headquarters; the use of informants; accountability of officers and a number of other issues such as recruitment, promotion and discipline. Of particular concern was the management of the Donegal division through Garda headquarters. Justice Morris called for a requirement to be placed on superintendents, chief superintendents and assistant commissioners to periodically review files of inspectors, sergeants and Gardaí.[22] He called for a change to management culture by inserting 'a barrier of distrust'. Management should assume 'that fault, deceit, negligence and cover-up will happen'.[23] A new system of review for 'important cases', such as explosives finds, was required as a matter of urgency.[24] While not examining the role of the Department of Justice, Justice Morris called on the Department to address 'the structural deficits and deficiencies' identified in the reports.[25]

Morris called for a formatted document for reporting of major incidents to Garda Headquarters to assist members to submit truthful accounts, including all key details.[26] HQ needs to take an ongoing interest in major incidents with follow-up communications set as a minimum requirement, which should form part of the case file.[27] A new system for handling informants is required, involving: a manual for all members; proper training; refresher courses; an independent audit of the policy and its implementation by someone with the necessary security clearance; periodic audits; a compulsory system of registration of informants and assessments of informants who would have individual files maintained and updated. Crime and security needs to be resourced sufficiently. Failure to comply with procedures should merit disciplinary action.

The blue wall which Justice Morris encountered necessitated that the previously repealed requirement of officers to maintain a journal be reinstated.[28] These should not be destroyed without approval from an assistant commissioner and should be regularly inspected. Added to this was the need to impose an obligation on members to account for any action taken as a member or while on duty, breach of which should be an offence meriting dismissal.[29]

REPORT TWO: THE BARRON INVESTIGATION

The second report, nearly 700 pages, published in June 2005, examined the investigation of Mr Barron's death and extortion calls made to the Peoples family. At 01.05 hours, 14 October 1996, the Garda Communications Centre was notified by a resident that Mr Barron was injured on a roadside in Raphoe, County Donegal and that an ambulance had been called. The on-duty Garda in Raphoe, Garda Mulligan, could not be contacted as he had, the Tribunal found, left the station to consume alcohol in a public house with Garda O'Dowd, in breach of disciplinary regulations.[30] The Gardaí in Lifford, the next closest town, refused to respond until they had finished meal-break,[31] by which time the ambulance had arrived and they had been phoned again. They did not arrive at the scene until 01.35, after the ambulance had removed Mr Barron from the road and brought him to hospital, where he died on arrival, a fact described by Justice Morris as 'scandalous'.[32]

It was raining heavily when Gardaí arrived at the scene. A search found nothing beyond a large quantity of blood and a decision was made not to preserve the scene, contrary to Garda codes. One officer found a piece of skin with hair attached but did not preserve it. A scenes of crime officer was not called to attend the scene to conduct a forensic search, as required by Garda codes. The one Garda notebook in which a description was made of the scene was missing when requested, a fact the Tribunal viewed with 'great suspicion'.[33] Justice Morris identified fifteen faults in how the Gardaí present responded at the scene.[34]

The hospital pathologist, not the State pathologist as would be the norm in suspicious cases, examined the remains and determined the cause of death to be head injuries. By his own admission, he was not sufficiently expert to express an opinion as to how these injuries were caused. He believed the injuries were caused by a blunt instrument and could not definitively say they were caused by a car. It was claimed by Gardaí that the State pathologist reviewed this report and determined that a further examination was not necessary.[35] The State pathologist had no recollection of this at the Tribunal[36] and stated that he is contractually obliged to attend an examination if requested by the Gardaí. As outlined previously, it was not until July 2001 that a State autopsy was conducted and concluded that death was most likely the result of a hit-and-run accident.

Rumours circulating at Mr Barron's wake that he had been murdered were quickly given credence by the chief superintendent, who formulated the belief that the murder had been committed by two cousins, Frank McBrearty Jnr and Mark McConnell. When an incident room was established a witness, 'Mr X', came forward and told how he saw the two men coming from the scene and further witnesses provided statements saying the two men 'were behaving very strangely on the night of the death'.[37] This was reinforced by a number of other statements from local residents.[38] However, some statements were later withdrawn and others were discredited. Mr X was revealed as Robert Noel McBride, a Garda informer who was coerced into making a statement which was then doctored by the Gardaí involved, Garda Collins and Garda O'Dowd. This was 'grossly improper and constituted grave misconduct'.[39] Justice Morris went so far as to say it was 'corruptly obtained', with the effect that the subsequent arrests, for which this was the basis, were unlawful.

A month after the death, Michael and Charlotte Peoples, residents in the area, received five phone calls from a man claiming to know that Michael had killed Mr Barron and demanded a sum of £1,000 to keep quiet. Mr Peoples went to the meeting place in order to see if he could identify the caller, action interpreted by Gardaí as indicative of involvement in the murder and he was arrested. Four of the calls came from a previously convicted criminal, William O'Doherty, a Garda informer, and the final came from the house of Garda John O'Dowd. The Tribunal found Garda O'Dowd, assisted by Superintendent Lennon, fabricated statements 'with a view to diverting the Garda investigation' into the calls.[40]

On 4 December 1996, Mr McBrearty Jnr, Mr McConnell and Mr Peoples were detained in Garda custody on suspicion of murder.[41] It was alleged they met, travelled the distance to the crime scene, committed the murder, cleaned up and returned to work at Mr McBrearty's father's nightclub in the space of fifteen minutes. Evidence available to the Gardaí prior to the detention of these men indicated that at the time that Mr Barron was hit/attacked, Mr McBrearty Jnr was expelling someone from the nightclub. Justice Morris found that this investigation was 'corrupt in its leadership. It was prejudiced, tendentious and utterly negligent in the highest degree'.[42]

The Tribunal found that the immediate response in the investigation was a 'catalogue of errors' and 'is indicative of the general undermining of morale within An Garda Síochána'.[43] The response of superiors to this initial response was 'shockingly inadequate and dilatory'. Where disciplinary action should have been taken, 'the matter was swept under the carpet'. The ability of Gardaí to ignore requests from superiors to account for their actions was exceptionally evident in this module. Garda Mulligan refused to divulge, for a number of years, the fact that he was in a pub while on duty.[44] Garda O'Dowd lied about the extortion calls.

The investigation of Mr McBrearty Jnr and Mr McConnell without evidence represented 'gross negligence on the part of senior officers and other members'.[45] There was a 'total failure of objectivity'. This 'emotionally driven' investigation, characterised by 'tunnel vision', meant Gardaí failed to examine other avenues. The failure to follow established procedures was at the heart of the case: 'Had there been a postmortem examination conducted by a forensic pathologist in the days immediately after the late Mr Barron's death, no murder investigation would have been launched.'[46] The investigation itself proceeded with the unwavering belief in the guilt of the two men, to the extent that suggestions of alternative possibilities were dismissed without consideration, questionable witness statements were accepted in blind faith and suspects were unacceptably interrogated. Justice Morris was forced to conclude: 'It is impossible not to see that negligence of the most astonishing kind, amounting to recklessness of the highest degree characterised the investigation.'[47] This did not just involve the investigating officers but all superiors: Chief Superintendent Denis Fitzpatrick, Superintendent John Fitzgerald, Detective Superintendent Joseph Shelley and Superintendent John McGinley all received scathing criticism from the Tribunal. Similar to the previous reports, numerous points can be identified at which escalation could have been prevented.

The recommendations in this report spanned eleven different issues and included a reprint of the recommendations of the first module. Justice Morris recommended the establishment of a whistleblowers' charter and a review of the Garda Bill (as it was at that point) to ensure it took account of the concerns in this report. While action was being taken in relation to the first report, he was concerned there had not been a strengthening of the Internal Audit Section, particularly with members of other police forces. A 'fresh approach' in this area was required, along with 'experience, dynamism and honesty'.[48] To facilitate this, the entrance requirements for members from other police services should be amended.

The lack of feedback to HQ on progress and response to HQ advice was noted as the 'most clearly-identified problem'.[49] Justice Morris felt that a trained analyst could have provided great assistance and objective analysis. A discipline of crime analysis should be developed within the force, staffed by civilian analysts.

Justice Morris noted that the first report of the Tribunal had not been debated in the Oireachtas and called for a debate of both reports, which concerned a matter of 'urgent public importance'.[50] He felt it should not be possible to put a request for an exhumation order on hold once the application had been made to the Minister and that once a request has been made the Department should actively follow up on this and question the reasons for the order.[51]

In addition to the need for officers' journals, Justice Morris added that conferences should have a designated note-taker keeping a clear and reasonable account, forming part of the case papers.[52] There should be a revision of the disciplinary measures to make them more stream-lined[53] and a new means of removing officers should be considered.[54]

Another issue which arose in this module was the delay in Telecom Éireann responding to Garda queries of phone records. Justice Morris recommended that the Communications Regulator (ComReg) should make it a base requirement of future licences that Garda queries be answered within five days, twenty-four hours for urgent matters.[55] Failure to comply should result in a forfeiture of the licence. The Department should also consider the establishment of an independent databank that operators would be obliged to subscribe to and where records of traffic would be held. An independent body could assist the Gardaí in queries.[56] Justice Morris also believed it would be helpful for a super-intendent to be able to establish specialist units on a temporary basis if necessary for the policing of an area. That superintendent should also have the power to transfer a member who would benefit from experience in another division.[57]

By way of an afterword, Justice Morris stated that this report alone could not undo the harm done to the various families concerned but that 'it is hoped that with this reporting of what has occurred, that the poisoning by hatred of sections of the community will begin to be brought to an end.'[58] Finally, Justice Morris called for a new system of promotion and for recruitment from ethnic and religious minorities, which would break down the monolithic attitudes and prevent atti-tudes such as Garda Leonard's, who declared 'you don't hang your own', from being expressed.[59] When anyone is posted to a new position it should be on condition of a minimum period of service in that post so as to benefit their colleagues and the organisation.[60]

REPORT THREE: ARREST AND DETENTION OF THE PEOPLES (THE SILVER BULLET MODULE)

The third report of the Tribunal dealt with the arrest and detention of Mark McConnell on 1 October 1998 and Michael Peoples on 6 May 1999, for allegedly threatening Bernard Conlon for giving evidence against the McBreartys in a prosecution for breach of their liquor licence. At the heart of this module was the relationship between Conlon, a Garda informer, and Detective Sergeant John White. The two men had met in Raphoe in July 1997 when Conlon complained to Sergeant White at not having been provided with a meal in Frankie's (the McBreartys' establishment), as required under the licence.[61] It was alleged that Conlon and White conspired to build a case against Frank McBrearty for breaches of liquor licence regulations. The suggestion was that Mr Conlon agreed to remain on the premises on 30 August 1997, drinking after hours, so that Detective Sergeant White could 'find him on' and prosecute the McBreartys. A week after this occurred, as planned, Conlon attended Sligo Garda station, where Nicholson, the arresting officer, was based, and made a statement in relation to the event.

Justice Morris held that Bernard Conlon was 'found on' the premises on 30 August on the instruction of Garda Nicholson, who had been asked by White to arrange this.[62] Justice Morris did not believe that Conlon's decision to provide a statement was made out of a sense of civic duty, but that it was part 'of a plan to use Bernard Conlon as an agent against Frank McBrearty'.[63] As payment, White and Nicholson arranged 'inflated' expenses payments for attendance at court on over twenty days and submitted seven forged work certificates.[64] Their determination to gather the evidence necessary to secure a conviction led to a complete disregard for policing standards.

Mr Conlon claimed that during the course of the trial, two men threatened him with a silver bullet at his home on 20 July 1998. He later identified these men as Mr McConnell and Mr Peoples, who were arrested. Mr Conlon also claimed that a letter of bribery was sent to him by Willie Flynn, Mr McBrearty's private investigator, in the hope of preventing him from testifying. Conlon claimed to the Carty inquiry that he had been put up to making these claims by Sergeant White, for which White was later charged and acquitted. When it emerged that White had known of Mr McConnell's alibi, it was found that this was not properly investigated and not relayed to officers who were investigating the case.[65] Justice Morris could not, however, find that White had encouraged Mr Conlon to make the silver bullet allegations due to a lack of corroborating evidence.[66]

In relation to the arrests of McConnell and Peoples, instigated by Superintendent Lennon and Detective Sergeant White, Justice Morris found that: 'It is likely that because their actions and decisions were under attack and scrutiny elsewhere, they were happy enough that trouble should be caused and/or exist for Mark McConnell and Michael Peoples in relation to the Bernard Conlon allegations. This is shocking.'[67]

The Tribunal held that the decision of Lennon not to call Conlon as a witness at the prosecution of McConnell and Peoples indicated that he knew Conlon had been used as an agent of the investigating Gardaí.[68] In doing this, Lennon's 'tactics were calculated to suppress the emergence of the true facts concerning the use of Bernard Conlon ... contrary to his obligation as a prosecutor to the court and improper'.[69] Saving face for An Garda Síochána was more important than pursuing wrongful prosecutions. When it appeared nonetheless that Conlon would be called as a defence witness the following day, White and Nicholson met him for the purpose of rehearsing questions and ensuring that he kept to the account in his statement. In relation to the evidence given in court that day, which aligned with the prepared statement, Morris said: 'Both their behaviour and Bernard Conlon's in the procurement and giving of this evidence was scandalous and calculated to undermine the integrity and fairness of the trial at which it was given. It was disgraceful conduct. I am shocked.'[70] A miscarriage of justice could easily have occurred in this case had it, as will be seen in the discussion of the seventh report, not later been dropped by the DPP.

Arrested on 21 March, White entered 'a series of lies' on the custody record. Nicholson's evidence to the Tribunal was described as 'a further example of the deceitful and underhand way in which he dealt with the tribunal and the Garda inquiry'.[71] He came in for further criticism, having named an officer who was now deceased as having supplied receipts for Conlon's witness expenses: 'That [he] has abused this man's name in death and tried to hide behind him is disgraceful.'[72] Nicholson pleaded guilty to three counts of uttering forged documents in July 2000. Of particular concern was White's response when questioned by the Carty inquiry on this matter, which involved refusing to answer questions, seeking to tape the interview, consulting with a solicitor and mentioning previously taped interviews. Such 'insubordination ... cannot be allowed to pass without sanction if discipline is to be maintained in the force'.[73]

Discovering the truth was a difficult task in this module as 'unhappily many lies were told to the Tribunal', lengthening its work significantly.[74] White had concocted 'extraordinary and sinister' lies in relation to the actions of colleagues whom he claimed were setting him up.[75] The blue wall of silence provided an almost insurmountable stumbling block, as did the complete disregard for criminal procedure by the Gardaí, of both senior and junior ranks.

The recommendations in this short report involved a reiteration of the need to streamline disciplinary proceedings, the need to chronicle the use of civilians as Garda agents and to produce regulations on their use, and to urgently consider changes in ethics, training and composition of the force to prevent these from reoccurring and to enhance the effectiveness of An Garda Síochána.

REPORT FOUR: ARDARA ATTACK

The fourth, and shortest, report concerned the investigation of an arson attack on a telecommunications mast in Ardara, Donegal in November 1996, which resulted in the arrest and prosecution of three individuals. Locals were protesting at a communication mast's site where the provider was to be changed, with the result that local residents would have to pay for a service that previously was free. Equipment was moved onto the site by way of a 'sleight of hand' whereby the protestors were tricked into leaving the site for negotiations, increasing the intensity of pickets. Nails and barbed wire were placed on the approach road to prevent Gardaí from reaching the site. Access could only be gained through the Shovlins' land, which was gated. Gardaí had access to the necessary keys. On occasion these locks were filled with glue. Garda patrols were conducted a number of times a day but an arson attack on 7 November 1996 caused £50,000 worth of damage.[76]

Sergeant White was brought to Ardara the following day to investigate the attack and adopted a confrontational approach. He was found by Justice Morris to have explored the Shovlin lands and removed a pot of some substance, which he thought might be glue, from a shed.[77] White was not truthful to the Tribunal on this matter. A number of days later, investigating officers, in the absence of White, obtained search warrants for the Diver and Shovlin properties in the belief that equipment used in the arson attack would be found. On White's return he complained of the relatively brief detention periods provided under the legislation used for the warrants. He had hoped to exercise powers under the Offences Against the State Act, which attracted longer periods of detention. The warrants were not used.

When the mast was being replaced on 19 November workers noticed a crude hoax bomb taped to the side. Justice Morris did not accept that this was placed there by protestors, who in the main had been peaceful.[78] The reaction of Sergeant White, the first on the scene, did not involve any of the activities which Justice Morris would have expected from a Guard. On return to the station, while the device was being packaged to be sent to the forensic laboratory, White tampered with it, removing a teaspoon of powder, and conducted a 'test' in the yard to see if it was explosive.[79] The other investigating officers should have expressed concerns to senior officers. Justice Morris accepted their explanations that they were concerned at the consequences of making such allegations and 'that structures of An Garda Síochána did not then allow for confidential communications to be made'.[80] Three arrests were made that night under the Offences Against the State Act.

The Tribunal found that the evidence of White on this matter was 'so riddled with inconsistencies' that it could not be accepted.[81] Sergeant White was responsible for the device being on the mast, either having put it there himself or having had it done, in an effort to secure arrests of certain individuals under the Offences Against the State Act 1939.

In the recommendations Morris restated his call for the establishment of a whistleblowers system. He pointed to the high standards which should be required for anyone to serve as a superintendent and stated that at no time should any individual appointed to this rank be 'overawed' by someone serving under them, as happened with Sergeant White. Again, the low number of members from minorities groups was deemed in need of redress. Continuous training and periodic temporary transfers to areas of specialisations were suggested as a method to prevent these events from reoccurring. This was also related to the noted need to increase experience in Donegal following the resignations occurring in light of the Tribunal.[82]

REPORT FIVE: BURNFOOT ARRESTS

The fifth report concerned the arrest and detention of seven members of the Traveller community in Burnfoot, County Donegal on 23 May 1998. Hearings for this module were held in private as criminal proceedings against Sergeant White were ongoing. The Tribunal was forced to engage in a process of 'peeling away the layers of deception that have been falsely laid over an essentially simple but repulsive series of events'.[83] The body of a Mr Fitzmaurice was found in his home in Mayo in May 1998. The investigation produced numerous suspects, including members of the Travelling community who had moved to Burnfoot, Donegal. The suggestion came from Sergeant White, who claimed to have received this information from informants who also told him these Travellers were in possession of a shotgun. On 22 May White made arrangements to conduct a search of the site the next morning. A sawn-off shotgun was found and seven men were arrested. Three years later, Garda Kilcoyne stated that White had planted the gun the night before the search and that he had been present.[84]

The Tribunal found that White had received some information as to the involvement of these individuals in the death of Mr Fitzmaurice and as to possession of a weapon, although there was disagreement as to the exact nature of that information.[85] As regards the search itself, which no member took responsibility for authorising, the Tribunal held it was White's idea.[86] The Tribunal was satisfied that the night before the search White conveyed to Garda Kilcoyne the need to ensure that a gun was found at the site.[87] White alleged that he secured the necessary search warrants from Lennon that night. Justice Morris was not satisfied of the evidence on this and felt that either White had access to blank warrants signed by Lennon or, alternatively, that somewere issued subsequent to the search.[88] Not only is it highly disturbing that White would consider planting dangerous evidence, but that the warrant procedure, in place to act as a safeguard against this behaviour, could be so easily circumvented. That White knew it could be is most worrying.

During the search, one member of the camp asked to see a search warrant but none was produced. Seven men were unlawfully arrested. Each detainee made allegations of mistreatment in custody. The investigation of these allegations was seriously hampered by the delay in making the allegations and by the unwillingness of Gardaí 'to deviate from the party line' in their evidence.[89] Morris found it 'entirely unacceptable' that derogatory remarks were made about the culture of these individuals and that a number were shown autopsy photos of Mr Fitzmaurice.[90]

No file was prepared on this finding, a fact Morris declared to be 'unacceptable', that it would have been done if it was a legitimate policing operation, 'The fact that no such file was ever produced leads the Tribunal to conclude that the finding of the firearm was in a fact a charade designed to ensure that the Travellers were taken into custody where they would be amenable to questioning in relation to the murder of Mr Edward Fitzmaurice.'[91]

White was found to have falsified theories in an attempt to explain the location of the gun, on a hook two and a half feet off the ground, which was dangerous considering the presence of children, and impractical for a defence weapon.[92] The Tribunal was 'shocked' that the gun was not properly stored at the station for the best part of the day. The cartridges with the gun had been 'mislaid' since arrival at the Garda Technical Bureau and no satisfactory account was provided as to the whereabouts of the bag and clothes found with the gun. Thirty-nine original notes of interviews with the detainees that day had gone missing. While no finding could be made that they had been deliberately destroyed, the Tribunal was left with 'considerable unease in relation to Garda procedures'.[93]

When Sergeant White was arrested in June 2001 on suspicion of illegal possession of the firearm, three officers conspired to 'corruptly invent a story' in his defence.[94] This involved the making of allegations against two innocent members, implying they had confessed to planting the gun. That the serious misconduct of one officer would prompt others to blame innocent men evidences further the decayed state of trust and integrity within the force.

Beginning the section of recommendations, Justice Morris declared 'proper discipline has been lost from the Garda Síochána' and to ensure that the events in Donegal are not repeated a management structure needs to be restored to the force which emphasises 'strict compliance with orders and immediate accountability'.[95] To ensure that An Garda Síochána is not 'a playground for the mischievous', the disciplinary system needs to be revised and the employment discipline model might be appropriate for the force.[96] Justice Morris further pointed to the need to select the right people for management. Again, he called for all of the previous recommendations to be implemented to ensure the future of the Gardaí.

Meriting specific attention was the power of a superintendent to issue a search warrant under s.29 of the Offences Against the State Act 1939, which Morris viewed as an exceptional power requiring justification and which he did not believe, in this case, existed. With modern communication there was no reason why a warrant could not be secured from a judge in speedy enough time.[97] He called for the issuing authority to be informed of the execution or non-execution of the warrant.

The publication of this report was delayed due to the ongoing criminal prosecution of Sergeant White for possession of a firearm. This prosecution had caused these hearings to be held in private and had been significantly delayed by a judicial review against the case. Justice Morris commented on this delay,[98] calling for new case management structures to assist in the disposal of judicial reviews more efficiently, given their potential to delay the procedure of cases, and thereby neg-atively impact on the administration of justice.

The sixth report, released in May 2008 and arguably the most distress-ing of all the reports, dealt with the treatment of twelve persons in custody in the Barron investigation and ran to nearly 1,300 pages, necessitating three volumes. At the outset Justice Morris stressed how difficult the determination of truth had been in this module, with substantive discrepancies between Garda and complainant accounts of interviews. Many officers involved attempted 'to thwart inquiries', controls operating within the force were 'demonstrably weak' and the Complaints Board 'woefully inadequate'.[99] He stressed the potential 'catastrophic injustice' of wrongful arrest and abuse in custody,

> ... that unhealthy focus or tunnel vision in the course of the Barron investigation led to manufactured evidence, wrongful arrests and completely improper behaviour by Gardaí towards prisoners in their custody. It cheapened the presumption of innocence and undermined the truthful resolution of a very tragic case. It domi-nated the lives and struck at the reputation of two families ... it did serious damage to the reputation of An Garda Síochána and its integrity and professionalism. It contributed towards social division in the town of Raphoe.[100]

The report proceeds by considering the experiences of each individual in turn.

Michael Peoples was arrested on two separate occasions, 4 December 1996 and 6 May 1999. Mr Peoples provided the police with state-ments after the death of Mr Barron and the extortion phone calls. Inconsistencies emerged between his statement and those provided by others, and there was a particular question concerning a phone call made to the hospital from his home on the night of the accident. These issues were the basis for the first arrest, though could have been clarified without an arrest.[101] He was arrested at home at 8 a.m. for the murder of Mr Barron, having been contacted the previous night by someone claiming to be from the Forensic Department asking if he was free to meet the next day. Justice Morris found that this arrest was unlawful and the reasons provided 'weak to tendentious'.[102]

Peoples alleged that he suffered verbal abuse on the way to the station. Following an initial refusal, he had a ten-minute telephone consultation with his solicitor during the first interview. Mr Peoples was interviewed four times in custody. Interviews 2 and 4, conducted by Detective Inspector (DI) Keane and Garda Collins, elicited complaints of misconduct and verbal abuse. The second interview was aggressive from the moment it began:

> I wouldn't get possibly time to answer the question and he'd 'answer up you lying murdering bastard' and then he would go on to the next question and just keep repeating that ... I was sitting terrified ... it was a hateful, hateful situation to be in ... There was no threat of physical violence but I was waiting on it to happen.[103]

Photographs from Mr Barron's autopsy were mentioned in the fourth interview and Garda Collins left the room to get them. In his absence, DI Keane raised the leg of the chair, which Peoples interpreted as a threat, though Justice Morris did not believe it was meant as one.[104] He was threatened with being charged and told he would serve fifteen years for the crime. Overall, Justice Morris found that Garda Collins failed to give a truthful account of these interviews and his answers to questions concerning the postmortem photographs were 'tantamount to an obstruction'.[105] There exists just one page of notes covering these two interviews, lasting a total of four hours and fifteen minutes. Justice Morris doubted these were made during the interview. Procedure was breached by failing to read them to the detainee.

The second arrest in May 1999 should not have occurred and Justice Morris placed much of the blame on the failure of Donegal Gardaí to share information with the Sligo Gardaí, who were involved in the silver bullet allegations.[106] This arrest was characterised by humiliation, conducted publicly with a large Garda presence. Mr Peoples alleged he was shouted at in the car, that he was asked to sign a pre-prepared statement and that an identification parade was unfairly conducted. While Justice Morris did not uphold all of these complaints, he did accept that Mr Peoples may have genuinely believed 'something more sinister was afoot' and that this could be 'readily understood in light of the completely shocking and appalling behaviour of other Gardaí which he and his family had experienced'.[107] Justice Morris stressed the overall impact which the previous three years had had on Mr Peoples, stating that he had been left feeling 'frightened, isolated and dejected', and outlined the need for An Garda Síochána to understand the 'real human cost' of this behaviour, an impact which is 'all too easy to trivialise or ignore'.[108]

Róisín McConnell's arrest on 4 December 1996, as an accessory to murder, was unlawful as not only was there insufficient evidence to support the charge, but since she was accused of assisting her husband she fell under the marital exemption to the charge.[109] Her arrest lasted for twelve hours, and involved five interviews and visits from her mother and her solicitor. Mrs McConnell's experiences were described by the Tribunal as 'repulsive' and 'shocking'.[110] She was verbally abused in the car on the way to the station, which officers explained as a technique to test the waters. She was initially denied information on who was caring for her child. Denying her a phone-call to inquire on this matter was 'senseless' and 'deeply disturbing'.[111] The most substantial complaints arise from interviews conducted by Gardaí White and Dooley. She was verbally abused throughout and instructed not to smoke. She was told at times to stand and on one occasion she was 'shouldered' between the officers five or six times. She had photographs from Mr Barron's autopsy pushed close to her face. She was told that her husband had been unfaithful. She was called names, including Satan. She was told that she would be stabbed and they would spit on her grave. She was told that her son would be taken into care. The lights were switched on and off in the room. She claimed she was told to pray on her father's grave and that Garda White passed wind twice in front of her. Notes were not taken during this interview. The result of her treatment in custody was the need for hospitalisation within weeks due to mental illness. Justice Morris believed that some involved had hoped that her illness would prevent her from testifying and he praised her strength in giving evidence, concluding that the 'ultimate act of courage in upholding the truth has been that of Mrs Mc-Connell'.[112]

Mark McConnell, husband of Róisín, was arrested on three separate occasions, twice in relation to the murder (4 December 1996 and 25 January 1997) and once in relation to the silver bullet affair (1 October 1998). His first arrest was unlawful. Five officers attended and his child was present and distressed. A forensic examination of his car was conducted, for which Justice Morris found no legal power.[113] When Mr McConnell alleged in a phone call to his solicitor that he was being verbally and physically abused, his solicitor attended the station but was refused a consultation. It emerged that Gardaí had listened to Mark's phone-call with his solicitor, in breach of his rights.[114] Justice Morris found that while it may have been minor in nature, Mark was pushed during this first interview.[115]

The Tribunal expressed serious concern that the application for extension of the detention was made by the member in charge, Garda Leonard. This was 'entirely inappropriate' as the member in charge should at all times remain independent of the investigation, 'to ensure diligently that the custody regulations are applied'.[116] Garda Leonard also adopted a 'dismissive' attitude towards a complaint of assault.[117] Justice Morris found that no physical abuse occurred, but expressed concern at the lack of notes for parts of this interview. Most seriously, 'when notes became unavailable or "lost" there was no explanation required of the person whose responsibility it was to make and preserve the notes.'[118]

Mr McConnell described the fourth interview as being traumatic and stated that he was shown autopsy photos, kicked in the shins, pulled by the ear and hair, had fingers poked in his eyes, digs in his ribs and called a murderer. Significantly, he was in a position to describe the photos, which Justice Morris was 'satisfied' that he was shown. The evidence of interviewing officers was rejected on this detention.[119] Justice Morris held that those involved failed to comply with regulations concerning note-taking and that 'it is utterly unacceptable in any criminal investigation, but especially in a murder inquiry, that experienced investigators would show such disregard for the keeping of essential records.'[120] Moreover, the Tribunal found that Inspector McGinley created a bogus statement from Frank McBrearty Jnr to show Mr McConnell, in an effort to 'trick him into admitting his own involvement'.[121] Garda Fowley stated she saw McGinley practising Mr McBrearty Jnr's signature beforehand. In all, Justice Morris noted the difficulties which existed to even 'unravel who was present in the final interview', and does not believe that those officers involved were truthful, naming officers whose behaviour was 'unprofessional and shocking'.[122] Justice Morris went to great pains to express the unacceptability of the treatment of Mr McConnell:

> This arrest marked the commencement of a personal nightmare for Mr McConnell. It had the most serious, social and personal consequences for Mr McConnell ... Their lives were twice turned

upside down by the actions of An Garda Síochána and events over which they had no control. This must have been physically and mentally draining. It is disgraceful and shocking that Mark Mc-Connell, an innocent citizen, was subjected to these arrests and detentions and that he and his family have had to live under their shadow for in excess of ten years.[123]

He continued:

The senior rank and experience of the personnel involved convinced me that there was a deliberate flouting of Mr McConnell's rights as a detainee ... Behind the veneer of propriety suggested by the entries in the custody record, there was the raw reality of Garda ill-treatment and misconduct. It was encouraged and motivated by the unquestioning and unquestioned conviction by senior officers leading this inquiry that Mark McConnell was guilty of the murder of the late Richard Barron. They were entirely wrong.[124]

Mr McConnell was rearrested on 25 June 1997, an action which requires an application to be made to a judge under the Criminal Justice Act 1984, in which the superintendent swears on oath that further information has come to light. Detective Inspector Joe Shelley[125] presented the confession of Frank McBrearty Jnr, taken just five minutes after Mr McConnell's release in December, as the necessary evidence. Suspicions were emerging over Witness X's (McBride) statement, the basis for the first arrest, and Frank McBrearty Jnr was challenging the confession of 4 December. Justice Morris concluded that had the judge to whom this evidence was presented known of 'these shocking matters' he would not have authorised the second arrest, and it was therefore unlawful.[126]

Notes for these interviews could not be located, for which no-one was held to account.[127] Inducements were made, that if Mr McConnell verified Mr McBrearty Jnr's confession, assigning him a smaller role in the killing, he would receive a lighter sentence. He was told that, if he did not, then the Barron family would come after him and he would not receive Garda protection. These comments 'should not have been said'.[128] Justice Morris determined that the aim of this arrest was to put Frank's statement to Mark and gauge his response.

The third time Mr McConnell was arrested, on 1 October 1998, under the Offences Against the State Act, was in connection with the silver bullet incident. He was detained for forty-eight hours and interviewed thirteen times. An allegation of assault against Garda Joseph Foley was withdrawn by Mr McConnell the day after it was made. Justice Morris 'condemned' this allegation and found that it was made out of anger at his arrest.[129] Justice Morris did not uphold a claim that McConnell's leg was pushed off a chair but stated that whatever did happen 'was borne out of frustration or annoyance at what was perceived to be his arrogance'.[130] The Tribunal would not find that a gun was placed on the table at any point, as Mr McConnell alleged, especially as he had not made a complaint at the time.[131] In relation to his claim that his wedding ring had been taken from him, it was found that Mark had himself removed it while washing but that his reaction was 'indicative of the highly charged nature of the interviews'.[132] Justice Morris was most sympathetic to the fact that this was Mr McConnell's third unlawful arrest, each of which 'brought with it its own disruption of his work and his personal and social life' and that his wife was still recovering from her experiences.[133]

Edel Quinn, sister of Róisín McConnell and Katrina Brolly, was arrested on 4 December 1996 and charged with being an accessory after the fact. Her arrest was unlawful as her alleged actions did not amount to the offence charged. Her twelve-hour detention involved four interviews. Justice Morris accepted that these arrests 'changed her life for the worse', to the extent that she moved away from Raphoe.[134] During the interviews she was asked whether she had gone to confession, told that Róisín had confessed, asked if she wanted to see postmortem photos, told she would be blacklisted, called a liar, had her actions compared to individuals in the Veronica Guerin murder case, and threatened with fourteen years' imprisonment. The reference to confession was deemed by Justice Morris to be 'unnecessarily strident'. Overall Justice Morris was 'disturbed' by the efforts of Gardaí at 'sanitising the evidence'.[135] At times Gardaí challenged statements made by Edel Quinn when the conduct did not amount to improper or illegal treatment, stemming, Justice Morris found, 'from an uncertainty in the minds of An Garda Síochána as to what is and what is not acceptable when someone is in Garda custody'.[136] It is worrying that Gardaí would challenge evidence of acceptable conduct.

Charlotte Peoples was unlawfully arrested on 6 December 1996 as an accessory after the fact. She became very distressed during interviews as she could hear roaring and shouting emanating from the room where

Róisín, her sister, was being interviewed. She asked for something to be done. Sergeant Henry stated before the Tribunal that he raised this with the member in charge. Justice Morris expressed particular concern at his limited efforts to intervene, stating: 'It is only when experienced and honourable Gardaí stand back and do nothing of an effective nature that abuse of the kind which has been admitted in respect of Róisín McConnell can take place.'[137] When her mother attended the station to provide her with necessary medication she herself was treated rudely and refused a visit with her daughter by the member in charge. This was not in fact a decision for Garda Leonard to make; he should have consulted with the investigating officers. Further, he failed to record the request. Garda Leonard failed to ask Mrs Peoples if she wished to consult with a solicitor on the second occasion that her husband phoned inquiring about this, with the result that she did not speak with a solicitor during her twelve hours of detention. While there was no evidence of a 'calculated or devious motive ... they are yet again another example of a somewhat cavalier, and unfortunate, attitude on the part of Garda Leonard to the provisions of the custody regulations.'[138]

Frank McBrearty Jnr was arrested on two occasions: on 4 December 1996 on suspicion of murder and on 4 February 1997 on suspicion of assaulting Edmond Moss. This was a difficult section to examine due to the unwillingness of witnesses to tell the truth. Every statement of evidence in this sub-module was contested by every witness. Justice Morris described Mr McBrearty Jnr as 'a most truculent and difficult witness' who was at times 'belligerent, threatening abusive or sullen'.[139]

Justice Morris did not accept allegations from Mr McBrearty Jnr concerning the first arrest, that he was called a murderer in front of his children and physically and verbally abused on the way to the station,[140] that he had been pushed on arrival at the station,[141] that he was abused in early interviews[142] or that notes of the third interview were fabricated to support the confession made later.[143] Mr McBrearty Jnr denied that at the end of the fourth interview he said he would think about making a statement and that he proceeded to do so in the fifth interview. He claimed that he was assaulted in the course of these interviews,[144] a claim not upheld by Justice Morris, who accepted there was a change of tone from McBrearty Jnr in these interviews. Justice Morris determined that local Gardaí made efforts to distance themselves from the confession which was made in the fifth interview by denying the claims of Dublin Gardaí that a conference was held after the fourth interview.[145] Mr McBrearty Jnr was shown postmortem photos, verbally abused and treated inappropriately in the fifth interview but this was 'grossly exaggerated' by Mr McBrearty Jnr.[146] He was not shown a fake confession from Mark McConnell.

A confession was produced in that interview, signed by McBrearty Jnr. Four handwriting experts all agreed before the Tribunal that the statement was signed by Frank McBrearty Jnr and their evidence was not challenged. The chair expressed concern that the details of the confession reflected the line of questioning and the Garda theory that had been pursued in interviews earlier that day. He did not accept that McBrearty Jnr became contrite while providing the confession. Justice Morris considered four possible ways in which this confession came about and decided that it represented a crumbling of Mr McBrearty Jnr's will, rather than a voluntary confession as suggested by Gardaí. Mr McBrearty Jnr did not provide evidence on why he made this confession, but the conclusion was supported by how terrified he became when next arrested.[147]

Mr McBrearty Jnr was released as it was believed there was more investigating to be done before charging him. Justice Morris expressed concern that Gardaí were 'happy to rely upon' this false confession:

> The task which An Garda Síochána must set itself is to ensure that nobody in the future is put in this appalling position due to police deceit, negligence and tunnel vision … The personal pain and trauma to the victim of a false confession and their family and the damage done to their status in the community are enormous … An Garda Síochána must robustly embrace change.[148]

Frank McBrearty Jnr was prosecuted in 1997 for an assault on Edmond Moss which occurred on 30 December 1996, for which the trial judge directed the jury to return a verdict of not guilty. Justice Morris examined how this investigation was conducted by the Gardaí and found that, while everything which was done by the Gardaí was lawful and proper, he was 'unconvinced that their motivation was unconnected to their antipathy towards the accused'.[149] Gardaí may have used their discretion to target McBrearty Jnr in some way.

McBrearty Jnr's arrest on 4 February 1997 was alleged by Gardaí to have been impromptu, on his visit to the station, although the presence of a video camera to record it suggested otherwise.[150] McBrearty Jnr was distressed when his solicitor arrived, alleged assault and claimed he was going to hurt himself and blame the Gardaí. The solicitor raised his concerns to the member in charge, who failed to respond appropriately. The interrogation continued and Mr McBrearty Jnr, who was extremely distressed at this point, proceeded to bang his head against the wall a number of times, causing injury.[151] Garda O'Dowd's statement shows that, rather than intervene and prevent McBrearty Jnr causing injury, he opened the door to get someone else to witness what happened. A request of the solicitor for a suspension was refused. McBrearty Jnr continued to maintain that he had been assaulted and it was only in 2003 that he admitted that he had injured himself.

Video tape footage of the final interviews showing Mr McBrearty Jnr lying on the floor, silent throughout, was described by Justice Morris as 'disturbing', evidencing 'a scenario totally at variance with what should occur in a Garda station'.[152] Mr McBrearty Jnr was called names and ridiculed while lying on the floor. Sergeant White used the video camera without permission from a superior officer; this should not have happened.[153] As he was leaving the station, McBrearty Jnr was served with two notices of intention to prosecute for dangerous driving, a step Justice Morris believed was 'calculated to enflame an already difficult situation and it was at least provocative'.[154] The whole experience was 'indicative of an inappropriate zeal'.[155]

Mark Quinn was arrested on 4 December 1996 due to dissatisfaction with information in his initial statement, which could have been resolved without arrest. Justice Morris was highly critical of the note-taking on the decision to arrest Mark Quinn, and even more so of the failure to explain the decision in tribunal hearings: 'Rather than lift during the course of these hearings, the fog, which initially obscured what should have been a relatively simple process, became thicker and more impenetrable.'[156] The arrest itself was 'unnecessarily robust'.[157] Mr Quinn claimed he was told that members of the Murder Squad were going to interview him to get back for what happened in the 1980s when one of their colleagues became embroiled in allegations that he had bribed Frank McBrearty Snr in return for not raiding his premises. Justice Morris was not convinced this had been said to Quinn.[158] The detention period was marked by a failure of the Gardaí to keep accurate interview notes, and the failure to demand explanation for this 'suggests a culture of indifference to the proper application of the custody regulations'.[159] The statement in the legislation that failure to observe the regulations would not lead to criminal proceedings 'does little to engender a culture of observance of these regulations by Gardaí and probably militates against close compliance'.[160]

Quinn made a number of allegations of abuse, including the removal of his shoes for the entirety of the detention, being dragged, verbally abused, shown postmortem photos and physically assaulted. He also claimed that one officer shook bullets in his hand while another tapped a gun on the table. He told the Tribunal of being very disturbed afterwards, engaging in heavy drinking and having recurring nightmares. Justice Morris accepted that he had been shown the photographs, given food while they were on the table, and told he should think about the photos as he ate, which Garda O'Dowd admitted saying in 2003.[161] This whole encounter showed a 'complete disregard for the well-being and dignity of Mr Quinn and very little respect for the memory of the late Mr Barron'.[162] There was not enough evidence to satisfy Justice Morris that the incidents relating to the bullets and the gun, and the assault, had occurred. All of this was again made difficult due to the lack of accurate notes, which left Justice Morris 'utterly dismayed' and believing that some officers were both 'negligent and deceitful'.[163]

The detention of Katrina Brolly on 4/5 December 1996 presented the Tribunal with a 'web of allegations and counter-allegations'.[164] Her arrest, as an accessory after the fact, was unlawful. Early in her detention her husband was refused a visit, a 'flagrant disregard of the provisions'.[165] During an interview held between 02.45 and 04.00, having made a remark which was deemed to indicate that she was too comfortable, Brolly was made stand in the centre of the room, the lights were flicked on and off, postmortem photos were pushed in her face, her hair was pulled sharply twice and she was called names.[166] In summer 2005 Garda Dooley confirmed all that had been alleged, having previously denied it to the Complaints Board. Sergeant White showed 'utter disdain for the prisoners ... he was prepared to use whatever tactics he could to achieve what he thought were the desired results for the investigation team.'[167] Justice Morris expressed concern that the extension and continuation of interviews past midnight was dealt with lightly by the investigation team and the member in charge. He stressed that for the previous ten years Katrina Brolly had been deemed a liar, and the chair congratulated her for her courage in giving evidence.[168]

Frank McBrearty Snr, arrested on 5 December 1996 following a search of his home, was charged under the Conspiracy and Protection of Property Act 1875 on the allegation that he had been following people to make them stop co-operating with the police. Justice Morris held that the arrest was largely based on unreliable evidence from Noel McBride and therefore unlawful, although the arresting officer acted in good faith.[169]

Frank McBrearty Snr requested a doctor attend, while his home was being searched, as he was feeling unwell. The doctor confirmed his blood pressure was high and advised that he not get any more stressed, but did not specifically state he was not able for interrogation. Ninety minutes after Mr McBrearty Snr's arrival at the station a doctor was called. In the meantime the detainee was interviewed. Claims of abuse at this point were not sustained. The doctor stated that Mr McBrearty Snr needed to attend a hospital as he was at high risk of a heart attack or stroke. He remained in hospital for a week. At the end of this period his physician advised that 'it would not be in his best interest to be interrogated at this time.'[170] The investigating officers saw this note but proceeded with the interview, without sharing this information with the member in charge. His solicitor submitted a letter of complaint. That they continued to interrogate at this point was a complete disregard for his rights and the reasoning was 'disingenuous in the extreme'.[171] Justice Morris found himself 'astounded' that the views of the physician could be ignored in this way. The Guards contacted the hospital where tests had been done and received a further report, in violation of Mr McBrearty Snr's right to privacy, action which was 'underhand'.[172] No-one admitted having done this, a familiar theme of the investigation.

Efforts were made to continue interrogations and Mr McBrearty was told that his son had made a confession to the murder. Justice Morris did not uphold a claim that McBrearty was asked to sign a blank piece of paper. Frank McBrearty was taken back to hospital less than twenty-four hours later where he would remain under Garda supervision for the following six days. On release from hospital he was released from custody but it was 'regrettable that his release did not occur some days earlier'.[173]

Perhaps the least controversial arrest was that of Martin McCallion, a doorman at Frankie's nightclub, on 8 December 1996 in relation to conflicting statements he had made about the night of the death. He was arrested on suspicion of withholding information. Some problems with note-taking were highlighted by Justice Morris, and in the second interview McCallion was shown the postmortem photos, which Justice Morris felt betrayed 'a lack of discipline and restraint'.[174] As McCallion was being released someone questioned how much Mr McBrearty

Snr had paid him, which Justice Morris held to be an 'insulting, gratuitous remark'.[175]

Seán Crossan was arrested on 11 December 1996, as the statements which he had given contradicted what McBride, the key witness known as Mr X who was later revealed to have lied, had said. He withdrew his statement during his detention, after, he claimed, he was abused and shown the photographs. Justice Morris found that there was some exaggeration in his testimony but accepted that he had been told he would be prosecuted for fraud and that his children would be taken away, and that he was shoved, poked and pushed around. This treatment was 'appalling', as was the fact that Garda Keane witnessed this and did not take action.[176]

The arrest of Damian McDaid on 17 December 1996 was for being an accessory after the fact and for failing to reveal that he had information. McDaid denied he was in Raphoe on the night Mr Barron died and claimed that he could not remember what happened as he was highly intoxicated. Justice Morris held that he was lying, possibly to protect some supposed IRA members that his statement might mention.[177] The tone of the arrest, which involved a car chase, his van being surrounded and his younger brother being kicked, created an 'unnecessary tension'.[178] McDaid made a number of claims of abuse which for the most part Justice Morris did not uphold. Notes for the interviews did not represent a complete record of the arrest. The decision to arrest 'was made haphazardly by an investigation team which had completely lost the capacity to analyse objectively the information before it'.[179]

Within the module, Justice Morris also examined allegations that certain interviews in Letterkenny Garda Station on 4 December 1996 had been bugged. These claims were made by White's solicitor. He stated that a specialist had been brought in to the station from Dublin to record interviews between detainees and solicitors. White claimed that upon entering a room he saw Inspector McGlinchey listening to a tape of one interview. He claimed to have raised the issue with Assistant Commissioner Carty but nothing had been done. Justice Morris held that these allegations were false and an effort to buy immunity from prosecution.[180] He found that the making of these allegations constituted a self-serving tactic by Sergeant White in an attempt to divert the focus of investigations from his own behaviour. His claim that he had taken this action out of a sense of injustice and wrongdoing was discredited by his unwillingness for years to admit his own abuse of Róisín McConnell and Katrina Brolly.[181]

That said, Justice Morris was obliged to consider the veracity of the allegations. Detective Sergeant Costello, from the Technical Support Section, was called to Letterkenny Station in December 1996 at the request of Shelly. There was nothing sinister in bringing him to Letterkenny, but Shelly was criticised for failing to follow the appropriate route for requesting a member of the Technical Support Section to attend.[182] The shortcomings, however, were not supportive of White's allegations, which Justice Morris held to be false.[183]

The extent of abuse of detainees chronicled by this substantial report is shocking, particularly given that all were made on the basis of a statement which Gardaí had conspired to secure. It could be argued that at times the techniques used by the interrogation officers strayed into the realm of inhuman and degrading treatment, particularly with physical abuse, sensory deprivation through the switching on and off of lights, and the deliberate efforts to traumatise detainees by showing graphic autopsy photographs. Such abuses of human rights should not occur. The role of the member in charge is to safeguard the rights of the detainee, but it clearly failed, and many of those interrogated suffered long-term pschological damage as a result of their experiences. The continued lying regarding how detainees had been treated, even during the Tribunal, is additional distressing evidence of the impact of the blue wall of silence, as is the failure of other officers to question the behaviour.

The recommendations of this module relate almost entirely to the treatment of individuals in custody. Justice Morris was primarily concerned with methods adopted in the interviewing of witnesses and suspects and he called for the PEACE[184] model of interviewing, used in the UK, to be implemented fully in An Garda Síochána.[185] Full training, leadership and resourcing would be required for this. A national committee should review strategies and develop proposals to be implemented by a national co-ordinator. The avoidance of a tunnel vision approach to interviews was deemed to be 'of paramount importance'.[186] Any confessions received should be very carefully analysed against other evidence. The best technology available should be used for audio-visual recording and the failure to record an interview should result in exclusion of evidence in the courts. The use of CCTV in waiting areas should be extended throughout all Garda stations. Permissible lengths of detention required higher standards of hygiene, sanitation and accommodation, including provision of exercise facilities.[187] Interviews should be externally monitored for advisory purposes. The Judges' Rules should still apply to admissions made outside of the interview rooms, but that regulation could be considered for recording on hand-held devices. The caution given in interviews needs changing as it is now outdated.[188] The Garda Commissioner needs to formulate guidelines on covert surveillance and the Law Reform Commission report on surveillance should be reviewed with a view to enactment,[189] under which monitoring of visits from solicitors should not be permitted and any authorisation for surveillance should have to come from a judge.

Of great concern to Justice Morris was the statement in Garda codes that advises refuting allegations where possible. This needs to be revised so as to require full, detailed and truthful accounts from members whenever allegations are made[190] and senior officers must show leadership in this regard.

The recommendations from the fourth report on the power of a superintendent to issue a search warrant were reiterated[191] before the Tribunal moved on to the procedure for the extension of detention, which had come to be viewed as a rubberstamp exercise. The superintendent making the decision should acquaint himself with all the relevant facts and record the decision taken in their journal with all necessary details. This was linked to Justice Morris's recommendations on the role of the member in charge, who should always be of the rank of sergeant or above and should be of 'considerable independence' from the investigating Gardaí.[192] The role, he maintained, is in need of being reinvigorated by senior members of the force, and training and refresher courses are required. Fundamentally, if the role is to be of any service, 'the Member in Charge must be regarded, by virtue of his appointment, and the statutory and regulatory duties imposed on him, as having an important, independent and active role in overseeing the treatment of prisoners in custody.'[193]

Finally, Justice Morris called for the provisions on questioning after midnight to be reviewed and clarified, so that this did not occur save in very exceptional circumstances.[194]

REPORT SEVEN: ALLEGATIONS OF HARASSMENT AND EFFECTIVE-
NESS OF THE GARDA SÍOCHÁNA COMPLAINTS BOARD

The seventh module dealt with the allegations of harassment of the

McBreartys and the effectiveness of the Garda Síochána Complaints Board. The examination was hampered by the level of co-operation provided by the McBrearty family. Justice Morris was nevertheless satisfied that he was in a position to 'reach a fair and balanced opinion on the issues'.[195]

The McBreartys alleged that they had been subject to a campaign of harassment by the Gardaí of Raphoe, which was at its worst in 1997 and focused on raids of their licensed premises, Frankie's nightclub. Justice Morris acknowledged that a number of events could have led to a change of policing strategy in the area and enhanced attention on the McBrearty family, including: the death of Mr Barron; the attack on Edmond Moss; the assault of a taxi driver; the statement by Frank McBrearty Snr that he was conducting his own investigation into the death and the arrests.[196] Prior to the period under consideration, the Gardaí and the McBreartys held a poor view of each other.

Superintendent Fitzgerald reported that public order was an increasing problem in Raphoe on 6 January 1997 and requested additional manpower.[197] An order issued in relation to public order policing for Letterkenny caused confusion. Some officers claimed they were instructed to inspect premises much more frequently, while the superintendent stated that it was meant to be flexible. One sergeant distributed the order with a letter describing it as a 'get tough policy and no nonsense should be taken from anybody.'[198] Sergeant White was transferred to Raphoe in January 1997, a move Justice Morris determined was only ever intended as a temporary transfer.[199] White was known to be a 'strict disciplinarian' and sending him to Raphoe where 'there had been virtually no Garda control for a significant period of time', without consideration of the existing relationship with Frank McBrearty Snr, ignored the fact that the 'two strong-headed men ... would come into conflict with one another'.[200]

The issuing of summonses to the McBreartys began on 6 January 1997. Garda O'Dowd, on the premises in relation to a separate matter, issued a summons for breach of the licensing laws. When White arrived at the station five days later he instituted a new regime[201] and that night he introduced himself to all the local publicans. His meeting with McBrearty resulted in a summons. The McBreartys began keeping a log of inspections that night. Throughout January there was a marked increase in the number of inspections of licensed premises in Donegal. Sergeant White engaged in a practice of lengthy visits to premises, sometimes lasting over an hour. Frank McBrearty Snr complained at the erection of roadblocks outside his premises, in the belief that these were an attempt to damage his business; Justice Morris held they were a genuine attempt to deal with traffic.[202]

In February the provisions of meals on the premises, as required by the terms of the licence, became a focus of attention for Sergeant White. On one occasion this involved a lengthy discussion of how long it would take to cook a sausage, and White began checking the cooking oil to see if anything had been cooked prior to his visit. White tried to produce a witness to testify as to McBrearty's efforts to avoid cooking the meals, indicating the 'lengths to which Sergeant White was prepared to go to obtain evidence that he thought might be useful against Frank McBrearty Senior'.[203] Justice Morris concluded that White was engaged in a 'tit for tat campaign' and that with the concerns he had he should have objected to the renewal of Mr McBrearty's licence.[204]

In February the McBreartys began making complaints about the treatment through their solicitor. Frank McBrearty Jnr was arrested for the second time in February, in the presence of White, adding to the tension. Later that month, four summonses were issued arising from the one night. Frank McBrearty Snr had installed a CCTV system as an early warning mechanism, enabling him to close the bar as the Gardaí were approaching and to re-open it after they left. On direction, White desisted from prolonged inspections, instead conducting multiple inspections in the one evening. At the Tribunal, O'Dowd, who had accompanied White on many of these inspections, conceded that there was a disproportionate focus on Frankie's.[205] In the 'middle period' of March to May 1997, the key events involving the ongoing inspections included an application by the McBreartys for an injunction against the inspections, the use of undercover agents by the Gardaí and the handling of hoax bomb threats made to the premises. Mark McConnell, who was not an employee at Frankie's, was issued a summons after an encounter with White on the premises. That same evening, White also issued a warning regarding the emergency doors which were not operational. Justice Morris found this to be an entirely appropriate policing action.[206] Regular and multiple inspections continued throughout April. Mark McConnell was served with the summons arising out of the previous incident, at home, close to midnight, which Justice Morris deemed to be 'inappropriate'.[207]

Hoax bomb calls began in May and on each occasion the McBreartys refused to evacuate the pub, for which they were criticised by Justice Morris.[208] Events reached a particular height in June when Frank McBrearty decided to run a '£1 a pint' promotion. This was, in Justice Morris's view, a form of 'reprisal' against Gardaí.[209] Around a thousand people left the premises when the club closed, leading to what White described as the most troublesome experience in Raphoe that year. McBrearty submitted a complaint as to how the Gardaí had handled the situation, though White claimed that the McBreartys had watched and laughed. Inspector Lyons was sent to Raphoe the following weekend to prepare an independent report on the disturbances in the town. Lyons' report on the state of lawlessness in Raphoe after the closing of Frankie's was of such an extreme nature that Justice Morris concluded the only correct recourse for the Gardaí was to object to the renewal of a licence. By not doing so, 'Superintendent Lennon was in grave dereliction of his duty.'[210] This was evidenced by the fact that on 20 July a total of eight summonses were issued on the one night, three stemming from a nine-minute period, a number which Justice Morris deemed to be 'inappropriate' and 'excessive'.[211]

Lennon subsequently spoke with Frank McBrearty Snr and issued an order that only one inspection a night was to be conducted. This resulted in a general calming of the situation. White was transferred to Letterkenny in August, though a delay in processing on his part meant that a further twenty-two summonses were issued in September, which Justice Morris accepted was a 'nasty shock' and would have 'reinforced [McBrearty's] perception that the Gardaí were mounting a campaign of harassment against him'.[212] The prosecution of summonses began in April 1997 and over the next two years would continue to be adjourned and added to. A settlement meeting was held between Chief Superintendent Fitzpatrick and McBrearty's legal team in January 1999. Justice Morris concluded that this was held as an 'attempt to prevent the emergence of the so-called wider issue' which the McBreartys continually referred to and which was about to be examined by Assistant Commissioner Carty.[213] Frank McBrearty Snr was unwilling to plead guilty to any of the offences and so the efforts failed. The investigation by Carty led in June 2000 to the DPP dropping all charges. Justice Morris concluded that the individual charges were warranted given that licensing laws had been broken but, when looked at in totality the sixty-eight summonses issued against the McBreartys was 'excessive' and the Gardaí should have selected a number of cases to pursue in the courts 'in a balanced and proportionate manner'.[214]

In a related allegation Justice Morris found that Paul Quinn was falsely arrested by Sergeant White on a drugs charge on 9 February 1997, in a situation where he could not have held genuine suspicion. Justice Morris was satisfied beyond any reasonable doubt[215] that White planted drugs on Mr Quinn while processing the arrest. It was not however part of a campaign against the McBreartys but rather 'a desire to "put manners" on Mr Quinn' after he had been disrespectful to a Garda.[216] Six other individuals in Raphoe alleged harassment by Gardaí in this period and Justice Morris found basis to some of these claims. Paddy Lynch, an employee of Mr McBrearty's, was served a summons by White for having swerved to avoid a pedestrian on the street. This was, according to Justice Morris, 'an incident of harassment or reprisal'.[217] A similar finding on the allegation made by William Logan, who was charged with breach of the peace 'in a disproportionate way', amounted to 'harassment of Mr Logan'.[218]

Justice Morris concluded that White was sent to Raphoe as a disciplinarian because senior officers 'wanted someone to deal with Frank McBrearty Senior'.[219] Senior officers, such as Inspector Lennon, then tried to distance themselves from what was happening in what was 'an appalling dereliction of duty'.[220] Lennon's evidence suggesting otherwise was rejected by the Tribunal. What ensued 'was not so much an orchestrated campaign of harassment against Mr McBrearty Senior but rather a bitter and escalating conflict'.[221] What occurred in Raphoe was not 'fair, balanced and proportionate' policing. It was 'not commensurate with proper policing in a rural area'.[222] On occasion Sergeant White's behaviour went 'completely beyond the realms of proper policing'. Justice Morris did apportion some blame to Frank McBrearty Snr for his unwillingness to obey the law. He 'must accordingly bear a share of the responsibility for the consequences which flowed'.[223]

The behaviour of Sergeant White in Justice Morris' final review is described as 'obsessive', engaging in 'cat and mouse' games and reaching 'farcical lengths'. The attention paid to Frankie's was 'excessive' and 'over the top', and Justice Morris was 'satisfied that the actions taken by the Gardaí in Raphoe in the period January 1997 to August 1997, under the directing hand of Sergeant John White, constituted harassment'.[224]

This is the third report which finds Sergeant White fundamentally at fault for the events in Donegal, and the temptation may arise to directly blame him. In each situation, however, senior officers should have exercised greater oversight. At no time should Sergeant White have believed that he had the power to engage in this conduct.

The second part of the seventh report dealt with the handling of complaints by the Garda Síochána Complaints Board.[225] A total of sixty-one complaints were made between 1996 and 2001, beginning the week after the arrests in December 1996. In the first seven months, eight individual complaints were made but not connected by the board. In October 1997, Superintendent Lennon forwarded eight letters of complaint of a very serious nature stemming from the previous December. The delay, the connections and the severity of the allegations were a 'cause of deep concern in the office' and led to swift action being taken to respond.[226] A special meeting was held in relation to this group of complaints and the chief executive officer (CEO) of the Board, Mr O'Brien, made the unusual decision to travel to Donegal to meet the complainants. Prior to this meeting, Frank McBrearty Snr faxed a letter containing further complaints to Mr O'Brien. He also met with the officers concerned, who gave 'a heavily edited version of the state of play', limiting the investigation.

The Commissioner appointed Chief Superintendent Carey of the Mayo division as investigating officer in November 1997, in addition to his existing workload. Carey was assigned an assistant, an unusual step, deemed warranted given the volume of complaints and the delay already incurred. Carey began his investigation in February and, breaking from standard procedure, updated the Board a number of times during the summer, to advise on when the Board would need to free time to consider the report. Frank McBrearty Snr complained of the delay in the process in October 1998: it was almost two years since the first complaints were submitted.

Carey's report of 1,000 pages, with 2,000 pages of appendices, as opposed to the standard 3–5 page reports, was collected by the CEO in mid-November 1998. Of the sixty-one complaints, nineteen were declared inadmissible due to time limits or failure to meet the requisite standard of behaviour. A further ten failed to proceed due to a 'stalemate', because one party refused to co-operate with the investigating officer, in most cases the complainant. This left thirty-two allegations which were investigated by Carey. Justice Morris found that Carey met with the 'Blue Wall of Garda denial … [and] was being fed a particular line by many of the Gardaí'.[227] Further, in a number of instances, such as the complaints of Róisín McConnell, they were 'pretty awful allegations', and 'he candidly admitted that he simply did not believe that any member of An Garda Síochána would have abused women to the degree alleged by the complainants.'[228] Carey, Justice Morris felt, 'was trapped in a system that did not and could not give effective redress to complainants'.[229]

The Board read the entirety of the reports, as opposed to summaries, further adding to the delay. It considered the complaints for the first time in May 1999 and, controversially, decided to defer decision-making until there was an outcome from both the prosecutions for licensing breaches and Assistant Commissioner Carty's internal investigation. The GSCB process allowed the investigator to ask questions but not to challenge answers. In effect, Carey's report comprised two conflicting sets of statements, in complete disagreement as to the facts. The Gardaí involved had denied every accusation. The chair of the Board, Mr McKenna, stood by the decision, stating that they were aware that if they got their decision wrong the outcome would be worse than not making any decision. Justice Morris observed that this decision 'demonstrated a very shrewd analysis of the circumstances'.[230]

The McBreartys continued to complain of the delay as it reached three years since the first complaints were made. The CEO attended a number of the court hearings for the prosecutions, which were dropped by the DPP in June 2000. The Board decided to contact the Carty inquiry in August with regard to information sharing, though a letter was not sent until March 2001. Carty informed them in July that there was no overlap in the investigations. The path was clear for the Board to take action but before they could consider the cases Frank McBrearty withdrew the complaints, now five years old, in October 2001. This brought an end to the matter for the GSCB.

Justice Morris found that the scale of the complaints received by the GSCB went 'far beyond its capability'.[231] The legislation could not deal with corruption at the level being investigated in Donegal. The delay in contacting the Carty inquiry was the sole basis for concern, though he found no 'culpable negligence' in this regard. The GSCB had asked for a new body to be created; this had now been done, and Justice Morris expressed the hope that this situation would 'not again be experienced by any group of complainants in this jurisdiction'.[232]

Closing this report, Justice Morris considered an allegation that the leader of Fine Gael had interfered with Deputy Higgins' efforts to raise the issue of corruption in Donegal on the floor of the Dáil. It was held by the Tribunal that the leader, John Bruton, had heard of the view expressed by a member of the GSCB, Mr O'Callaghan, who had read Carey's report, that Higgins should exercise caution in his approach to this case. Mr Bruton contacted Deputy Higgins to confirm that he could support the line he was adopting. When satisfied that Deputy Higgins could do so, Mr Bruton said no more. Justice Morris felt that while he was perhaps too uninformed on the matter to have become involved, Mr Bruton could not be criticised for his response given the inside knowledge of the source.

No specific recommendations were made in this report, largely as the Garda Ombudsman Commission had replaced the board. Whether or not the legislation for the new body managed to address the flaws identified in the old system by this report will be assessed in Chapter 5.

REPORT EIGHT: ANONYMOUS ALLEGATIONS

The final report of the Tribunal concerned allegations made anonymously about members of the Carty team to Deputies Higgins and Howlin. On 25 May 2000, Deputy Higgins received an anonymous fax and Deputy Howlin received a phone call from Mr McBrearty Snr's senior counsel, who suggested his information came from a Garda in Donegal. A second fax was received by Deputy Higgins on 15 July 2000. The allegations suggested that Sergeant White had information of misconduct on the part of Assistant Commissioners Carty and Hickey and that if the investigation into White's behaviour was conducted properly he would use this against them. It was alleged that concern existed regarding White's expenses and that he had access to stolen property which he could plant on individuals. After White was arrested for unlawful possession of a gun he was suspended but this was terminated after seventy-two hours. He then applied for and was granted a transfer. Concern was expressed at these decisions.[233] Justice Morris and his team found no evidence to support the allegations and concluded that the faxes were written by Frank McBrearty Snr,[234] with the aim of increasing pressure on the Minister for Justice to establish a Tribunal. Justice Morris felt it was related to the withdrawal of prosecutions by the DPP, and the fear that this 'closed the door of a forum where they hoped to explore the "wider issue"'.[235] Mr McBrearty was assisted by P.J. Togher, a retired Garda, who had worked for Mr McBrearty Snr for a number of years.

In relation to the allegation regarding White's transfer, Justice Morris found that while it was not unreasonable to suspect something 'mysterious' had occurred, it had not.[236] The module centred on 'an elaborate hoax' in which 'innuendo, rumour and half truths were drawn together'.[237] The actions of McBrearty Snr were described as 'disgraceful, shocking and unfair to those whose reputations he deliberately besmirched for his own ends'. That said, he found that in making the decision on White's transfer application, 'due regard was not had to the nature of the offence under investigation.'[238]

In handling the allegations, the Tribunal accepted that the deputies acted in a 'bona fide manner' and while they could have gone to the Garda Commissioner or made further inquiries before going to the Minister, 'they were, to an extent, manipulated by those furnishing the information.'[239] Caution had to be exercised in any response where allegations have been made anonymously. The assertion of privilege with regard to sources, when the Minister established an investigation, was, in Justice Morris' view, 'premature' as they had not consulted with their source to establish if they would co-operate with the Tribunal.[240] Given the source of the information, the deputies 'owed it to themselves, to the Minister and to those who were the subject of the allegations to explore the information furnished to them somewhat further'.[241]

Two issues merited recommendations at the end of this module: Garda disciplinary regulations and how public representatives should handle anonymous allegations. On the former, Justice Morris called for an amendment to regulations so that suspensions were dealt with before transfers were considered, and also for the criteria for suspension to be clarified and included in Garda regulations.[242] He recommended that the Committee on Practice and Procedure of Dáil and Seanad review how anonymous allegations be dealt with, as a matter of urgency, as he did not feel that sufficient inquiry was conducted by the members concerned.[243]

Concluding the Tribunal, Justice Morris called again for full implementation of all recommendations made across all reports and expressed the hope that these reforms, and a strong adherence to accountability, would prevent repetition of the 'shocking scandals' the Tribunal was required to investigate.[244]

IMPLICATIONS

There is much that is astounding about the above reports, but perhaps of central importance is the extent of criticism. This is the first time that An Garda Síochána have been condemned in a public tribunal. In past years a number of judgements in the courts have led to individual members of the force incurring substantial criticism for their behaviour. But the reports of this one tribunal hint at institutional problems which individual cases do not necessarily have the capacity to identify, including poor management, bullying, indiscipline and the blue wall of silence. The fear, apparent from the Tribunal, is that the failings in terms of each have now, due to apathy, become part of 'routine' policing in Ireland, that is to say, they have been institutionalised. The Tribunal did not produce a concluding report, but a number of central themes can be extrapolated from these reports.

Management

Inherent in many of the reports is the fact that, had it not been for the negligent management of the division, many of the events should have been prevented. It was not simply about rotten apples. This was evident in the supervision of investigations and informers, in the lacklustre response to irregularities as they arose and outright support of some of the misconduct. This management problem was compounded by the promotion system: 'The Tribunal regards with disquiet the promotion to senior ranks of persons who were unwilling or unable to give their vocation the energy and aptitude that it demands.'[245] Those in supervisory roles were not capable enough to prevent what happened or to deal with it effectively once it was uncovered. Unsuitable candidates were being promoted into positions for which they were not capable, and no system of review existed whereby management could later revisit this position. Just as damaging is the fact that talent within the lower ranks was being wasted. Those left behind were resentful of superiors, whom they believed had been unfairly promoted. Some were being driven, as has been shown by the Morris Tribunal, to extreme measures in an effort to secure promotion. The lack of independent involvement in the promotion system within the force ensured that nepotism could thrive.

It also enabled problems of bullying to thrive. The prime example in the Morris Tribunal was the occasion on which Garda McMahon pointed a gun at the head of a member who had asked to become involved in the case of Adrienne McGlinchey. There have been increasing reports in the media throughout the past decade of a bullying culture within the Gardaí. It has affected individual officers, with some retiring early[246] and others suing senior officers.[247] In addition, the Association of Garda Sergeants and Inspectors argued that senior management were abusing their authority and that 'top Gardaí were bullying them into pursuing certain lines of inquiry.'[248] Bullying is problematic in any organisation, symptomatic of indiscipline and will contribute to non-disclosure of problems.

Internal Discipline

> The sorry sequence of events in respect of this matter which was important to the investigating Gardaí is an appalling reflection on the standards of integrity, efficiency, management, discipline and trust between the various members and ranks of the Garda Síochána ... The public interest in resolving important issues of fact concerning the death of the late Mr Barron was subsumed under an inflexible legal blanket ... Gardaí looked to protect their own interests. The truth was to be buried. The public interest was of no concern.[249]

> An Garda Síochána is losing its character as a disciplined force ... Ultimately the gradual erosion of discipline within An Garda Síochána is a developing situation that will, sooner or later, lead to disaster.[250]

The behaviour detailed by Justice Morris breached most aspects of the disciplinary code of conduct: discreditable conduct; misconduct towards a member; disobedience of orders; falsehood or prevarication; neglect of duty; breach of confidence; corrupt or improper practice; abuse of authority; misuse of Garda property; drinking on duty without good or sufficient cause; criminal conduct; failure to co-operate with disciplinary investigations; and accessory to a breach of discipline. Only four breaches of discipline were not evidenced, two of which related to off-duty activities and so were not the concern of the Tribunal, and one of which is unauthorised entry of a licensed premises. This scale of misconduct within one region in a short number of years raises deep concerns as to the heart of discipline within An Garda Síochána. Justice Morris determined that without sufficient reform it was possible that this could occur again:

> Without a management structure being restored to the Gardaí that

is based on strict compliance with orders and immediate accountability, the danger is extreme that what the Tribunal has reported
on in Donegal will be repeated; and that such conduct will multi-
ply if allowed to go unchecked.[251]

He does not, however, suggest there were any reasons why it happened
in Donegal and not anywhere else: 'Of the Gardaí serving in Donegal it
cannot be said that they are unrepresentative or an aberration from the
generality. All of them were trained as Gardaí and served under a uniform structure of administration and discipline that is standardised.'[252]
    Certainly the proximity to the border had a particular relevance in
the context of the first report and the corrupt planting of hoax IRA
bomb finds. McCullagh explains that 'the context of a terrorist threat
and of the over-riding political need to be seen to be defeating terrorism contributed significantly to the kind of corruption that took place
in Donegal.'[253] McMahon and Lennon took advantage of this context
to further their own ends. When it came to policing the IRA, An Garda
Síochána have been supported and, as the discussion in the introduction
of the 'heavy gang' would suggest, were given a degree of leeway.
McMahon and Lennon knew that if they were reporting finds of IRA
weaponry, the 'how' would most likely not be questioned. In this way,
it was not a coincidence that those events occurred in a border county,
and that IRA bombs were a tool of their corruption. This was of more
indirect relevance in other modules where we saw individuals being
arrested under the Offences Against the State Act 1939, a policing tool
designed to tackle paramilitary organisations. On the other hand, while
there may have been peculiarities within the district which may have
enabled such conduct, there is no reason to believe that misconduct
does not occur throughout the State. Punch warns of 'danger zones' in
policing which are by their very nature vulnerable to corruption.[254] He
includes drugs, vice, undercover work, informant-handling and
licensing, a list which overlaps with much of what occurred in Donegal.
Universally these are areas of concern.
    Of particular concern in terms of misconduct is the treatment of
detainees during interrogation. As previously outlined, this has histor-
ically been a site of misconduct within An Garda Síochána, but the scale
of abuse of detainees' rights, including physical abuse, documented in
the sixth report is deeply disturbing. Great emphasis is placed on the
role of the member in charge to safeguard the rights of detainees, but

this clearly failed in the situations under examination. These detentions occurred before the Recording of Interview Regulations came into effect, which would have limited the potential for abuse experienced by these detainees. However, that does not alter the policing belief in the value of these interrogation methods, and raises real concerns that they could still be utilised outside of the interview room.

The Blue Wall of Silence
The blue wall of silence was found by Justice Morris to be a strong feature of life in An Garda Síochána. The Tribunal experienced it in every module, at every turn. McMahon and Lennon fed the Tribunal a 'tissue of lies'. Garda Martin Leonard, in explaining his unwillingness to reveal what his colleagues had done, infamously stated to the first stage of the Tribunal: 'You don't hang your own.'[255] The blue wall emerged over the preservation of the crime scene after Mr Barron's death, the falsification of records on the extortion calls, in relation to each detention, regarding the authorisation of the search warrant for Burnfoot and the subsequent attempt by officers to cover up the wrongdoing of Sergeant White as well as throughout the Garda Síochána Complaints Board investigations. Justice Morris was critical: 'It is clear that members of An Garda Síochána adopted a thoroughly uncooperative manner with my investigations. The Tribunal noted the same attitude in testimony.' Equally, 'The enquiries by the Tribunal have been lengthy and difficult. Let it be clearly stated that this happened because so many witnesses determined to persistently lie.'[256] But even before the Tribunal began its work, the blue wall had prevented all the misconduct from coming to light and stalled every investigation – internal Garda investigations, GSCB investigations, DPP prosecution – driving the situation forward to the necessity of a tribunal. Vaughan notes that 'one reason why the incidents in Donegal snowballed was that those in authority were too credulous of claims of serving officers.'[257] What is perhaps most galling is that even when the Tribunal was established officers still lied, suggesting that they believed they could evade discovery and sanction. Further, the institutional response to such an attitude was criticised. Justice Morris repeatedly expressed his dismay that the 'absence' of notes and notebooks was not investigated or sanctioned by senior officers. The GRA also had a hand to play and in the first report Justice Morris was forced to find that 'members of the Garda Representative Association set out to destroy an investigation ordered by the Garda Commissioner.'[258]

When an officer becomes aware of corrupt or unlawful activities taking place within a police force it is a difficult position. To come forward almost certainly guarantees alienation and ostracisation, and their position may become untenable.[259] Not coming forward will most likely mean the continuance of the behaviour.[260] Both options are problematic for the officer, for as Kleinig outlines, 'It brings into conflict two strong commitments: on the one hand, the professional (and personal) commitment to integrity; and on the other hand, the institutional or fraternal commitment to loyalty. Both of these may be felt as moral requirements.'[261] The whistleblowing options for a police officer are multiple. They may decide to approach superiors, co-operate with investigating officers, go public, resign or, as is becoming more common, report the information confidentially.[262] Whistleblowing can lead to loss of confidence in the institution, affecting public confidence and employee morale.[263] The benefit to the public of revealing the information may not be perceived as worth the consequences[264] and so the motive of the whistleblower also needs to be considered to militate against revenge of some sort.[265] Whistleblowing therefore is not automatically a morally justifiable action and it has to be considered whether it is being done for the 'appropriate moral motive', on sound grounds, after all other avenues have been exhausted.[266] For this reason, it is best to have mechanisms for dealing with whistleblowing, providing options beyond approaching the media. The leading example of whistleblowing in the police is Serpico, who exposed corruption in the New York Police Department (NYPD) in the early 1970s.[267] On coming forward, he effectively sealed his fate and resigned having given evidence to the Knapp Commission. If anything, his tale is likely to discourage others from coming forward. Protection needs to be provided if corruption is to be discovered and rooted out early. What the case of Serpico does show is that blowing the whistle can in actuality be the ultimate expression of loyalty to the institution, motivated by a belief that the organisation can be better.[268]

In the context of An Garda Síochána, and given the presence of bullying as well as the blue wall of silence, the unwillingness to come forward and speak about the problems within the force is unsurprising. The information which led to the establishment of the Morris Tribunal came not from a member of the force, but from a tenacious family and an officer's wife. There were numerous people not directly involved in the activities in question who could have spoken up but did not. This was due in part to the lack of a safe mechanism and a knowledge that doing so would make their position in the force untenable. When Garda Fowley spoke to the Carty inquiry she endured harassment and bullying for her actions, as well as a suspension which she perceived as unjustified.

Each of these issues identified by the Tribunal is in fact a manifestation of the culture of the police, which is well documented as espousing values such as machismo, conservatism, loyalty to each other, isolation from others, cynicism, a sense of mission, racism and pragmatism.[269] Police officers are bound up in these beliefs and values as to what is right and what is appropriate within that job. They inform decision-making and use of discretion. They are inextricably linked to the problems of bullying, indiscipline and the blue wall of silence evidenced by the Tribunal. This moves the challenge of reform into difficult territory, where rules and regulations can be implemented but fail to impact. Indeed, one of the characteristics of the police culture is a resistance to change (conservatism). Changing beliefs, inbuilt stereotypes and interpretations of their role in society is notoriously difficult, yet this is the task facing Ireland in the wake of the Morris reports.

NOTES

1. For instance, Justice Morris decided that term of reference (b), which covered the investigation into the death of Richard Barron, related arrests and the management of the investigation with a particular emphasis on the handling of informants, involved three separate sub-issues. He decided to deal with it across two modules (reports two and six).
2. At the time of writing this remains unknown, and the case open within An Garda Síochána.
3. Peter Charleton SC, Paul McDermott SC and Anthony Barr BL, with Bernadette Crombie, solicitor.
4. The Tribunal will be referenced according to report number and paragraph number. IV/2.16 would thereby refer to the fourth report, paragraph 2.16.
5. I/4.99.
6. The Tribunal had difficulty in relation to these stages, determining what actually happened. Adrienne's sister has since written a book (K. McGlinchey, *Charades* (Dublin: Gill & Macmillan, 2005) in which Adrienne maintains that her version of events is accurate.
7. I/5.12, 5.23, 5.37, 5.42, 5.65.
8. Such as being seen in possession of weaponry and being drunk and disorderly in public.
9. I/6.18, 6.76, 6.115, 8.61, 9.04.
10. Further details on each of these finds was also provided by C. McCullagh, 'The Global in the Local: Police Corruption in Donegal', unpublished, 2005.
11. I/7.141.
12. I/9.160.
13. I/14.30.

14. I/1.21.
15. I/5.55.
16. I/5.62.
17. I/6.32.
18. I/1.40.
19. I/1.43.
20. I/14.59.
21. I/14.96.
22. I/13.10.
23. I/13.13.
24. I/13.14.
25. I/13.96.
26. I/13.19, such as dates, times, locations of finds, details of search warrants, legislative provisions being used and so on. These very specifically stem from finds of explosives.
27. I/13.22.
28. I/13.93.
29. I/13.114.
30. II/3.158.
31. II/3.53.
32. II/1.13.
33. II/3.86.
34. II/3.122.
35. II/4.24.
36. II/4.31.
37. II/1.07.
38. II/5.53.
39. II/1.32.
40. II/6.86.
41. II/5.215; the treatment in custody was subject to examination in the sixth module.
42. II/1.40.
43. II/3.615.
44. II/3.163.
45. II/3.165.
46. II/4.79.
47. II/5.208.
48. II/9.08.
49. II/9.11.
50. II/9.18.
51. II/9.24.
52. II/9.29.
53. II/9.43.
54. II/9.45.
55. II/9.32.
56. II/9.32.
57. II/9.35.
58. II/afterword (p.617).
59. I/13.124.
60. I/13.127.
61. As will be seen below, the issue of serving meals in Frankie's was of particular interest to Sergeant White.
62. III/1.37.
63. III/2.60.
64. III/1.41. Exactly who had forged the signatures remained unclear despite forensic examina-

tion, though Justice Morris was satisfied that at the very least both officers were aware that these were not genuine certificates and that it was probable that Nicholson had forged some of the documents, III/2.166.

65. III/3.99.
66. III/1.69.
67. III/1.72.
68. III/2.86.
69. III/2.86.
70. III/2.110.
71. III/2.101.
72. III/2.171.
73. III/3.163.
74. III/1.18.
75. III/1.55.
76. IV/1.15.
77. IV/1.30.
78. IV/1.41.
79. IV/1.58.
80. IV/1.65.
81. IV/1.96.15.
82. IV/recommendations.
83. V/1.07.
84. The full statement is reproduced in the report at V/2.29.
85. V/3.47.
86. V/3.49.
87. V/3.61.
88. V/3.100.
89. V/5.45.
90. V/5, Conclusions 15.
91. V/3.142.
92. V/3.147.
93. V/3.156.
94. V/4, Conclusions 6.
95. V/6.05.
96. V/6.10.
97. V/6.24.
98. VI/6.27.
99. VI/1.37.
100. VI/1.89.
101. VI/2.09.
102. VI/2.63.
103. VI/2.29.
104. VI/2.49.
105. VI/2.43.
106. VI/2.64.
107. VI/2.95. The treatment of his wife will be outlined below.
108. VI/2.99.
109. VI/3.106.
110. VI/3.144.
111. VI/3.39.
112. VI/3.144.
113. VI/4.16.
114. VI/4.39.

115. VI/4.41.
116. VI/4.54.
117. VI/4.66.
118. VI/4.87.
119. VI/4.108.
120. VI/4.183.23.
121. VI/4.183.17.
122. VI/4.182.
123. VI/4.183.2.
124. VI/4.183.24.
125. Who had been involved in the events considered in the Kerry Babies case and the Abbey-lara investigation.
126. VI/4.193.
127. VI/4.197.
128. VI/4.215.
129. VI/4.258.
130. VI/4.274.
131. VI/4.286.
132. VI/4.293.
133. VI/4.294.2.
134. VI/5.17.
135. VI/5.39.
136. VI/5.56.14.
137. VI/6.55.
138. VI/6.35.
139. VI/7.07.
140. VI/7.73.
141. VI/7.76.
142. VI/7.110. Justice Morris referred to one such claim as a 'wild allegation'.
143. VI/7.144.
144. VI/7.151.
145. VI/7.197.
146. VI/7.390.
147. VI/7.390.31.
148. VI/7.390.40.
149. VI/7.451.6.
150. VI/7.459. McBrearty had attended the Garda station to obtain a new tax book for his car. Following a heated discussion with members in the station he left but returned soon to complain of being followed by members of the Barron family. It was as he was leaving after this trip to the station that he was arrested.
151. VI/7.476.
152. VI/7.519.10.
153. VI/7.519.11.
154. VI/7.519.12.
155. VI/7.519.13.
156. VI/8.13.
157. VI/8.22.
158. VI/8.27.
159. VI/8.64.
160. VI/8.64.
161. VI/8.108.
162. VI/8.111.
163. VI/8.134.15.

164. VI/9.06.
165. VI/9.33.
166. VI/9.40.
167. VI/9.98.
168. VI/Chapter 9, Conclusions 16.
169. VI/10.67.
170. VI/10.163.
171. VI/10/193.
172. VI/10.203.
173. VI/10/279.
174. VI/11.37.
175. VI/11.36.
176. VI/12.52.8.
177. VI/13.09.
178. VI/13.22.
179. VI/13.51.
180. VI/14.14.
181. VI/14.63.
182. VI/14.124.
183. VI/14.200.
184. PEACE stands for Planning and preparation, Engage and explain, Account and clarification, Closure, Evaluate evidence obtained through questioning.
185. VI/16.03.
186. VI/16.06.
187. VI/16.14.
188. VI/16.21.
189. VI/16.31.
190. VI/16.33.
191. VI/16.34.
192. VI/16.37.
193. VI/16.39.
194. VI/16.42.
195. VII/1.35.
196. VII/2.26–.31.
197. VII/3.03.
198. VII/3.07.
199. VII/3.14.
200. VII/3.24.
201. VII/3.26.
202. VII/3.54.
203. VII/3.74.
204. VII/3.81.
205. VII/3.118.
206. VII/4.20.
207. VII/4.54.
208. VII/4.70.
209. VII/5.09.
210. Ibid.
211. VII/5.50.
212. VII/6.07.
213. VII/6.53.
214. VII/6.61. This is a prime example of how an operational decision which is legal can be a bad policing decision, highlighting the problems that can be created by the exercise of discretion.

215. Notably using the terminology of the criminal burden of proof, rather than the required civil burden, suggesting a higher level of belief.
216. VII/7.121.
217. VII/8.87.
218. VII/8.107.
219. VII/9.03.
220. VII/9.14.
221. VII/9.21.
222. VII/9.22.
223. VII/9.25.
224. VII/9.37.
225. For a thorough review of the operation of the Complaints Board see D. Walsh, 'Twenty Years of Handling Police Complaints in Ireland: A Critical Assessment of the Supervisory Board Model', *Legal Studies*, 29, 2 (2009), p.305.
226. VII/11.13.
227. VII/12.54/56.
228. VII/12.104.
229. VII/12.109.4.
230. VII/11.70.
231. VII/11.104.1.
232. VII/11.104.8.
233. VIII/2.61.
234. This discovery was a prime example of a fact that could not have been uncovered save for the High Court-like powers invested in the Tribunal under the legislation. See further VIII/3.250 and the discussion of the Tribunal in the Conclusion.
235. VIII/3.34.
236. VIII/2.68.
237. VIII/1.16.
238. VIII/2.120.
239. VIII/3.112.
240. VIII/3.121.
241. VIII/3.130.
242. VIII/4.05.
243. VIII/4.09.
244. VIII/4.10.
245. I/1.43.
246. *Irish Examiner*, 19 December 2005.
247. *Irish Times*, 30 December 2004.
248. *Irish News*, 14 November 2005.
249. I/3.179.
250. I/13.102.
251. V/6.05.
252. V/6.02.
253. McCullagh, 'The Global in the Local: Police Corruption in Donegal', p.9.
254. Punch, 'Police Corruption and its Prevention', p.319.
255. I/1.49.
256. I/1.08.
257. B. Vaughan, 'A New System of Police Accountability: The Garda Síochána Act 2005', *Irish Criminal Law Journal*, 15, 4 (2005), p.18.
258. I/12.110.
259. J. Moran, 'Blue walls, grey areas and cleanups: Issues in the Control of Police Corruption in England and Wales, *Crime, Law and Social Change*, 43, 57 (2005), p.66; W. DeMaria, 'The Whistleblower Protection Bill: A Shield Too Small, *Crime, Law and Social Change*,

27, 139 (1997), p.145; L. Westmarland, 'Blowing the Whistle on Police Violence', *British Journal of Criminology*, no. 41 (2001), p.523.

260. W. Knapp, *The Commission to Investigate Alleged Police Corruption* (New York, 1972).
261. Cited in Newburn, *Understanding Police Corruption*, p.613.
262. Westmarland, 'Blowing the Whistle on Police Violence', p.530; Kleinig, *The Ethics of Policing*, p.88.
263. N. Bowie, *Business Ethics* (London: Prentice Hall, 1982), p.224.
264. Kleinig, *The Ethics of Policing*, p.132.
265. J.P. Near and M.P. Miceli, 'Organizational Dissidence: The Case of Whistleblowing', *Journal of Business Ethics*, no. 4 (1984), p.1.
266. Bowie, *Business Ethics*, p.226.
267. Knapp, *Commission on Alleged Police Corruption*.
268. R. Larmer, 'Whistleblowing and Employee Loyalty', *Journal of Business Ethics*, no. 11 (1992), p.225.
269. For a detailed discussion of police occupational subculture see Reiner, *The Politics of the Police*; P.A.J. Waddington, 'Police (Canteen) Culture', *British Journal of Criminology*, 39, 2 (1999), p.287; J. Chan, 'Changing Police Culture', *British Journal of Criminology*, 36, 1 (1996), p.109.

Chapter Four

The Morris Discourse

The findings made by Justice Morris represent the first occasion on which such a critical examination has been conducted of the force by an official authority. These sit in stark contrast with the traditionally supportive official line and the high levels of confidence in the police expressed by the public. That the police could engage in such activities contradicted traditional views of the Irish police, particular police in border counties, who had been engaged in the process of defending the State against subversive challenges. If these findings were not to create a crisis of confidence and legitimacy in the police, discourses would have to enable society to excuse, explain, disregard or accept these findings in a way that would allow the consensus view of policing in Ireland to be maintained. These discourses emerged through the media coverage, as well as political and Garda responses to the findings and recommendations of the Tribunal. These would all have a role in how the work of the Tribunal was interpreted, digested and transformed into a means of accepting the findings while retaining fundamental confidence in the force. From the public perspective, the media played an important role in this process, as public attendance at the Tribunal was low. The public were reliant on others to inform them of the findings. This chapter will firstly consider that media discourse, examining how the reports and findings of the Tribunal were interpreted and represented across newspapers. The discussion will then turn to how Garda officials, particularly the Commissioner and the Garda Representative Association, responded. Their voices would be particularly important, not just for the public interpretation, but also for members of the force whose morale would need to be addressed for the organisation to move forward and for reforms to be accepted.

MEDIA DISCOURSE

The Morris Tribunal, from conception to completion, was 'big news'. Consider the findings: police pretending that a local woman is a key

IRA informer, planting bombs to claim policing successes in relation to highly politicised events, threatening another officer with a gun, having tunnel vision in the conduct of an investigation to the extent that they frame two innocent men, abusing detainees including young mothers, securing a false confession, planting evidence such as drugs and guns, fabricating statements, harassing citizens and continually lying to senior officers as well as a senior member of the judiciary. Being classified as big news involves a complex process, for, as Philo explains, 'news is not "found" or even "gathered" so much as made. It is a *creation* of a journalistic process, an artefact, a commodity even.'[1] Given the number of events occurring nationally and internationally on a daily basis,[2] for any event to be selected as a news feature it is required to align with what are perceived to be key features of a news story, or what are often called 'news values'. These are the gatekeepers to the news, determining what is admitted and excluded by journalist and newsmakers at the selection stage. Gatlung and Ruge have produced a list of these 'news values':

- frequency (a singular event rather than a long-term process is more likely to be reported),
- threshold (refers to the scale of the event for it to be included e.g. a ten-car pileup is more newsworthy than a two-car collision),
- unambiguity (ease of accessibility to readers),
- meaningfulness (will the event be considered both culturally proximate and relevant to the public? For example, domestic events may be of more interest to Irish people unless the international events have a significant relevance to Irish life),
- consonance (is it an event that people expect or want to happen?),
- unexpectedness (not expected to happen or unusual),
- continuity (once defined as newsworthy an item will continue to be reported on),
- composition (how does it relate to what else is to be reported that day? Is it overshadowed by other events or repetitive of other news?),
- reference to elite nations,
- reference to elite peoples,
- reference to persons (if a story is expressed in personal terms we can see the consequences of an event for a personified subject),
- reference to something negative (this is perhaps, they suggest,

because it accords with the above criteria more fully than positive news tends to).[3]

In terms of Gatlung and Ruge's set of news values, the work of the Morris Tribunal merited selection as it aligned with a significant number of these values: the scale reaches the necessary threshold (the number of officers involved, the number of individuals affected, the amount of money and time consumed in the inquiry); it had achieved continuity ('the McBrearty affair' was defined as 'news' years previously at the allegations stage and continued to be reported; see Chapter 2); it is unambiguous (Morris's findings were concrete and clear, naming particular individuals); it is meaningful for the public ('ordinary' Irish people – fathers, mothers and children – had been mistreated by Gardaí whom we believed we could trust, the Troubles was used for personal gain and the investigation was at enormous cost to the taxpayer); it is unexpected (the Irish public have exceptionally high confidence in their police and indeed, as a scandal, these are behaviours which the original actors did not wish us to know about); it makes reference to both elite people (senior, powerful Gardaí and politicians) and persons (numerous characters such as Frank McBrearty Jnr and Adrienne McGlinchey emerged through the Tribunal); and is negative (in a democratic state innocent people should not be framed by the police for crimes they have not committed and the police should not abuse their powers and position for personal gain). In addition to this the media had been more reactive than proactive in breaking the scandal, as outlined in Chapter 2. O'Brien has written that the Irish focus on crime and zero tolerance in the late 1990s (Richard Barron's death came just months after the deaths of Veronica Guerin and Detective Garda Jerry McCabe) blinded the media as to what was occurring within An Garda Síochána:

> Such was the enthusiasm for dramatic stories of the criminal underworld that corruption within the Garda Síochána went unnoticed and unreported. It is instructive that no crime correspondent broke the story of the corruption within the Donegal division of the Garda Síochána. Instead it fell to two Dáil deputies, Jim Higgins and Brendan Howlin, to use Dáil privilege to bring the corruption to public attention.[4]

It was a news story which had caught the media off-guard. Whereas the activities of the 'heavy gang' were 'broken' by the *Irish Times*, the siege in Abbeylara which ended with the death of John Carthy was instantaneously being reported by the media and the May Day protest violence was filmed and broadcast, the media had in effect been duped in Donegal, as had the public. The death of Richard Barron and subsequent arrests were reported in all papers. The arms finds across Donegal were widely reported in papers and on television, thereby contributing to the attention and resultant benefits stemming from the Garda misconduct. The findings of the Morris Tribunal were, therefore, inherently newsworthy, although they would still have to be subjected to the processes of the construction of news. Hall et al. describe this stage:

> This involves the presentation of the item to its assumed audience, in terms which, as far as the presenters of the item can judge, will make it comprehensible to that audience. If the world is not to be represented as a jumble of random and chaotic events, then they must be identified (i.e. named, defined, related to other events known to the audience), and assigned to a social context (i.e. placed within a frame of meanings familiar to the audience).[5]

This 'framing' process enables readers to make sense of the story as presented to them. Reporting should not, therefore, be taken as a mirror image or objective replication of the findings of the Tribunal. Discretion remained in terms of how much space to dedicate to the reports, where in a paper to place it, what findings to focus on and how to represent the implications of these. Gatlung and Ruge also suggest that 'once a news item has been selected what makes it newsworthy according to the factors will be accentuated.'[6] Even the language used to describe the findings is important, for as Fowler describes, 'anything that is said about the world is articulated from a particular ideological position: language is not a clear window but a refracting, structuring medium.'[7] McCombs develops this area and examines what influence the media's presentation of a story has on a reader, once established as news:

> Newspapers communicate a host of cues about the relevant salience of the topics on their daily agenda. The lead story on page 1, front page versus inside page, the size of the headline and even the length of the story communicate the salience of topics on the news agenda ... The public uses these salience cues from the media to organize their own agendas and decide which issues are most

important. Over time, the issues emphasized in news reports become the issues regarded as most important by the public. The agenda of the news media becomes, to a considerable degree, the agenda of the public. In other words the news media set the public agenda.[8]

McCombs is describing here the power that the news media have to tell us what issues to think about. They cannot, of course, determine what we think about these issues, but the information they provide will certainly form the basis of those opinions.

There remains, then, much to be analysed about how the media reported the Tribunal. Added to the power of the media to influence public opinion is the context outlined by Hall et al., in which 'the media are often presenting information about events which occur outside the direct experience of the majority of society. The media thus represent the primary and often the only source of information about many important events and topics.'[9] This was true in relation to the Morris Tribunal. The first hearings were held in Donegal, as Justice Morris believed the people of that county were so directly affected by the events under investigation. Proceedings were transmitted to a room in a hotel near the courthouse to serve as an overflow for members of the public who wished to attend, but there was very limited attendance.[10] The lack of public attendance at the Tribunal, throughout its Dublin sittings, was a source of comment by Justice Morris in his reports. The Tribunal operated an impressively transparent system, with all reports, rulings and even transcripts being posted on its website.[11] The length of these presumably militated against a thorough reading by the public. Counsel's opening statement and the first report of the Tribunal were over 500 pages in length, the second report was close to 700 pages and the sixth more than 1,300. The public was therefore reliant on the media representations in newspapers, and on the radio, television and internet. The media outlets appeared to be aware of this from the moment the Tribunal began its first hearings in November 2002:

> The phones never stopped ringing. There were TV and radio interviews and newspapers calling to look for quotes. The internet was constantly being checked for the latest update of the Morris Tribunal's opening statement, published on the Tribunal website ... During breaks in the proceedings, and at the end of the day, the just delivered parts of the statement are handed out to queuing

reporters by the Tribunal registrar … It is the hottest publication in the country.[12]

The first ten days of the Tribunal were taken up with counsel for the Tribunal presenting their opening statement, which reviewed the findings of the preliminary investigation. In spite of the fact that much of this replicated what had been reported in the press in the build-up to the creation of the Tribunal, this received extensive coverage. It also emerged during the first week that one of the investigators for the Tribunal was a former Garda sergeant, Michael Finn, who had been named in the Nicky Kelly case as being in the 'heavy gang' and as having abused Kelly while he was detained in police custody. This was controversial on two counts: first, the Tribunal was established because internal investigations had been unsuccessful, so having a Guard investigate the Guards was not viewed as independent; second, to have a Guard accused of such misconduct himself investigating Garda misconduct brought the Tribunal into controversy. The Tribunal issued a statement on the matter in which it defended the record of Sergeant Finn and explained the benefits of having a member of the team who understood the internal workings and standards of An Garda Síochána.

How the media framed the reports would be key for how the public ingested and responded to the Tribunal. There were a number of frames which could have been applied to the reports, stemming from the positions adopted by other stakeholders. The Tribunal could have been perceived as an attack on the venerable institution of An Garda Síochána (a position adopted by the Garda Representative Association), as exposing the reality of long-term abuse and ill-discipline within the force (as believed by many academics and civil liberties groups) or as rooting out a number of rotten apples while reasserting the solid grounds for confidence in our police force (the view held by the key political parties and senior Garda management). Leishman and Mason tell how 'there has been a historical tendency for the media to recast the police institution in a favourable light – the "one bad apple in an otherwise clean barrel narrative" … This appears to be linked inextricably to the working ideology of news reporters, who see themselves as having a fundamental moral duty to support "goodies" over "baddies".'[13]

This chapter involves a review of Irish broadsheets to assess how the Tribunal was presented. The daily papers selected for the review include the *Irish Independent*, *Irish Times* and *Irish Examiner*, which account in the relevant years for more than half of all daily papers purchased in Ireland.[14] In terms of Sunday papers the *Sunday Times, Sunday Tribune, Sunday Business Post* and *Sunday Independent* were consulted. These papers were selected for a number of reasons. They cover a range of political spectrums, have national readership (as opposed to local papers which would only influence opinions at that level) and would be accessed by social elites in Ireland, those with power to impact on reform processes within An Garda Síochána. Also, they are the most easily accessed and researched media outlets in Ireland. The Tribunal was also widely covered by television and radio, often with re-enactments of extracts from proceedings, but this work will be limited to reviewing print media.

Articles from these papers were gathered through a combination of collecting them on a daily basis while the Tribunal was ongoing and supplementary searches of their online databases, where possible. Searches of newspaper databases online also identified coverage of the Tribunal in Northern Irish and English outlets, which added a further dimension to the work and highlighted the appeal of the 'story' beyond the regional national press. In the print media, four themes emerge from a review of the broadsheet coverage of the Tribunal;[15] the events as fiction; playing down or denial of events; focus on the political issues arising through the Tribunal; and declarations of revolutionary change.

A FICTITIOUS TALE

Much of the events established by the Morris Tribunal had a somewhat fictional quality. As McCullagh has written, 'the detail of the corruption has a certain hypnotic effect and the Tribunal report reads in places like a high quality but improbable thriller.'[16] The characters, the events, what the police were alleged to have done, all appeared to defy reality. This was strongly represented in media headlines, many of which drew heavily on the less than real qualities. Some of the headlines focused upon the environment and context of the story, hinting at its unsolved and bizarre nature: 'Murder, mystery and mayhem in Donegal' (*Sunday Business Post*, 17 November 2002); 'The murder that NEVER WAS' (*Sunday Business Post*, 4 October 2005). Others identify the extreme characters of the story and how their actions became interwoven: 'The whistleblower, the spy and the explosive tale of Garda corruption' (*Irish*

Examiner, 16 July 2004); 'An arch-manipulator tripped up on his own tangled web of lies' (*Irish Independent*, 20 August 2006); 'A morass of corruption: intimidation, lies, planted evidence. Indiscipline and bully-boy officers' (*Daily Mail*, 18 August 2006); 'The disgraced detective' (*Irish News*, 8 October 2008). A number highlighted the dark and almost seedy nature of their actions: 'Shameful web of lies and deceit' (*Irish Independent*, 16 July 2004); 'Grisly tale of crime and corruption raises haunting questions' (*Irish Examiner*, 11 October 2008); 'Corruption, lies and wall of silence' (*Irish Examiner*, 8 May 2008); 'Arms, bullets and bombs: A litany of lies' (*Irish Examiner*, 16 July 2004). Throughout, media tools of alliteration and word-play were used to add to the impact. The fiction theme was often expanded on further within the newspaper articles themselves. The *Irish Independent*, reporting on the first Morris report to be published, wrote: 'A tissue of lies and ludicrous excuses, involving animal feed and home-made fertiliser explosives, constituted the so-called "findings" designed to make two shamed Gardaí appear to be crack detectives' (16 July 2004). Others focused on the 'volatile' relationship between Garda McMahon and his wife and how this led to the Tribunal.

Such headlines read like film or novel titles and informed little about the findings of the Tribunal. The use of heavily loaded words, playing on the extremity of the findings, which run counter to usual descriptions of An Garda Síochána, are themselves attention grabbing, which in turn distorts the facts into a different narrative. At times the headlines stray into direct fictional references, with Adrienne McGlinchey being described as a 'Walter Mitty-type' (*Irish Examiner*, 16 July 2004) and the McBrearty family being referred to as 'the Don Corleones' (*Irish Examiner*, 24 September 2004). One article referred to some of the officers involved as 'The Incredibles' when they continued to serve in the force months after the first reports were produced (*Village*, 15 April 2005) whereas another identified the heroes of the 'story': 'Mum and Garda the true heroines of Morris inquiry' (*Irish Independent*, 11 May 2008, referring to Tina Fowley). This link to fiction has been reinforced with the reporting that this story merits dramatisation: 'Garda Scandal Set to Hit Big Screen' (*Irish Examiner*, 18 April 2009). A number of personal accounts have been published, including that of Adrienne McGlinchey (entitled *Charades*) and a forthcoming book by Frank McBrearty Jnr (provisionally entitled *Tell Them Daddy's Not a Murderer*).

Specific aspects of the Tribunal have been pulled out in a similar fashion to draw on the more human features, with one report on Sheenagh McMahon citing, 'I'm lucky to be alive, says whistleblower' (*Irish Examiner*, 19 July 2004) and referring to Mr Barron's death as 'Death on a lonely road that set probe in motion' (*Irish Independent*, 16 July 2004). The former, as a headline, implies that Mrs McMahon's life was at risk as a result of her whistleblowing, when in fact the article centres on the abusive behaviour of her husband, a private matter that was not relevant to the work of the Tribunal. The latter twists the reality to suggest Mr Barron died on a road that has been dramatised as lonely solely for the purposes of the story. This type of reporting creates an interpretation of the events so close to fiction that they are seen as extreme and thereby fail to penetrate as genuine problems, supporting the notion of a few bad apples who need to be purged. They appear so far-fetched and unimaginable that there cannot possibly be a continued risk of such behaviour. Justice Morris warned time and again, however, that unless serious reforms were introduced the events of Donegal could be repeated elsewhere. This was only reinforced by another theme of the media reports which was to play down the damage or the extent of the problem, discussed below.

At the same time, while the 'shock factor' is highly visible in the coverage of the first number of reports, by 2006 and the publication of reports three to eight, this fictional aspect is far less apparent, even when particularly disturbing details emerged. For instance, the sixth report, which arguably contained the most shocking details of the Tribunal, upholding specific allegations of the appalling treatment of detainees, was met with quite passive headlines which made, somewhat surprisingly, no effort to play on the salacious details: 'Crude attempt to put pressure on the chief suspects' and 'Clear abuse of power of arrest' (*Irish Times*, 8 May 2008) and 'Gardaí abused suspect, tribunal finds' (*Irish Times*, 8 May 2008). This on a report which found that women had been shown postmortem pictures. On Morris' finding that Frank McBrearty Jnr made a false confession, it was blandly written: 'Garda O'Dowd knowingly took false statement, tribunal concluded' (*Irish Times*, 8 May 2008). It may be that abuse of detainees by Gardaí is not an entirely new story, with similar allegations being made on a regular basis throughout the last number of decades. It is clear that from a media perspective the treatment of young mothers, the showing of autopsy photos, the use of sensory deprivation tactics and the religious references all provided significant fodder. Presumably, then, there was an increasing sense of Morris fatigue. For instance, when the *Irish Examiner* reported 'Five reports and counting but the criticisms of the Gardaí are the same' (19 August 2006), it was specifically written that 'if the language used in the latest Morris Tribunal reports sounded familiar, it's because many of the comments and criticisms made by Justice Frederick Morris also featured in his first report two years ago.' Not only does this hint that there is nothing of additional value in the later reports, it ignores the reality of the findings of each report, which have highlighted very different problems within An Garda Síochána.

PLAYING DOWN THE DAMAGE

At the same time that the findings were being presented as fictional, the media also at times downplayed the extent of the problem. The headline in the *Irish Times* the day after the first report was published announced that 'Tribunal finds two Gardaí offered a "tissue of lies"' (16 July 2004). The article goes on to detail how nineteen officers had been seriously criticised by the Tribunal, but the headline would not suggest to a passing reader that there was a large-scale problem. The headline would give credence to those who wished to believe that the problems were caused by a number of rotten apples.

The review of the print media also revealed presentations that challenged what Morris had found: 'Disgraced superintendent rejects findings of report' (*Irish Examiner*, 21 September 2004), one lawyer suggested that 'Morris has agenda to destroy officer' (*Irish Examiner*, 15 June 2005) and once action was taken we are then informed that 'Morris Tribunal Garda may take legal action over sacking' (*Irish Examiner*, 7 October 2004). These headlines serve to diminish, and even discredit, the findings of the misconduct. Again, on the publication of the fifth report on the arrests of members of the Travelling community, RTÉ reported: 'Adverse tribunal finding on Sgt John White', suggesting an individual bad apple and ignoring the broader aspects of the report such as the issuing of search warrants.[17] This was added to by the fact that the third, fourth and fifth reports were all published on the same day and Sergeant White was a key figure in each. Indeed, the following day the *Irish Times* ran short pieces on White and four other Gardaí named in the reports, making it seem all about a number of individuals rather than a large-scale problem. White's behaviour received attention beyond Ireland too. In England *The Sun* decried 'You are a bent cop, Sgt White' (18 August 2006) and the *Mirror* ran the headline 'Garda did plant gun' (18 August 2006). Meanwhile the *Belfast Telegraph* said: 'Blackest day for disgraced Garda'. At the same time, other stories challenged the findings: 'GRA criticises treatment of White', 'White calls findings perverse' (*Irish Times*, 18 August 2006) and 'Suspended officer claims he's the subject of a vendetta' (*Irish Independent*, 18 August 2006). This continued to the extent that, during applications for costs, Justice Morris responded that 'the findings I made in the report I am absolutely satisfied are correct.'[18] The newspapers equally focused on White's pension entitlements following dismissal: 'Det. Sgt White set to keep Garda pension' (*Irish Times*, 21 August 2006); 'White's pension terms revealed' (*Irish Independent*, 21 August 2006). All of this kept the attention stemming from the third, fourth and fifth reports on the actions of one officer, while numerous other officers were criticised and broader issues identified.

A further development was then to use this singular focus to argue that while there may be rotten apples, the barrel was fine and in fact being unfairly maligned: 'Cops still doing a good job' (*The Sun*, 23 August 2006); 'Insubordination not widespread, says Garda chief' (*Irish Times*, 2 September 2006); 'Actions of some Garda officers a "dark period"' (*Belfast Telegraph*, 8 October 2008); 'Garda morale affected by recent Morris Tribunal reports' (*Irish Independent*, 23 August 2006); and 'Rank and file Gardaí feel maligned by Morris reports' (*Irish Times*, 25 August 2006). The public were being in this way advised that the body of the force could still be trusted and, indeed, that we should perhaps have sympathy for the officers who continue to work hard and serve society.

There were also efforts to tarnish those who had made allegations against the Gardaí. Following publication of the sixth report, in which Justice Morris had criticised Frank McBrearty Jnr, one paper ran the headline: 'His own worst enemy' (*Sunday Times*, 11 May 2008) and the Irish edition of the *Daily Mail* reported: 'The man who made those original allegations, and has subsequently received €5.5 million in compensation from the taxpayer, publican Frank McBrearty, was himself involved in concocting and then leaking completely untrue allegations about two senior Gardaí to politicians' (8 October 2008). The 'innocence' of this particularly high-profile victim of Garda misconduct was called into question and it was queried whether he deserved the level of compensation received. This did not pass without challenge: 'Victims slam Morris report as a "fudge"' (*Sunday Tribune*, 20 August 2006) and 'McBrearty criticises report and denies he exaggerated abuse' (*Irish Times*, 8 May 2008). The protectionism of Gardaí was taken further by the *Evening Herald*: 'Garda's finest finally get the all clear as TDs' claims blasted' (8 October 2008).

One further attempt to detract from the work of the Tribunal was the occasional focus on its cost. This was an ongoing issue in relation to the numerous tribunals sitting in Ireland during the lifespan of the Morris Tribunal. In February 2004 the *Sunday Tribune* reported on the '€101m payout for tribunal lawyers', while a similar theme was picked up by the *Irish Examiner* months later: 'Lawyers get €250,000 to watch tribunal' (1 November 2004). The same paper reported the following summer that 'McBrearty scandal set to cost taxpayer over €15m' (9 June 2005). The article is accompanied by a picture of Frank McBrearty, mentions both the civil actions and the costs to be paid to him for the Tribunal, and indicates the extent of the bill the 'taxpayers' will face. It mentions the general points for which payment will be made but fails to mention any single Garda or detail any of the treatment the victims suffered. At no point is Frank McBrearty presented as the meritorious victim, but as a financial burden on the State.

A POLITICAL HOTCAKE

While not a direct attempt to downplay the findings of Morris, the focus on the political issues emerging diverted attention away from the severity of the findings. Political points-scoring was inevitable in such a situation. The opposition availed of the publication of the reports and the recommendations contained therein to criticise the government's plans for Garda reform which had in fact been announced prior to the publication of the first Morris report: 'Reform of the force more crucial than ever, says opposition' (*Irish Independent*, 16 July 2004); 'Immediate reforms urged by opposition parties' (*Irish Examiner*, 16 July 2004); 'Opposition continues attack on govt over Garda reform' (*Irish Examiner*, 16 June 2005). It became a political issue to the extent that 'McDowell defends record on Garda affair' (*Irish Examiner*, 9 June 2005) and 'Pressure grows to publish Carty report' (*Irish Examiner*, 18 June 2005), though this never did happen. Even after the reforms had been implemented the opposition's dissatisfaction merited attention:

'Rainbow to shake up Garda body' (*Sunday Times*, 3 September 2006).
A number of very specific issues arose as political points worth reporting.

The first of these related to the long-standing request from the
McBreartys to have their costs paid by the State: 'Pay McBrearty legal
bill, says FG' (*Irish Independent*, 16 July 2004) and 'Trouble ahead for
McDowell over McBrearty legal costs decision' (*Sunday Business Post*,
24 October 2004). Others called for attention to be paid to the pensions issue, 'Call for Garda pensions review' (*Irish Independent*, 19 July
2004) or the restrictions on admission to the force: 'Abolish Garda age
limit, says TD' (*Irish Examiner*, 19 July 2004). Others undermined the
whole process of reform that had been implemented: 'Patten, Hayes
should review Garda Síochána, says Labour' (*Irish Examiner*, 21 July
2004). This was media attention which ostensibly related to the Morris
Tribunal but, in actuality, did not.

The sixth report of the Tribunal, containing, as the reader will be
aware, some of the most disconcerting findings, was published on the
day that Brian Cowen became Taoiseach, taking over from Bertie
Ahern, and announced his new cabinet. Accusations abounded that this
was an attempt to bury the report and this particular accusation merited as many column inches, if not more, than the contents of the reports themselves: 'Minister accused of burying report' (*Metro*, Dublin,
8 May 2008); 'Lenihan accused of burying report' (*Irish Examiner*, 8
May 2008); 'Government criticised over timing of report' (*Irish Times*,
8 May 2008); 'Coughlan denies trying to bury Morris' (*Irish Independent*, 9 May 2008); 'Coughlan denies Morris timing a stroke' (*Irish
Times*, 9 May 2008). The media decision to focus on this issue, as well
as downplaying the conclusions as discussed above, detracted substantially from the findings. Without question, this report received substantially less space in the print media than the previous reports.

Similarly, when the seventh and eight reports were published, telling
of the Garda campaign of harassment against the McBreartys, the planting of drugs on Mark McConnell and the inadequacies of the Complaints Board, all focus was on the anonymous allegations and the
relatively slight criticism of the politicians involved: 'Howlin and Higgins criticised in report' (*Irish Examiner*, 8 October 2008); 'Tribunal
judge raps TDs over handling of claims' (*Irish Independent*, 8 October
2008); 'Howlin and Higgins reject criticism by Morris Tribunal' (*Irish
Times*, 8 October 2008); 'Parties hit out at Morris report's criticism
of TDs' (*Irish Independent*, 9 October 2008); 'Concern over tribunal

criticisms' (*Irish Times*, 9 October 2008); 'Gilmore defends two TDs criticised by Morris Tribunal' (*Irish Times*, 9 October 2008); 'Morris Tribunal blows whistle in wrong direction' (*Sunday Times*, 12 October 2008). The TDs in question received general support for their actions: 'Without our intervention abuses would still be going on, say politicians' (*Irish Times*, 8 October 2008). Quite possibly this received such media attention because it was unusual to hear politicians criticised in this way, but also because journalists see the exposure of stories as a function they can relate to. Irrespective, this political focus diverted all attention away from the findings relating to Garda misconduct.

DRAMATIC STATEMENTS OF CHANGE

Immediately after the publication of the reports, the media were informing the public that swift action would be taken to overhaul the systems in place to ensure that this would not happen again. The Commissioner was quoted on the day the first Morris report was published as being concerned about the findings and announced the establishment of a working group to examine the report and begin the process of addressing the points made.[19] We were informed that 'Morris fallout sparks overhaul' (*Irish Examiner*, 22 June 2005), that 'McDowell pledges action on "frightening" findings' (*Irish Independent*, 16 July 2004) and that 'Corrupt offenders face swift justice' (*Irish Independent*, 16 July 2004).

The public was reassured that those at fault were to be removed from the force and would not be policing the country again: 'Senior Garda to retire after tribunal findings' (*Irish Times*, 17 July 2004); 'Morris: senior Garda retires, detective faces dismissal' (*Irish Examiner*, 17 July 2004); 'Garda sacked over fake explosives finds' (*Irish Examiner*, 6 October 2004); 'Gardaí sacked in wake of corruption probe revelations' (*Irish Examiner*, 8 December 2004); 'Disgraced detective set to leave Donegal Garda' (*Irish Independent*, 19 August 2006); 'Key Morris Tribunal garda to retire' (*Irish Examiner*, 24 July 2007); 'Six Gardaí face dismissal over Morris reports' (*Irish Independent*, 11 May 2008). On one of the rare occasions where the Taoiseach spoke about the affair, his reassurance to the public was reported: 'More Gardaí to leave, says Ahern' (*Irish Examiner*, 1 July 2005).

Details then emerged of plans to reform the Gardaí, picking up on very specific issues which Morris had alluded to: 'Major reforms ordered after tribunal lifts lid on widespread misconduct in force' (*Belfast Telegraph*, 18 August 2006); 'Commissioner's powers expanded to include summary dismissal' (*Irish Times*, 18 August 2006); 'Gardaí to get training on handling of informants' (*Irish Examiner*, 23 March 2005); 'Gardaí set to blow the whistle on malpractice' (*Irish Examiner*, 14 April 2004);'Comreg set for talks over Morris recommendations' (*Irish Examiner*, 14 June 2005). At the same time, we were told that these were not changes that were simply being imposed on the force. The Commissioner and senior management solidly informed the public that they were ready, willing and able to ensure that Donegal would not repeat itself and that An Garda Síochána could be the kind of force the public wanted: 'Gardaí not afraid of accountability – Conroy' (*RTÉ*, 24 June 2005); 'Senior Garda officers "would welcome any outside expertise"' (*Irish Times*, 21 August 2006); 'Garda changes aim to prevent abuse' (*Irish Examiner*, 3 March 2006); 'Gross abuses of power "unacceptable"' (*Irish Times*, 18 August 2006).

Certainly, much legislative change quickly followed the publication of the reports but, substantively, it could be said that little happened. There was no major shake-up at the higher ranks of the force, and little change even in terms of those officers who had been named and shamed by the Tribunal. These statements gave the public the impression that something *would* be done, that changes *would* be made, that problems *would* be rooted out. Justice was not swiftly served for those officers involved. Those that resigned escaped disciplinary proceedings and, where disciplinary action is being pursued, it will be a lengthy and drawn out process. Instead of the 'swift justice' promised, there was 'No date set for disciplining Donegal Gardaí' (*Irish Examiner*, 6 August 2004) and it was 'Revealed: why Donegal Gardaí won't be prosecuted' (*Sunday Business Post*, 18 July 2004). Almost a year after the first report was published it was revealed that 'Gardaí who misled Morris Tribunal still serving in the force' (*Irish Examiner*, 18 April 2005). Still later that year 'Morris Gardaí still not moved from Donegal' (*Irish Examiner*, 15 September 2005). But no media frenzy was whipped up over this – crazy things had happened, the government had responded, the public believed it would not happen again, end of story; a *story* being exactly what this was.

GARDA STATEMENTS

An equally important discourse for how the police organisation moved forward would be that which emanated from the organisation itself. Garda management had two tasks to achieve: the public had to be convinced that this would not happen again, that the police could be trusted and members of the force, in particular 'officers on the beat', had to believe they would be supported in their work and that any reforms introduced would not make their working life too difficult. Rank and file officers would need the systemic failures within the organisation to be recognised and remedied, if they were not to be blamed and distrusted for what happened. There is a well documented tension between the views of 'street cops' and 'management cops', which Reuss-Ianni has documented as being increasingly in conflict, a conflict which can 'isolate the precinct functionally, if not structurally, from headquarters'.[20] After reports which indicated that headquarters was already isolated from policing districts, the challenge for Garda management would be to bring all members with them as they moved forward. The Commissioner issued statements in relation to each of the reports, which will now be considered alongside the comments of members of the GRA. The wording is often sophisticated, presenting a particular interpretation of events, emphasising issues which reflect well on the Gardaí, and limiting any potential admissions or statements which could be interpreted as penetrating the image of the force as strong and proud.

The Commissioner took swift action following the first report, informing the media that he had established a working group under Deputy Commissioner Fitzgerald to examine the report and feed back to him quickly. Some newspapers were reporting on specific planned reforms the day the report was published.[21] The Commissioner expressed concern at 'the possible impact this report's findings will have on all members of the organisation and public alike'.[22] This places the emphasis on future harm, which could be caused by the *report*, rather than accepting the damage that has already been done or admonishing the behaviour of the Gardaí involved, who effectively took advantage of the Troubles and the ongoing security alerts for their career development.

On the same day, a Garda spokesperson said: 'I certainly don't believe there is anything out there of the magnitude of behaviour as happened up in Donegal. No doubt if there was, somebody would come forward and tell us.'[23] Of course, as later reports would show, if other people had been trying to come forward to tell the Guards of similar problems, there was no effective method in place for them to do so. The GRA, in response, spoke of how the management failings found by Morris merited 'grave concern', also stressing that it would be a pity if all Gardaí were 'tarnished' by the report.[24] The Minister referred to it as a 'dark day' for the Gardaí, and continued:

> I will stand by the Gardaí rather than dump on them. The force has the respect of the public ... By and large, since the foundation of the State, An Garda Síochána has served our community well – sadly too often at great personal cost. We would do well to remember that the bad behaviour of the few should not be allowed traduce the reputation of the many members of the force who will continue to serve us in the best traditions of dedication, efficiency and loyalty to the State.[25]

This statement reasserts the dangers Gardaí face and minimises the extent of the problem by relying on the rotten apples theory. Further, his statement also made assurance of disciplinary action for those involved, when, as has already been considered, this would in fact be quite limited.

Following publication of the second report, the Minister was asked on national radio whether the State should apologise to the McBreartys. His reply indicated his intention to concede liability in the upcoming civil case. This, of course, is not an apology. The Commissioner's response to the second report was equally limited, stating that all the problems which occurred stemmed from the failure to preserve the scene, which he described as a 'cock up'.[26] Again, this reduces the entirety of the findings of the second report to the decision taken by three officers at the scene. Such a view ignores the problems that occurred in getting an officer to the scene, itself indicative of much broader complacency within the force. It implies that had the right decision been made at the scene, then no opportunity for 'tunnel vision' would have arisen. But that does not deal with the fact that the sequence of events in Donegal shows that it was more engrained than that position permits.

On the silver bullet module, published in the summer of 2006, the Minister spoke strongly about 'the gross abuses of power and fabrication of evidence' being 'completely unacceptable and deplorable'. He declared that An Garda Síochána could not be 'a playground for mischief makers'.[27] The GRA, on the other hand, expressed serious concerns at the treatment of Sergeant White: 'no citizen of the country would have their rights tramped on in this fashion' and reiterated that White had not been found guilty in the criminal trial.[28] The GRA felt that rank and file officers were being scapegoated when failures lay with senior management and rejected the findings accordingly. This reveals a state of discontent between ranks and low morale and directly reflects the type of conflict Reuss-Ianni described. P.J. Stone of the GRA further undermined the reports, in an opinion piece in the *Irish Times*, stating that the Tribunal 'can ultimately only report on what probably happened … one of the things that hurts the force so deeply, particularly those of Garda rank, is that these events under Tribunal scrutiny occurred ten years ago and we are all still suffering from the fallout of these regrettable events.'[29] In the immediate aftermath of the silver bullet report a Garda spokesperson emphasised that 'the vast majority of Gardaí … are trying to do the right thing.'[30] He spoke of how 'tonight [members are] running a gauntlet of threats, abuse and belittlement … our members feel even more isolated and demoralised.' This presentation of Gardaí as victims of the process, by both the GRA and the spokesperson, undermines the message of the Tribunal but also shows that Garda efforts to argue that the force was reforming, that these problems would not arise again, and that rank and file officers had the support of Garda management was not overcoming the isolation and low morale felt by members. The Commissioner cut short his holidays when this report was published and issued a statement two weeks after its publication, the same day the report on the Dean Lyons inquiry was published. He rejected Morris's finding that insubordination was widespread throughout the force and stressed that, in an organisation the size of An Garda Síochána, it was inevitable that some would perform below standard.[31] He further pointed to the level of reform that had been implemented since the Tribunal began its work: 'This organisation has changed so much in the last number of years that you would not really know it.' The Commissioner spoke to the magazine of the GRA in September 2006 and, while advocating a 'more open police force', there is in the interview much reliance on the rotten apples theory:

While I would accept from reading the reports that some people were clearly in breach of discipline I also say that we have over 12,500 sworn officers around the country and it is not unusual in an organisation of that size that there are some people who do not comply with the discipline regulations and who are sometimes in breach of the criminal code. I am not saying it was completely confined to Donegal. We have experienced it in different parts of the country, but I want to emphasise that it is not a major problem. It is not a major problem throughout the country.[32]

The response of the Commissioner to the sixth report, which, it has been suggested, is the most serious in terms of the form and scale of abuse disclosed, contains a strong apology to victims of Garda abuse. On the other hand, it could be said to combine minimisation of the problem, careful non-reference to specifics and an assertion of the rotten apples thesis:

The powers of arrest and detention bestowed on members of An Garda Síochána carry profound responsibility and the community is entitled to expect that Gardaí will exercise those powers appropriately and that every member of An Garda Síochána will work to protect and uphold the rights and dignity of the people they encounter in the course of their duty.

It is a matter of profound regret to me and to An Garda Síochána that this was not the experience of the individuals whom this report finds to have been mistreated by members of the organisation as identified by Mr Justice Morris. I want to take this opportunity to apologise to those people. It is also deeply disappointing that the Tribunal found that some members of An Garda Síochána were less than forthright in their dealings with the Tribunal ...

The vast majority of Gardaí perform their duties in an ethical manner, never violating or abusing the authority granted to them and working at all times to meet the needs of the communities they serve. The small minority who fail to observe those professional standards do a grave disservice to their colleagues and dishonour the history and tradition of a proud organisation.

The way in which this second paragraph is phrased in its issuing of an apology is quite limited. In describing this as mistreatment it also reduces what could otherwise be described as 'inhuman and degrading treatment'. The apology does not condemn the behaviour of the officers, give assurances that they will be dealt with or declare that their behaviour is unacceptable within the force. Continuing, and asserting the depth of reform which the organisation is undergoing, important in a time of scandal, the Commissioner states:

> Our resolve to do so [to address failings identified by Morris] is evidenced by the extensive change and modernisation programme upon which we have embarked in recent years. The reform programme has been greatly assisted by recommendations from the Morris Tribunal and further steps will be guided by the firm recommendations of this report.

Concluding, Commissioner Murphy stated:

> I am determined to lead this organisation through the daily challenges of meeting the needs of modern policing and I am committed to ensuring it meets those challenges in a way which respects the dignity of all persons and works closely with communities to solve their problems. We are fortunate to have thousands of men and women working in An Garda Síochána who are committed to securing safe streets in our cities and towns and a peaceful countryside. My priority is to ensure those dedicated individuals have the policies, resources and leadership required to enable them to fulfil that important role.

For the morale of officers, which the GRA's statement following the silver bullet module had shown to be low, this concluding point could be important. On the other hand, it does not resonate with coming a day after publication of the most serious review of endemic problems in the history of the Irish police force.

The final reports were published the following October, at which point the Commissioner stated that 'the unacceptable actions of individual members … represent a dark period in the history of a proud organisation.'[33] Again, there is no acceptance of any endemic problem. He reiterated his apology, which is not directed to any individual persons so it is unclear whether it includes the Barron family. On the final reports, his only comment was to express his gratitude that the reputations of senior police officers had been 'vindicated'. He concluded by thanking Justice Morris, whose work had 'enhanced' the reform programme, and describes how An Garda Síochána is ready to move forward.

CONCLUSION

Given the low public attendance at the Tribunal and the prohibitive size of the reports, the Irish public was, by and large, reliant on the media for information. This power of the media, to set the agenda on the importance to be attributed to the Tribunal as well as the identification of the important issues emerging from it, could directly shape and determine the impact which it had. Two points are unveiled in this context. First, while the earlier reports received substantial coverage, this waned in terms of the later reports, undermining their potential to take a key place in the public agenda. So while the public may know that there is a problem of some corrupt officers in Ireland (first report), the extent of abuse of detainees may not have penetrated to the same degree (sixth report), particularly given the publication of that report on the same day that Brian Cowen assumed the position of Taoiseach.

Second, this chapter has examined the different frames that were placed on the reports and how the findings were represented and shaped to align with certain interpretations. Through emphasising the less than real characteristics of the findings and playing down the extent of the problem, the idea was prompted that the level of concern which the Tribunal necessitated was limited. Whatever problems did exist were being remedied, we were informed, by fundamental reforms. And by focusing on the political aspects, attention was diverted from issues within the police force. Accepting the power of the media to set agendas, any discussions that would take place in the public had been shaped and limited by these frames.

Finally then, this chapter considered the Garda response to the reports, both at the management and at the representative level. The Commissioner was forthright in his apology for Garda actions after the publication of the sixth report. His statements spoke of the extent of reform that was being introduced and how the proud record of the force would be maintained. He denied Justice Morris' finding of widespread ill-discipline however, and outlined that a small number were responsible for the abuse of powers. The limitation of Justice Morris' inquiry to one policing district did, perhaps, facilitate this position but it is nonetheless difficult to reconcile with the amount of evidence the Tribunal heard. Of importance as well are the statements from the GRA which express the dissatisfaction of members with the response to the Tribunal. It is not questioned here whether this dissatisfaction was justified: its presence signals that difficulties will be experienced in ensuring rank and file officers internalise and operationalise reform.

No studies have specifically been conducted on public attitudes to the Tribunal itself but in the following chapter the political and Garda discussions, as well as the results of surveys on public attitudes to the police, will be the subject of analysis, with special emphasis on how these discourses were converted into reform. What will be apparent in those discussions is how similar themes were used by politicians to divert attention from the true scale of the problem in An Garda Síochána. In the Dáil, there was limited dedicated discussion on the reports, but even in the reform debates members of the House made little mention of specifics arising, which resulted in minimisation of and distraction from the findings as well as a continuing effort to defend and support the Gardaí.

NOTES

1. G. Philo, 'Bias in the Media', in D. Coates and G. Johnston (eds), *Socialist Arguments* (Oxford: Martin Robertson, 1983), pp.130–45.
2. The dilemma which Gans identifies in the American context is that: 'In reporting the news about a nation of 200 million potential actors in news stories, journalists could, in theory, choose from billions of potential activities; and having limited air time and magazine space, they must select an even tinier fraction.' H. Gans, *Deciding What's News* (Constable: London, 1980).
3. J. Gatlung and M. Ruge, 'Structuring and Selecting News', in S. Cohen and J. Young (eds), *The Manufacture of News: Social Problems, Deviance and the Mass Media* (London: Constable, 1973), pp.62–72. There are other factors that are relevant at a more over-arching level as to what receives media attention, relating to social, historical and economic criteria. Certain newspapers will have certain political allegiances which through their reporting they will attempt to support. Further, in order to ensure a regular supply of news, certain agencies, institutions and events are constantly monitored as potential sources. (For a detailed list of these institutions see B. Whitaker, *News Limited: Why You Can't Read All About It* (London: Minority Press Group, 1981), pp.31–2.) These cover well-established, well-organised and well-resourced bodies that have the resources for public relations. Certain bodies then secure a louder voice in the media – these are often institutionalised bodies with an elite voice and a matching language. Fowler contends that this leads to 'intertextuality', whereby media reports replicate the language used by official reports, undermining any potential critique of that report: 'So specific powerful institutions, frequently accessed (with neglect of other sections of the population, and other organisations) provide the newspapers with modes of discourse which already encode the attitudes of the powerful elite. Newspapers in part adopt this language for their own and, in deploying it, reproduce the attitudes of the powerful.' R. Fowler, *Language in the News* (London: Routledge, 1991), p.23.
4. M. O'Brien, 'Selling Fear? The Changing Face of Crime Reporting', in Hordan et al., *Mapping Irish Media: Critical Explorations* (Dublin: University College Dublin Press, 2007).
5. S. Hall, C. Critcher, T. Jefferson, J. Clarke and B. Robert, *Policing the Crisis: Mugging, the State and Law and Order* (London: Palgrave Macmillan, 1978), p.54.
6. Gatlung and Ruge, 'Structuring and Selecting News', p.66.
7. Fowler, *Language in the News*, p.10.
8. M. McCombs, *Setting the Agenda: The Mass Media and Public Opinion* (Cambridge: Polity Press, 2004).
9. Hall et al., *Policing the Crisis*, p.34.

10. Paul Reynolds of RTÉ spoke of no members of the public in the morning session and five in the afternoon: http://www.rte.ie/news/2002/1104/morris.html.
11. www.morristribunal.ie; for some reason this became inaccessible from July 2009.
12. *Irish Independent,* 9 November 2002.
13. F. Leisman and P. Mason, *Policing and the Media: Facts, Fiction and Factions* (Devon: Willan, 2003), p.16.
14. See the results of the Joint National Readership Survey available at www.jnrs.ie.
15. The newspapers reviewed included the *Irish Times, Irish Examiner, Irish Independent* and *Sunday Business Post,* covering all the major broadsheets in Ireland.
16. McCullagh, 'The Global in the Local', p.5.
17. RTÉ News, 17 August 2006.
18. G. Cunningham, 'Tribunal chairman stands over report', *Irish Times,* 21 July 2004.
19. H. Bruce, 'Chastened Commissioner expresses concern', *Irish Independent,* 16 July 2004.
20. E. Reuss-Ianni, *Two Cultures of Policing: Street Cops and Management Cops* (New Brunswick, NJ: Transaction Publishers, 1983), p.4.
21. T. Brady, 'Reform will mean new system of promotion', *Irish Independent,* 16 July 2004.
22. Bruce, 'Chastened Commissioner expresses concern'.
23. C. O'Keeffe, 'Force promises to act on tribunal findings', *Irish Examiner,* 16 July 2004.
24. Bruce, 'Chastened Commissioner expresses concern'.
25. T. Brady, 'McDowell pledges to action frightening findings', *Irish Independent,* 16 July 2004.
26. C. O'Keeffe and P. O'Brien, 'Barron death probe a cock-up, says Garda chief', *Irish Examiner,* 18 June 2005.
27. C. Lally, 'Gross abuses of power "unacceptable"', *Irish Times,* 18 August 2006.
28. Anon, 'A morass of corruption', *Daily Mail,* 18 August 2006.
29. P.J. Stone, 'Rank and file Gardaí feel maligned by Morris findings', *Irish Times,* 25 August 2006.
30. S. Hogan, 'Morris reports are damaging to Gardaí', *Irish News,* 23 August 2006.
31. Anon, 'Garda chief: my hands were tied by courts over discipline', *Irish Independent,* 2 September 2006.
32. Interview with Commissioner, *Garda Review,* September 2006.
33. 'Statement by Garda Commissioner Fachtna Murphy on the Seventh and Eighth Reports of the Morris Tribunal', 7 October 2008 (Press Release 1163/08).

Chapter Five

The Reforms

The Morris Tribunal has been linked to the most significant reforms of An Garda Síochána since the foundation of the force. The Garda Síochána Act 2005 overhauled the legislative basis for internal discipline, promotions, complaints and accountability, standard-setting, community policing, auditing and international police co-operation. The timing of this legislation coincided with the early reports of the Morris Tribunal, and was proffered as resolving the problems identified. In addition to reforms imposed externally, the organisation itself implemented a programme of reform in the wake of the reports, about which a number of reports have now been published. This chapter will be broken into four parts, the first introducing the context of international debates on police reform, the second reviewing the legislation implemented, the third considering the internal Garda responses and the final part assessing to what extent these have addressed the problems identified by Morris. Justice Morris stated clearly that, without sufficient reform, what happened in Donegal could happen again elsewhere. Certainly, a substantive package of reform has been implemented but this chapter will argue that it has not given full effect to the reports. It is also suggested that the government and An Garda Síochána have created an anomalous situation whereby they can collectively claim to have addressed the problems identified by Morris, which they promote as representative of all problems within the force, when in fact they have not fully responded to Morris and all the problems of the force are as yet not known.

POLICE REFORM

The need to reform the police is not peculiar to An Garda Síochána. Similar processes have been undertaken in numerous jurisdictions: in England and Wales following the West Midlands 'Serious Crime' Squad controversy and again this decade following the Stephen Lawrence

inquiry; in New York in the 1970s following the infamous whistleblower
Serpico[1] and in the '90s subsequent to the Mollen Commission;[2] the
Wood Commission in New South Wales in the early 1990s following
serious allegations of endemic corruption, which led to the establishment of the Police Integrity Commission; the Fitzgerald Commission in
Queensland;[3] and of course Northern Ireland underwent a substantial
police reform process as part of the peace process of the late 1990s.
What prompts the reform can shape the nature of that reform and how
extensive it is. Stenning and Shearing differentiate the various drivers
for police reform:

  - External: states in transition, move to human rights, best practice
    policing (globalisation/harmonisation), population booms/
    demographic changes, changing concepts of justice/move to
    restorative justice.
  - Internal: efficiency, service not force, community policing/
    intelligence-led policing/evidence-based policy/reassurance
    policing, changes in police officer demographics, competition
    from private policing and scandals.[4]

A number of these could be seen to be influential in Ireland at the
beginning of the twenty-first century. Beyond the growing dissatisfaction
with existing accountability mechanisms,[5] the influence of events in
Northern Ireland, and indeed commitments under the Good Friday
Agreement to implement parity of human rights obligations, the growth
of Irish obligations to international human rights mechanisms (which
increasingly were of relevance to policing[6]) as well as the international
move towards civilian oversight mechanisms of accountability, had created a climate in which the government and the Gardaí had little option
but to reform accountability mechanisms. But, unquestionably, the
Morris Tribunal and the scandal it created was a monumental driver,
serving as a final catalyst. From the moment the Tribunal was established, the government, knowing that negative findings would be made
by the Tribunal, particularly in light of the various investigations which
had already been conducted, began working on the reform package. The
Irish process of reform, therefore, while influenced by other factors,
was, at its core, scandal driven.

    While by their nature seeming like a negative occurrence, 'scandals'
can create the necessary impetus, both internal and external to the
force, necessary to rectify the damage done to the force's relationship

with the public.[7] The problem with this response to corruption or misconduct is that it is so needs-driven it risks not getting to the heart of the real problem, addressing only those aspects that have caused greatest public alarm.[8] By their very nature scandals are reactionary. The calls for change can come before a full understanding of the problem has been achieved. Scandals prompt knee-jerk reactions, with short-term goals of instant improvement.[9] But the reality is that corruption is invariably engrained and interwoven with police subculture with the effect that it cannot be transformed overnight.[10]

A scandal indicates that both internal and external controls have failed, or have been manipulated and evaded by the institution. The invariable police response is that the problem has been caused by a number of bad apples, as will be present in any large organisation, deflecting attention away from the true extent of the problem.[11] The 'rotten apples' theory is based on the assumption 'that unlawful activity by police is a manifestation of personal moral weakness, a symptom of personality defects, or a result of recruitment of individuals unqualified for police work'.[12] The blame for corrupt activities rests solely with individuals rather than the force as a whole. All that is required of a reform process is to purge the force of those officers. Newburn dismisses this theory and points out that any time it has been relied upon, usually by police unions, the evidence suggests otherwise.[13] The Knapp Commission in New York in the 1970s, investigating widespread, institutionalised corruption in the NYPD, found that:

> According to this theory, which bordered on official Department doctrine, any policeman found to be corrupt must promptly be denounced as a rotten apple in an otherwise clean barrel. It must never be admitted that this individual corruption may be symptomatic of underlying disease ...
> The rotten-apple doctrine has in many ways been a basic obstacle to meaningful reform. To begin with it reinforced and gave respectability to the code of silence ... A high command unwilling to acknowledge that the problem of corruption is extensive cannot very well argue that drastic changes are necessary to deal with the problem.[14]

Whether it is through ignoring it, tolerating it or even encouraging it, there are organisational origins of police misconduct. It is not just down to a few rotten apples, and indeed Lundman goes so far as to argue that individual officers are marginal to organisations.[15] As Patrick Murphy, the NYPD commissioner at the time, explained, 'The task of corruption control is to examine the barrel, not just the apples – the organisation, not just the individuals in it – because corrupt police are made, not born.'[16]

If reform proceeds on the basis of the bad apples thesis then it will take an individualistic and not an organisational form and the evidence indicates that this will not be long-lasting as was the case in both New York and London. As Punch stated: 'When the sound and fury die away, it is all too often a case of returning sooner, or later, to business as usual.'[17] Newburn explains: 'The "heat" produced by major scandals can have a genuinely if often short-lived reformatory effect.'[18] The public perception that 'something has been done' can negate the potential for continued oversight created by the scandal.[19] Efforts at reform need to incorporate an awareness of the long-term nature of the problem. In fact, Punch suggests that scandal-driven reform can worsen the situation as it 'may confirm some policemen in their secondary deviance, may force "bent" police to be more devious and sophisticated to be successful and may simply push up the price of corruption'.[20]

So what is needed for effective, long-term reform? An overview of incidents of corruption internationally and how they were dealt with showed Punch that, to be successful, interventions had to comprise the following features: an energetic cleanup campaign; strong leadership; more powerful internal investigative capacity; enforcement of measures against police deviance either through internal disciplinary methods or criminal prosecutions; and a fundamental overhaul of the organisation, involving changes in personnel at all levels.[21] Efforts to curb corrupt behaviour will require changes in terms of human resource management, anti-corruption policies, internal controls and external controls.[22] More than anything, there will need to be police management responsibility for all of these. This can at times be most problematic. Punch describes his experience of the Dutch police:

> ... for within the Amsterdam Police there was a fatal ambivalence. Within the organisation you had the 'bureaucratic birds' that glided high in the sky without ever looking down; they believed in the sanctity of the rules and that no news must mean good news. Then there were the 'innovative hawks' that actively stim-ulated and encouraged rule-breaking ... The exciting new area of drugs enforcement (with heroin coming on the market for the first

time), the encouragement to get closely involved with criminals, the praise and encouragement for bringing in information or solving cases, all stimulated the rule-benders among the police to indulge in 'Miami Vice' behaviour ...

But when 'the shit hit the fan' the bureaucrats were horrified and demanded a ritual house-cleaning. Control was focused downwards – and not upwards. A number of scapegoats were hung out to dry. And the hawks cynically folded their wings to fight another day ...

In brief, the ambivalence within the organisation allowed the deviance to flourish, the organisation displayed no capacity for picking up the danger signals and the 'real' culprits got away with it.[23] (emphasis in original)

Widespread police corruption, therefore, is not about a few rotten apples. It is representative of problems at management level and a related failure of disciplinary controls.

Identifying what reforms need to occur is one thing, but implementing such reform within the police institution is difficult. Brogden et al. suggested there were two ways of viewing this change process.[24] Focus could be centred on rule tightening. This approach to change sees the police 'as a machine with faulty rules; be they external or internal'.[25] However, this method fails to adequately appreciate and problematise the particular intricacies of policing. The police are, at the end of the day, an organisation, and are inherently and sociologically much more problematic than this analysis allows. The alternative viewpoint sees this sociological aspect of all organisations, and focuses on transformation of culture. In this understanding of change, there is a more realistic conception of organisations which accepts that rule-change could actually be damaging if perceived by members of the organisation as punishment for past behaviour. For Brogden et al. this was the key; the relationship between formal rules and subcultural rules. Prenzler adopts the view that both the rules and the culture are incorporated in strategies for change and identifies twenty-five specific issues to be addressed in order to prevent corruption.[26]

Chan argues that police reform, particularly where any reform of culture is required, is a more complex process than this binary view permits. Her thesis requires acknowledgment of the role of the police officer, as an actor with influence over three elements: the structural conditions of policing, the cultural knowledge within the force and the police practice which occurs as a product.[27] To have the greatest chance of taking effect reform will have to address each of these factors: the conditions of policing, the culture of policing, the nature of officers who take action and the practice which results. The culture of policing, for Chan, is broader than others such as Reiner have contended. It is not a static body of characteristics but a fluid source of knowledge adapted by newer officers to their situations. It should be viewed 'in terms of the interaction between the social and political context of police work and the institutionalised perceptions, values, strategies and schemas'. This reconceptualisation allows for recognition of multiple cultures within the one police organisation and acknowledges the individual officers' role in structuring their culture. Reform should not be limited to rule-tightening or police training, but requires changes to the social and legal structures of policing as well as the knowledge of officers of policing. It must be recognised that when changing any of these areas the results will be 'unpredictable' particularly given the intersection with allocations of power and resources. Chan warns that 'change is traumatic, it has to be directed and continuous, people must be willing to change and, finally, planned change is difficult to achieve, especially where it is imposed by one group on another.'[28]

The challenge facing the Irish government and the Gardaí was to implement a system of reform which addressed the issues raised by the Morris reports; institutional rather than individualistic in nature, which tackled the deep problem of reforming culture, and which would be accepted by the Gardaí themselves, particularly recognising the traumatic affect of both the Tribunal and the reform process. This would all be dependent on the attitudes of those tasked with implementing reforms: politicians and senior Gardaí.

PLANNING REFORM

Reform of the governance and accountability of the police has been regularly raised by various members of the Dáil. In 1982 Garret FitzGerald included a Garda Authority in his programme for government, though the Kerry Babies case led instead to the establishment of the Complaints Board. The notion of an authority resurfaced in 1996[29] and in 1997,[30] at which point the Minister for Justice indicated that he had no intention of introducing one. In February 1998, by which time complaints were being made to the Complaints Board concerning Donegal, the Minister stated that he was reviewing the operation of the complaints system based on recommendations of the Board itself and the proposals of a steering group.[31] The government signed the Belfast Agreement in April 1998, committing to take comparable steps to those being implemented in Northern Ireland to improve human rights.[32] Reform was described as a legislative priority in October 1999,[33] and in June 2000, referring to proposals from the European Committee for the Prevention of Torture, Garda management and the Garda associations, the Minister outlined his intention to amend the legislation 'shortly'.[34] On that occasion the Minister refused to accept that the Complaints Board did not have the confidence of the public. Six months later, his position on this changed and he accepted the 'shortcomings' and 'dissatisfaction with its operation, in certain quarters'.[35] In May 2001, ten months before the Tribunal would be set up and before the government saw the Carty report, Minister O'Donoghue stated he was 'finalising proposals' for amendment.[36]

Brendan Howlin introduced a private member's motion on Garda reform in April 2001,[37] condemning the Minister for his failure to institute reforms of policing, calling for a Garda Authority, county policing liaison committees which would decide the policing plan and a Garda Ombudsman. Though these proposals were defeated after a lengthy debate, six months later the Minister announced a plan to produce a Garda Inspectorate Bill, rather than simply amended existing legislation. It was accepted in the period prior to the establishment of the Tribunal that reform would have to be more extensive than previously planned.

The heads of the Bill published in July 2003, prior to the publication of any Morris reports, proposed the creation of a Garda Inspectorate to handle complaints against the police, a Garda Reserve and local policing committees, and included a statement that the determination of policing priorities fell to the Minister for Justice and plans for a code of ethics. The Bill had some significant differences when presented to the Seanad in February 2004.[38] The Inspectorate was replaced by the Garda Ombudsman Commission. Local policing committees were renamed joint policing committees. When a year later the Bill reached the Dáil, by which time the first report of the Morris Tribunal had been published, the Minister had reinserted the Garda Inspectorate as a body which would examine areas of practice and procedure within the force.

What is particularly telling is how throughout the debates of the Bill, during which time the first two reports were published, Justice Morris' comments and findings were rarely mentioned, despite their inherent relevance and significant bearing on proceedings. There was no debate or Dáil discussion on the reports until the week before the final stage of the Bill. Presenting the Bill to the Dáil, Minister McDowell made just one mention of the Tribunal, explaining that the Inspectorate would address the knowledge gap between Garda HQ and the Department of Justice, identified by the Tribunal.[39] Despite the findings in the first Morris report of hoax bomb finds, negligent management of the division, an ability to keep Crime and Security in the dark, failed handling of informants, not to mention the blue wall which Justice Morris encountered in his work, opposition speeches lacked the emphasis on accountability that may have been expected. Jim O'Keeffe, Fine Gael's spokesperson for justice, criticised the Bill for being overly focused in that direction: 'The emphasis is on accountability and that is not enough.'

> The provisions as outlined by the Minister have to be examined against the backdrop of current realities in many areas, particularly that of resources, which are not provided for in the Bill. Day in day out our Gardaí are at the coalface of the darker side of society. When the Minister and I are sleeping in our beds the Gardaí are confronting dangerous situations and fighting crime. They deserve the best to match the willingness to put themselves on the line. From that point of view, the Minister has failed to win the battle for resources for Gardaí.[40]

Ignoring the report of Justice Morris on how officers had planted explosives on both sides of the border and the inadequacies of the system for handling informants, Deputy O'Keeffe proceeded to condemn the failure to provide a new radio system, the state of Garda stations around the country, the age of retirement, the Garda Reserve, and what he claimed to be the rising crime rates in Ireland. O'Keeffe finished by saying:

> There are achievements and advances in the Bill but it does not cover the essential problems of the force, such as lack of resources, the lack of input to modern technology and the kind of things that will allow us to have what I want for the Garda Síochána, namely, the best police force in the world.[41]

While correct in emphasising the importance of a well-resourced police force, to state in the wake of the most damning report ever published on An Garda Síochána that these constitute the 'essential problems of the force' and to fail to mention the Tribunal is to wholly undermine the seriousness and significance of its findings. Others made a more passing reference to the Morris reports. Deputy Ardagh, for instance, stated that 'recent events, particularly in Donegal, show that, while the structures operate well in many cases, they are too reliant on one person.'[42] Moreover, numerous deputies defended the Gardaí in their speeches, such as Deputy Keaveney:

> Coming from County Donegal where the Garda Síochána has received one of its greatest batterings in the history of the State, through the tribunals, this is a time when not only the people of the county but the Garda are getting a bad name and are being tarred with the one brush unnecessarily.[43]

The Gardaí are presented as passive recipients of abuse, while no mention is made of the hardship those involved caused for the deputy's own constituents. Replicating O'Keeffe's sentiment, Keaveney's speech proceeded to focus on the under-resourcing of the Gardaí, an issue also mentioned by Deputies Breen and Sargent.

This defensive theme was developed further by deputies such as Glennon who, in the course of the debate, detailed the dangers faced by Gardaí, and mentioned in particular Garda Richard Fallon who was killed in 1972, without reference to the Morris Tribunal.[44] Deputy Deenihan referred to the first ten Gardaí to be killed.[45] Deputy Gilmore raised the issue of the government considering for the early release scheme those who had killed Gardaí.[46] Many emphasised the inevitability of a few bad apples in any organisation, such as Deputy Hogan, who asserted that 'Certain individuals in the Garda Síochána have besmirched the good name of the force ... this is inevitable in every occupation',[47] while Deputy Durkan excused the fact that 'some of its members have fallen by the wayside ... no organisation is perfect.'[48] On similar lines, Deputy Timmins cautioned that 'while those few bad apples must be dealt with in the most severe terms, it is unhealthy for us as a society to regard their behaviour as a reflection on the general well-being of a particular force.'[49]

Perhaps of greater concern is that in this second-stage debate countless deputies contributed to the debate on the Bill without referring to the report, its findings or its recommendations.[50] Deputy Andrews outlined the background to the Bill without mentioning the Morris Tribunal. Equally, Deputy McGuinness, not referring to Morris, stated: 'The Garda has served the State well throughout its history. It is doing an excellent job, but it could do much better if its structures and its level of funding were much different.'[51] The issue was not what was wrong within An Garda Síochána, but the limitations placed on the force by external factors.

Others made statements which down-played and even challenged the findings of Morris. Deputy Haughey commented that the accountability measures would 'boost public confidence in our security forces following recent high-profile cases which do not reflect the organisation as a whole, but, sadly have led to its being tainted in the eyes of a few.'[52] Deputy Connaughton declared that 'it has become the in thing to do down the Garda, a dangerous path for society to take.'[53] This is in spite of the warning which Morris had given in the first report that discipline as a whole was disintegrating in the force and that the events in Donegal could happen again. Deputy Curran was also concerned with such critical views, noting that 'complaints against Gardaí are not an everyday occurrence',[54] despite the fact that in that year the Garda Complaints Board received, on average, 3.2 complaints a day.[55] Similarly, Deputy Carey stated that he recalled 'few enough examples of questionable practices in terms of management or accountability'.[56] The reality of police misconduct in Ireland, and the findings of the Tribunal, were being indirectly denied by those tasked with reform.

There were those who argued that the accountability provisions in the Bill were weak. The Labour party continued its calls for a Police Authority and, in that vein, Costello argued:

> The time has come for a root and branch review of the culture, role, structures and operations of the Garda. Unfortunately this is not what we have here ... A lasting new police culture of service can only be delivered if a strong sense of participation, responsibility and ownership is first engendered through the consultative process. The Minister has missed a golden opportunity by failing to establish such a commission.[57]

Dan Boyle of the Green Party similarly placed substantial emphasis on the report of the Tribunal:

Those who have listened to re-enactment of the Morris Tribunal would wonder why there is not a wider debate about what seem to be systemic problems regarding the Garda Síochána promotion system, the perceived need to provide high-profile so-called crime convictions which turn out not to involve crimes, and the development of networks in terms of how people can push themselves forward as individuals within the Garda Síochána ... the Minister has not responded properly to the Morris Tribunal findings.[58]

Such critical voices were in a minority and the Bill passed to the Select Committee on Justice, Equality, Defence and Women's Rights in April 2005, by which time the government had announced that an implementation group would be established for the legislation, chaired by Senator Maurice Hayes.[59] On the first day of committee discussions Deputy Costello asked the Minister to consider widening the implementation group into an independent commission on policing, without which 'we cannot change the culture the Morris Tribunal identified in County Donegal, where colleagues see their priority as standing by one another rather than standing by the truth or the code of ethics and conduct by the force.'[60] The acknowledgement that Morris had identified a culture in need of reform indicated a crucial realisation of the extremities of the report, but this was not widespread. Limited mention of the Tribunal was made in discussions save in relation to new provisions concerning the exchange of information with other police forces, the confidentiality of information emanating from An Garda Síochána and the offence of causing disaffection from An Garda Síochána. It became apparent in the discussion that deputies were not clear what Justice Morris meant by his comments on the state of discipline within the force.[61] This confusion may have been spared if a debate had been held on the reports. As it was, the legislature continued to push the Bill through the process, despite the lack of consensus on the actual contents of the reports.

A stark display of the influence of Morris on these debates came in the final two days of committee debates. On 31 May 2005, the penultimate day of discussions, the committee moved to consider the provisions relating to the Ombudsman Commission. To many, this part of the Bill was the lynchpin of accountability reforms, yet, again, throughout the discussion that day there was no mention of Morris or events in Donegal. The following day, the second Morris Tribunal report was published and the Tribunal suddenly had a much greater bearing on proceedings. The Minister announced that the only legislative change on foot of the Act would be the inclusion of a duty to account. He specifically stated that any debate on the reports should not delay the passing of the legislation 'because there is no point letting it go beyond that'.[62] Specific mentions of Morris on that day included whether Gardaí could make complaints to the Commission, access to telecommunications records and the extent to which the Inspectorate would improve the relationship between the Department and Garda HQ.

Prior to the final stage debate in the Dáil, time was dedicated in June 2005 to a discussion of the second Morris report (not the first). This was the first discussion on the work of the Tribunal in either house. Rather than a dedicated debate on the findings and recommendations, and what those meant for policing in Ireland, this took the form of statements from various parties on the report. The Minister began with a response to the reports in which he accepted the scale of abuse:

> The reality is – we have to accept this – that the whole system failed badly. The handful of corrupt Gardaí should not have been able to get away with their outrageous behaviour for so long, but they did. The fact that they even started out on their corrupt path indicates a certain confidence on their part that they would not be challenged or stopped. The damage inflicted on their victims is enormous and the damage inflicted on the force would be incalculable unless we respond decisively to address the management and system failures exposed by the Morris Tribunal.[63]

As his statement progressed it became clear that he would not address the intricacies of the report's findings. He discussed the political issue of the delay in establishing the Tribunal and in receiving the Carty report. This was followed by an outline of how the proposed legislation would address the shortcomings identified in the report. He bypassed a direct discussion of the reports and refocused the discussion on the legislation, which had been drafted prior to the reports being published. He spoke of his intention to reform the Bill in light of the second report and mentioned the working groups to be set up within An Garda Síochána. His speech, described by the opposition as 'defensive and narrow', did not encompass an open and engaged discussion of the issues raised by Justice Morris.

Opposition parties expressed particular concern with the finding of a blue wall of silence 'as impregnable as the Berlin Wall. Like the Berlin Wall, it must be torn down.'[64] Fine Gael called for the government to use the summer recess as a review period for the reports and the Bill, suggested the establishment of a select committee for security and called for the appointment of a 'commission of review for the Garda Síochána'. Both Labour and Fine Gael supported such a commission.

Deputy Costello focused on the political issues[65] and referred to the Ombudsman Commission as 'little more than the old Garda complaints body, with a coat of paint'.[66] Deputy Ferris was one of the few to mention the need to sanction those officers condemned by the reports and also raised other cases of Garda misconduct which did not fall under the remit of the Tribunal.[67] Deputy Ó Snodaigh continued in this vein: 'The Morris Tribunal will not bring us the whole truth even with the remaining eight modules. Many questions remain about serious Garda misconduct in all parts of the State.'[68] He questioned where else in the country those Gardaí implicated by Morris had served, a point discussed further by Dan Boyle:

> ... due to the limitations in the terms of reference of the Morris Tribunal, we have not been able to ask questions as to whether such people have practised in a corrupt way in other parts of this country, whether they learned to practise corruption in other parts of the country and whether a web of corruption has been established through their careers and the careers of others they have touched.[69]

Ciarán Cuffe of the Green Party called for the resignation of the Commissioner and for the withdrawal of the proposed legislation. All agreed time was needed to reconsider the Bill.

Others rose to the defence of the Gardaí, with Deputy Timmins of Fine Gael reminding the House that 'many members of the Garda Síochána have been murdered by organisations ... I suggest we should not be selective by using the Morris Tribunal to have a go at the Garda countrywide.'[70] He expressed a fear that the proposed reforms may do more harm than good: 'If we have too many groups looking over the shoulder of the Garda Commissioner he and his force will become introverted.'[71]

The Bill was before the House for the final stage one week later. A raft of amendments were introduced at this point, including provision for the creation of a Garda Professional Standards Unit (GPSU), a duty to account, the appointment of one member of the Commission as chairperson, the creation of a Garda Inspectorate to conduct examinations into the administration and effectiveness of An Garda Síochána and a Promotions Board, new disciplinary regulations (with the potential for a Disciplinary Board) and a whistleblowers' charter. None of these had been scrutinised in the second stage or by the committee. Dozens of further amendments were introduced the day before the final debate, which was guillotined to ensure passage before summer recess. Green Party TD Ciarán Cuffe commented:

> Over the past few days, my fax machine has been overheating as a result of the Minister's amendments. Like others, I have not even had a chance to count those amendments, let alone read them in detail. This makes a mockery of the parliamentary process ... It is at best infuriating and at worst impossible to deal with the complexity of the amendments before us.[72]

Of the 300 amendments proposed, only forty-two were discussed in the final debate. Many of the amendments were only distributed after the final stage debate had begun, and much anger was expressed at the Minister's absence for parts of the debate.[73] A number of issues received considerable attention in the limited time available, including the establishment of a reserve force, whether there should be a single ombudsman or a commission and when the government received the Carty report. There was little discussion beyond this of the substantive amendments or their relation to the Morris findings. One notable trend in this debate is the emerging willingness of deputies to be more critical of the force than they previously would have been. For instance, Deputy Crowe said that 'Gardaí have abused their positions and there have been criticisms in the past'[74] and Deputy McGrath noted that 'there is a major crisis of confidence in some sections of the force and on the broader issue of policing more generally.'[75] While this change would be a very welcome critical development were it to continue, the debate is marked by a lack of recognition generally of the cultural aspects to be reformed and the difficulties in doing so. Perhaps the strongest nod in that direction came from the Minister himself:

> There are many provisions I would like to include in the Bill such as a provision that every interview should be recorded or that the

scene of a crime should never again be left in the state that Justice Morris found regarding the accident involving Richie Barron. This legislation is not meant to be a series of aspirations or best practice guidelines given by legislators to the Gardaí. This is a constitutional framework for the Garda Síochána and it will be in the context of directives, annual policing plans, the professional standards units and the Inspectorate that best practice will evolve and that issues of this kind will be brought to the fore rather than by contenting ourselves that we have dealt with the matter because we have put something on the Statute Book.[76]

The following sections will examine all levels of reform introduced since this time and assess the extent to which they have contributed to reform at the necessary level. What can be said initially, though, is that inadequacies with accountability systems had long been recognised and the government did not act until the scandal of Donegal pushed it to the point of no return. It cannot be said with certainty that the Garda abuse in Donegal could have been prevented had action been taken sooner, but earlier action on the part of the government, even in the late 1990s, may certainly have minimised the harm caused to the victims of Garda abuse in Donegal. Rather than being proactive, the Irish government stalled until it was left with no alternative. The process which followed was needs-driven and, as the above analysis of the debates has shown, paid scant recognition to the work of Morris and failed to engage in discussions of deep cultural reform.

THE 2005 ACT

The Act, signed into law by the president on 10 July 2005, was heralded by the Minister as 'the most profound piece of legislation relating to An Garda Síochána in the history of the State'.[77] A lengthy Act of over 130 sections, it provided for a wide range of areas including internal affairs, whistleblowing, the relationship between Garda HQ and the Department, citizen complaints, public consultation and financial accountability. These will be examined in turn to assess how this Act, and each of the constituent elements, contributed to the reform of An Garda Síochána. Did the above political debates and concerns translate into a new 'constitutional framework' for the Irish police? This will be complimented with the subsequent discussion of statutory instruments and other legislative reforms of relevance, before considering what reforms were implemented within the organisation itself.

Internal Affairs

Both the first two reports had raised very particular issues relating to the internal handling of matters, from the negligence of senior management, to the failure of officers to answer questions, the need to 'streamline' disciplinary regulations making the process 'less cumbersome and swifter',[78] and the lack of resources attaching to the Internal Audit Section. The Act gave priority to the reform of the disciplinary codes and the process of investigation. The structuring of these provisions, particularly in terms of what was addressed by the legislation directly and what was delegated to the Minister and the Commissioner to regulate at a later date, is telling. Section 39 of the Act creates a duty for all members to account for an on-duty act or omission when requested to do so by an officer of a higher rank. Failure to do so is a breach of disciplinary regulations,[79] meriting dismissal.[80] This is a strict requirement to place on officers and is a direct effort to deconstruct the 'blue wall of silence' which Justice Morris encountered. That it was dealt with separately from the disciplinary regulations, and indeed quite far ahead of these in the Act (s.123), indicates the level of importance attached to that specific requirement. Section 123 makes provision for the revision of disciplinary regulations and the establishment of a more independent Disciplinary Board, tasks delegated to the Minister to be completed at a later date. The Act specifies provisions to be incorporated into the revised disciplinary code[81] and outlines some of the powers the Disciplinary Board is to have.[82] The details would come in statutory instruments, to be discussed below.

Morris expressed concern at the inability of the Commissioner to dismiss members summarily, and s.14(2) of the 2005 Act gives the Commissioner the power to do so, for a member not above the rank of inspector, in the following circumstances:

(1) the Commissioner must be of the opinion that due to their conduct, retention would undermine public confidence in the force and dismissal is necessary to maintain confidence,
(2) the member has been given an opportunity to be heard,
(3) this response has been considered but the Commissioner's view remains and the government consents.

This is a welcome provision that provides the Commissioner with a level of control which any individual leading such an organisation should have access to, although some appeal mechanisms should clearly apply.

Justice Morris concluded in his first report that what had occurred 'could not have succeeded but for the negligent manner in which the Donegal division was being managed'. A substantial element of this relates to a failure to provide clear definition of roles and responsibilities at senior and junior levels. This did not form part of the legislative response of the government and remains lacking. Two reports in 2007 drew attention to the issue.[83] The final report from the Advisory Group on Garda Management and Leadership Development (the Hayes report) emphasised that '... there should be performance measurement and appraisal at all levels and that proper arrangements are made for training and staff development to prepare them for their new or changed roles.'[84] Hayes felt this would require a delineation of the roles and responsibility of both the Minister and the Commissioner, a definition of the roles delegated by the Commissioner to others, and the identification of performance measurements that can be assessed against agreed benchmarks.[85] Increased training and support for those in management roles is required as well as an acknowledgement of different training requirements for recruits with primary degrees. Much of this was reiterated by the Garda Inspectorate report published the same year, particularly in relation to appropriate training and promotion of highly talented individuals.[86]

Section 124 of the Act states that the Minister, on consultation with the Commissioner, the Ombudsman Commission, the inspectorate and the government, will implement a charter containing guidelines and mechanisms to allow members of the force (Gardaí and civilians) to report allegations of corruption and malpractice in confidence. Details as to its operation were left to the regulations, which were published in April 2007 and will be discussed below.

New promotion regulations published in October 2006 contribute to development of this area. The Act requires the Minister to publish a code of ethics, although the organisation already had in place a Declaration of Professional Values and Ethical Standards and a Garda Customer Charter ('Putting People First'). Codes and charters, while valuable in clarifying the standards to be applied, run the risk of remaining a paper exercise. This new code will be complimented by the Professional Standards Unit created by the Act,[87] to be headed up by a chief superintendent. Its functions are to examine and review the operation, administration and management of the Gardaí, make recommendations for improvements and promote high standards of practice.[88] The unit was established in January 2006 with a staff of twenty. The three-year report from the Commissioner notes that in that period thirty-five Garda districts and Garda headquarter units were examined: no details on these reviews are yet available.[89] Walsh views this unit as 'undoubtedly a most necessary and valuable initiative in developing and promoting compliance with professional standards in An Garda Síochána', but he calls for the promotion and development of human rights within the force to be included in its remit.[90]

The functions of the Garda Inspectorate, created under the legislation, are intended to compliment the GPSU. The independent Inspectorate is tasked with ensuring that the resources of An Garda Síochána are used efficiently and effectively in the operation and administration of the force[91] and judged by best standards in comparable police forces. Its functions are to inspect or inquire into any particular aspects of the operation and administration of An Garda Síochána and report to the Minister on these matters advising him on best practice. To date the inspectorate, headed by Kathleen O'Toole,[92] has published five reports on barricade incidents, senior management structures, roads policing, missing persons and one overarching report which considers the policing of Ireland, broadly defined. Progress reports were published in the summer of 2009 which clearly indicate that these reports are considered by the force as requiring implementation, and that action is being taken to that end. The UK has long operated a system of inspectorates across the criminal justice system, so again, this is a welcome development for accountable,[93] modern and efficient policing.

Relationship Between Headquarters and the Department of Justice
This relationship came in for heavy criticism from Justice Morris and was subject to much political attention once it emerged that the department had serious difficulty securing a copy of the Carty report. The Act requires the Commissioner to account fully to the government and the Minister on any aspect of their functions, including providing any documents or records requested.[94] No limitations or conditions are laid down for the exercise of this power. In another clear bow to the Carty report incident, the Commissioner is also required to provide the Attorney General with any records or documents relating to ongoing

legal proceedings. This is the first time that the government has been given powers to demand records or documents from An Garda Síochána and while the reason for this may be evident, it may not be a welcome development that political individuals be able to make such demands of the national police force without constraint. As Walsh has stated, 'While there may be situations in which it would be legitimate and proper to place such a power in the hands of government, it must be acknowledged that, in the absence of express limitations, it can also be used for more sinister reasons.'[95] While An Garda Síochána should be accountable to a higher body, this power given to government needs to be regulated and it may be that, perhaps, the government is not the appropriate body to be vested with such powers.

Section 25 gives the Minister the power to issue directives to the Commissioner concerning *any* matter relating to An Garda Síochána and states that the Garda Commissioner shall comply with these directives. This is a considerable power for the Minister to be given and while the section states that it is not to interfere with the independence of any officer or any individual case, it does place serious political limitations on the exercise of control over the force by the Commissioner. For Walsh this section 'represents the most clear-cut break with the established theory of Garda independence from ministerial control'.[96] Section 41 requires the Commissioner to keep the Minister informed of a variety of policing matters, and in a direct reflection of the developments in Donegal, it specifically mentions 'significant developments that might reasonably be expected to affect adversely public confidence in the Garda Síochána'.[97] As Walsh notes, this is the first time in the history of the State that statutory obligations to report to government have been placed on the Commissioner.[98] The Minister is also given the power to appoint an individual to inquire into any aspect of the administration, practice or procedure of An Garda Síochána where public concern arises,[99] creating a new, and perhaps more internal, method of inquiry. The Minister's powers of control over the force have been definitively expanded in a way that is not in keeping with the concerns expressed by Justice Morris.

Citizen Complaints

Perhaps the reform that has received the greatest attention has been the replacement of the Garda Complaints Board with a new body, the Garda Síochána Ombudsman Commission. The Introduction to this book outlined the way in which the Complaints Board had been flailing in the years preceding the Tribunal.[100] We have also seen that the seventh report of the Tribunal examined the inadequacies of the Board.[101] The Garda Síochána Ombudsman Commission ('the Commission') began work in May 2007. It is a three-person commission, with members chosen by the government,[102] – a missed opportunity to establish an independent appointments panel, which would have given the Commission complete independence from political interference.[103] The current incumbents of the Commission are Conor Brady, former editor of the *Irish Times* and author of historical books on the Gardaí, Carmel Foley, the director for consumer affairs, and Dermot Gallagher, a former senior civil servant, who holds the position of chair of the Commission. Each has a parent who was a member of An Garda Síochána. The key functions of the Commission are:

- to receive complaints from the public about the conduct of members,
- to use its powers and perform its duties with regard to those complaints,
- to issue guidelines for informal resolution and set out procedures for investigations,
- to report on its investigations to the Garda Commissioner and possibly the DPP,
- to conduct other investigations into conduct of Gardaí where necessary,
- to examine the practices, policies and procedures of the Garda Síochána.[104]

Its functions are much broader in scope than its predecessor. The power to initiate investigations into the conduct of a member without a complaint having first been made is important. While research is yet to be done in Ireland, the Police Ombudsman's Office in Northern Ireland found in 2009 that, while 13 per cent of the public experienced unacceptable conduct from a police officer, only 14 per cent of those had made a complaint: 'The most frequent reasons given by those who had not complained were firstly a belief that nothing would be done about their complaint and secondly a belief that the incident would not be taken seriously.'[105] This is in spite of the fact that 88 per cent stated that they had heard of the Police Ombudsman and 83 per cent believed he was impartial in the performance of his functions. The power to initiate investigations without a complaint becomes paramount when the numbers willing to complain are so low. Also, the ability of the Commission to move beyond complaints of misconduct and look at the practices, policies and procedures of the force could allow intervention in a problematic area, either before complaints are made or where it is apparent through complaints that the problem is systemic and that dealing with complaints against individual officers will not resolve the issue.[106]

Members of the Garda Síochána or members of the police force of another state can be employed as officers of the Commission.[107] This power was used to recruit four superintendents from An Garda Síochána in 2008. Their investigatory experience and knowledge of the inner workings of the force may well support the Commission's work, but it can also undermine the semblance of independence. The Commission has a staff of just under 100 individuals.

A complaint about any behaviour of the Gardaí may be made by a person directly affected, someone on their behalf or a witness, to the Guards[108] or to the Commission[109] within six months, unless the Commission feels an extension is justified.[110] The Commission availed of this extension in relation to a complaint concerning the fatal shooting of two armed robbers in Lusk, County Dublin in May 2005.[111] If used frequently this could compensate for cases where individuals may have genuine reasons for a delay in complaining.[112]

The Commission first determines if the complaint is admissible,[113] excluding complaints where the member has retired or resigned. The conduct complained of must 'constitute an offence or a breach of discipline'.[114] Almost 20 per cent of complaints in 2008 were deemed inadmissible for failing to satisfy this condition. A disjuncture emerges whereby over 500 complaints have been made in one year about Garda behaviour which the system cannot consider. It is not satisfactory to simply dismiss such a high level of cases where people have felt sufficiently aggrieved to make the complaint. A very serious problem with the standard required emerges where, as Walsh has stated, 'the disciplinary code was not drawn up for the purposes of accountability to the public'.[115] An alternative standard could be produced for the Commission which takes into account matters that the public clearly deem unacceptable.

A complaint can be dealt with by way of informal resolution or mediation (s.90), investigation by the Gardaí, which may or may not be supervised (s.94), or the Commission will conduct its own investigation (s.95 or s.98). The primary appeal of informal resolution and mediation is that, where successful, the complaint will be expunged from the member's record.[116] Where a s.94 investigation is initiated, the Commission refers the complaint to the Garda Commissioner, who in turn appoints a member to conduct an internal investigation in the same manner as any internal disciplinary matter. The Commission may opt to supervise. This procedure can result in disciplinary action being taken or, if a criminal offence emerges, a s.98 investigation.

The Commission can conduct two types of investigations: where the conduct appears not to involve an offence (s.95) or where the conduct appears to involve an offence (s.98). In s.95 investigations the Commission gives the complainant and the member an opportunity to be heard and to present evidence and submissions, and it can also require the production of relevant information or documents relevant to the case from any person.[117] On completion of the investigation a report will be made to the Garda Commissioner recommending action to be taken. This method of investigation was used in relation to complaints regarding the Garda handling of a protest over the Corrib gas station in County Mayo, which resulted in a recommendation of 'less serious disciplinary action' to the Commissioner.[118]

In s.98 investigations the investigating officer of the Commission has all the powers, immunities, privileges and duties of a member of An Garda Síochána. Specifically, and significantly, they have the following powers:

- the entry and search of any place pursuant to a warrant and the seizure of authorised things,
- the arrest of the member under investigation,
- charging a member,
- the issuing of a summons to a member,
- the search of a member and the taking of photographs, finger-prints and palm prints,
- the detention and questioning of a member,
- the taking of bodily samples from the member.[119]

A search of a Garda station can be conducted with authorisation of the Commission where there is reasonable cause to suspect the member is guilty of an offence and that there is evidence in the station.[120] The Commission must notify the Garda Commissioner and the Minister in advance and, if they object for reasons of the security of the State, the Minister can direct a station be searched in part.[121]

These powers have been extended for use against members of the public. The Commission is also seeking an extension of the use of these powers to all investigations, not just s.98. The granting of such fundamental policing powers to non-police for the purpose of investigating the police is quite a departure for the investigation of complaints and marks a substantial difference from the types of investigations described in the seventh Morris Tribunal report. What is not clear is how an individual, either a member of the Gardaí or of the public, could complain about the Commission's use of these powers should the need arise. Section 109 states that a judge can be appointed to review the use of these powers. This is determined by the Minister and is not therefore accessible to the public.

The investigator reports to the Commission at the end of the s.98 investigation, which can result in no further action, resubmission for a s.95 investigation or the sending of a file to the DPP.[122] By the end of 2008, thirty-six files had been sent to the DPP by the Commission; one conviction has been secured and ten further directions for prosecution have been made. One of the prosecutions which went to court was dismissed when it appeared that the Commission had not followed proper procedures in the instituting of proceedings.[123]

The Commissioner is obliged to report, and the Commission is obliged to investigate, any case where death or serious harm to a person has occurred pursuant to Garda operations.[124] Also, without complaint, the Commission may instigate an investigation if it appears a member has committed an offence or behaved in a manner meriting disciplinary proceedings.[125]

In spite of these reforms, the Ombudsman Commission cannot as yet be said to be operating a fully independent system of police complaints. The Commission received 5,478 complaints and 416 referrals from the Commissioner in its first two years of operation.[126] The initial month saw the Commission receive a particularly high number of complaints (491[127]) but since then there has been an average of 216.8 complaints submitted per month, which is more than double the monthly average of the Complaints Board in 2006. Aggregating figures for 2007 and 2008, 34.6 per cent of cases have been deemed inadmissible.[128] Of those, 14 per cent have been dealt with by informal resolution, 37 per cent have undergone an unsupervised s.94 investigation, 8 per cent have undergone a supervised s.94 investigation, 0.2 per cent have been dealt with by way of a s.95 investigation and 40.5 per cent have led to a s.98 investigation. Wholly independent investigations are, therefore, being reserved for s.98 (conduct involving a criminal offence) cases, which account for less than half the workload.

The increase in the number of complaints may reflect an increased knowledge of the system in the wake of the publicity surrounding its creation: a similar phenomenon was witnessed in England and Wales following the creation of the Independent Police Complaints Commission (IPCC) in 2004.[129] It could be explained by a public belief in the independence of the system, irrespective of whether it is more independent, as supported by public surveys conducted by the Commission which found, in 2008, that 82 per cent of the public believe it is independent.[130] It could also be evidence of a cultural shift, whereby, in the wake of the Tribunal, there is an increased public willingness to complain about An Garda Síochána.

As it stands, the Commission has no involvement in one third of complaints investigated in its name, 45 per cent of complaints continue to be investigated by Gardaí and, as the seventh report of the Morris Tribunal showed, bias cannot be removed from those investigations. At the very least, the power of supervision should be utilised to a greater extent and has proven elsewhere to result in disciplinary action in more cases.[131] The Commission has sought an amendment to the legislation which would provide discretion to 'lease back' cases involving minor criminal offences to the Gardaí for investigation under s.94[132] (a call criticised by the chairman of the Complaints Board in his final report[133]), the Irish Council for Civil Liberties[134] and, at the international level, the UN Human Rights Committee.[135] In effect, the Commission could be described as an oversight agency rather than an investigatory one. It has been proffered nonetheless as a wholly independent body and the research indicates that the public have accepted this as being the case. The government have through these reforms managed to create the *semblance* of independent oversight, without the substance.

Justice Morris expressed the hope, in the seventh report, that the failings of the Complaints Board system would be rectified by the Commission such that the 'shortcomings' 'will not again be experienced by a group of complainants in this jurisdiction'. It is disappointing that the new system is not sufficiently independent with investigations being conducted by Gardaí in addition to pre-allocated work, and the additional investigatory powers attaching to the Commission do not apply. It was this lack of investigatory powers, combined with encountering the blue wall of silence and denial, which led to the failures of the Complaints Board to handle the Donegal cases. The new duty to account may prevent the blue wall of silence from bringing such investigations to a standstill but if this duty is not operationalised then the fundamental problem Justice Morris encountered with the complaints procedure may still remain for all cases investigated by Gardaí. And, according to Walsh, 'most critically, both the Garda Commissioner and the government had retained their stranglehold over resources available to the Ombudsman Commission.'[136]

Joint Policing Committees
The Act also introduced Joint Policing Committees (JPCs), forums for consultation, discussion and producing recommendations on policing matters affecting the local authority's administrative area.[137] These are tasked with considering levels and patterns of crime and anti-social behaviour, advising the local authority and An Garda Síochána on how best to perform its functions, arranging public meetings and establishing, as necessary, local policing forums for discussion of such matters.[138] The Act does not deal with the substantive details on the committees, save to say that the Minister is to issue regulations on these details; hence these will be discussed in greater detail below.

Garda Accounts
Finally, the 2005 Act sets out provisions relating to the financial accountability of An Garda Síochána. The Commissioner is now personally designated as accounting officer and is answerable to the Public Accounts Committee for matters of spending.[139] The Commissioner is required to establish an audit committee within the force, to advise and report to the Minister on financial matters, four members of which are not members of the force.[140] It is tasked with ensuring effective, efficient and appropriate use of Garda resources.

The Garda Síochána Act, through the wide range of reforms and initiatives introduced, certainly changes the context of policing in Ireland. On paper, the accountability mechanisms are stronger, though a discernable trend towards centralisation of power and increased control by government is evident in a number of provisions. The introduction of JPCs and a whistleblowers' charter are welcomed but their efficacy remains to be determined by the regulations and their implementation. The Inspectorate is proving an active body which can provide useful and realistic research and recommendations for the Gardaí. As has been outlined, however, the Ombudsman Commission, one of the defining features of the Act, has not as yet become the independent body that it could have been under the provisions and in fact, through calls for additional lease-back, it will regress further towards the Complaints Board mechanism. Vaughan criticises that the Act reduces the concept of policing to the public police, failing to recognise other factors which relate to 'community safety and security'.[141] Among these could be other government departments and health and education bodies.

REGULATING THE ACT

The previous discussion referred to numerous aspects of the legislation regarding which the details were relegated to be dealt with by way of regulation. A range of statutory instruments have since been introduced to that end. While it is usual for statutory instruments to provide supplementary detail to the parent act, it will be seen that many of the regulations arguably contain details which may be expected to feature in the Act. This would be worrying if, due to haste in the passing of the legislation, the democratic process for enacting provisions was by-passed. On the other hand, it may be that the provisions benefit from the additional framing time. The instruments relating to discipline, whistleblowing and JPCs will be reviewed here, providing a critical analysis as to how these key concepts in the Act will operate in practice.

Discipline

The required new disciplinary regulations were introduced in 2007, incorporating the new breaches of discipline from the 2005 Act relating to the duty to account, whistleblowing and the work of the Garda Ombudsman Commission, and amending the procedure for investigation and punishment of breaches. It remains the case that the disciplinary procedures cannot continue where the member has resigned. It should be possible to conduct an investigation and produce a report in such a case, even if sanctions will not result. This would legitimise the internal accountability mechanism and provide knowledge which can be used to improve the general operation of the force.

The regulations establish a partially independent Disciplinary Board. Previously, the Board consisted of three senior Gardaí appointed by the

Commissioner,[142] whereas now one member of the Board, the presiding officer, is selected from a panel of individuals nominated by the Minister for Justice,[143] and the other two will be senior Gardaí.[144] The power to impose less serious sanctions has been removed and the Board makes a recommendation to the Commissioner,[145] who must determine what action to take within fourteen days.[146] Should the member concerned wish to appeal the outcome of the disciplinary procedure, the Appeals Board will now be chaired by a District Court judge, or a barrister or solicitor of ten years' standing.

The summary dismissal power of the Commissioner is extended under regulation 40, and in addition to the provisions in the Act (dismissal permitted due to impact on public confidence, failure of hearing to affect Commissioner's view and government consent) can now be exercised,

(1) where the offence was so grave that holding a Disciplinary Board could not affect his decision, or
(2) where disclosure of the facts would breach state security or be 'a serious and unjustifiable infringement of the rights of another person', or
(3) where the member displays an intention to abandon membership.

The exercise of the power requires the consent of the Minister and cannot be used for a member above the rank of inspector. In such instances, the Minister decides on the basis of the Commissioner's recommendation. Beyond these situations, the Commissioner's decision to dismiss a member must be based on the recommendation of the Disciplinary Board, giving it a prominent role. And while the inclusion of a non-Garda member may have enhanced the independence of the Board, it could be questioned whether the inclusion of a judge or lawyer will make the process more adversarial. The Morris Tribunal showed how difficult it was previously to dismiss a Guard and such moves towards a more quasi-judicial system may not be in the spirit of his proposals for streamlining.

Whistleblowers' Charter

Regulations on the Confidential Reporting of Corruption or Malpractice were introduced by government, in April 2007, as required by s.124 of the Act.[147] The regulations direct the Commissioner, following consultation with the relevant parties, to establish a charter which provides details on its operation. The charter was distributed internally in July 2008. The regulations provide for the appointment by the Minister of an independent person, known as a confidential recipient,[148] to whom Gardaí and civilian members of the force can report any concerns in confidentiality, although they cannot be made anonymously. Brian McCarthy, a former secretary general to the president, was appointed as the first incumbent of the post in March 2008.[149]

Where it is determined that a report has been made in good faith and on reasonable grounds, three protections are afforded to the complainant. Their identity will be protected and only revealed where necessary for tackling the corruption. They cannot be disciplined for filing the report.[150] Anyone who bullies the individual for making a report will be subject to disciplinary proceedings. In February 2009, it was reported that an assistant commissioner had been appointed to investigate allegations of failure to investigate serious crimes in County Cavan.[151]

Joint Policing Committees

Guidelines for JPCs were issued in 2006, 2007 and 2008. JPCs initially operated on a pilot phase in twenty-nine local authority areas but, following a review,[152] they were extended to all 114 local authority areas in September 2008. The committees are comprised of local authority-elected members, members of the Oireachtas, the city or county manager, Garda officers, as well as community or voluntary sector representatives.[153] Each must hold four committee meetings and at least one public meeting a year. It is difficult to imagine that one public meeting a year can lead to real and effective consultation with the community. The District Policing Partnership Boards (DPPBs) in Northern Ireland meet at least six times a year, a viable way of forming solid communication and relationships between those involved.[154] Patten considered that public knowledge and understanding of policing was fundamental to achieving an accountable police force which deserved the trust of the public.[155] Further, it remains difficult to find information about the existing JPCs. Some, most particularly those in Dublin, have published detailed information on their council websites[156] while in other areas such as Limerick, Offaly and Galway there is no information, even times of meetings, to be found online.[157]

The practical impact these bodies can have remains limited. Their role is to provide a forum for discussion without an obligation on the police

to take the views expressed by the committee into account. This makes
the view of the Minister, that 'Joint Policing Committees are also a means
by which communities can have an increased sense that policing in their
areas reflects their concerns',[158] difficult to accept. The Northern Irish
model requires DPPBs to submit annual reports to their council, which
are then sent to the Policing Board.[159] The Policing Board can request
particular reports to be drawn up by the DPPB on specific issues. Most
significantly, the district commander within the police is obliged to consult with the DPPB in setting targets for the local policing plan. Herbert
is cynical about the potential of community policing fora: 'The empirical
record indicates that officers remain in effective control of such forums.'[160]

That said, evidence is beginning to emerge of efforts being made by
some JPCs to make the greatest impact possible. The JPC in Waterford
city has published a *Draft Strategy for Community Safety*, drawing on
crime-mapping, reviews of anti-social behaviour reports, population
statistics, mapping of childcare, youth and recreational facilities and
consultations with community interest groups. This led to the development of a multi-agency strategy to target the identifiable problems and
the document has gone to public consultation.[161] This holds the potential of engagement and contribution but is dependent on a proactive
JPC and a positive attitude to the process from Gardaí, something that
is unlikely to be repeated across all local authority areas.

Beyond the Act-Same Level as Resulting the Act
There are a range of statutory instruments and some legislation which
are unrelated to the 2005 Act but which also build on the findings of
Justice Morris. Some of these came as immediate responses and did not
require a legislative basis. Others came subsequent to the Act, as necessitated by later reports, indicating an acceptance, to some degree at
least, that the Act was not the final step in reform. Provisions relating
to admission to the force, promotion procedures, strategic management
and covert policing will now be discussed.

Admissions
Admission regulations were amended in 2005[162] in order to enhance
the recruitment of persons from minority ethnic backgrounds, something that Justice Morris saw as crucial to bringing an end to the 'them
and us' mentality which pervaded the force and contributed to the blue
wall of silence. The prohibitive Irish language requirements were

removed and Irish language is now covered within the training.[163] The citizenship requirement is reduced to a total residence in the State of four in the last eight years. The Garda Annual Reports for 2007 and 2008 show that thirty-nine trainees from non-Irish backgrounds were recruited and thirty-four more to the Garda Reserve. In 2008, An Garda Síochána had set out in its strategic goals an aim of 5 per cent of new recruits being from an ethnic minority background but achieved just 2.2 per cent. A Sikh member of the Reserve force sought and was denied permission to wear his turban while on duty in 2007.[164] Moving to increase the numbers of individuals from diverse back-grounds is not simply an issue of changing legislation but of changing culture within the force, and while work is being done to train commu-nity Gardaí to be ethnic liaison officers, the failure of An Garda Síochána to meet its own targets should raise concerns as to the prevailing culture within the force.[165] Chan has warned of the difficulties of ensuring acceptance of new recruits in the force, and also of the difficulties which ethnic minorities can face within their own communities for joining the police.[166] The ban on public sector recruitment in 2009, due to the economic recession, has put a halt on increasing the numbers of individuals from ethnic minority backgrounds in the force.

Promotions
New Garda Síochána promotions regulations were introduced in 2006.[167] Promotions were an internal decision and prompted internal distrust that the system was cliquish. Under the new regulations interview boards will now be composed of two civilians and one member of An Garda Síochána. This, it is hoped, will assist in ensuring professionalism in the promotions systems and negate any internal perceptions of nepotism in the system.

Strategic Management
Building directly on the recommendations of the Garda Síochána Act Implementation Group, chaired by Maurice Hayes, the government amended the 2005 Act, via the Criminal Justice Act 2007, to create an Executive Management Board, comprised of three executive (senior Garda) members and three non-executive members. These should be in-dividuals, selected by government with financial, executive and human resource management experience, who can advise on annual plans, budgetary matters, allocation of resources, equipment, technology and training, development and leadership within the force.

Covert Policing

The regulation of surveillance called for by Morris in the sixth report came by way of the Criminal Justice (Surveillance) Act 2009. The Act was introduced in the context of the 'fight' on organised crime, and a perceived need to expand the powers of the State to combat this issue, rather than being introduced as a mechanism to regulate a problematic area. The definition of 'surveillance' is broad and excludes tracking devices. While in the main judicial authorisation is required to conduct surveillance, a 72-hour permit can be granted by a superior officer and up to four months of tracking or monitoring can be conducted on the approval of a superior. Justice Morris specifically stated that there was no situation in which judicial authorisation was not practical. His recommendations have been ignored in this regard. A complaints procedure is created for surveillance, but of course this is dependent on an individual being aware that they are the subject of a surveillance order. The Act further regulates the use of this data in court as evidence. The data can be retained by the Gardaí for up to three years, which is probably in breach of EU laws on data retention, given a recent decision which limits retention to two years.[168]

Despite the publication of reports three to eight since the passing of the Act, this represents the totality of government-initiated reform in the five years since. This ignores important recommendations made by Justice Morris relating to issues such as the use of Garda agents, treatment of persons in custody including the role of the member in charge and the use of the PEACE interrogation method, changes to the caution, mention of suspensions in the disciplinary regulations, and the issuing of search warrants. The government simply falls back on the reforms introduced in the 2005 Act when the reports and Justice Morris' calls for reform are mentioned.

INTERNAL REFORM

While much of the above legislation and regulation was a necessary response to the Tribunal, it was clear from the reports that problems lay in the internal workings. Noel Conroy, as Commissioner at the time of publication of the first report, accepted its findings and appointed Deputy Commissioner T.P. Fitzgerald[169] to conduct a review of the findings and compile a report on the implications for An Garda Síochána. In reviewing this work as it has progressed to date, this section will consider not just the actual reforms implemented but the emerging philosophy underpinning this work. It was seen in the discussion at the beginning of this chapter that reform of culture is a difficult process, which often necessitates a 'reforming chief'. Punch has argued that these leaders can in fact, drawing on infamous cases in London and New York, be characterised as follows:

> Both displayed steely determination in tackling the organisation and its deviants; they displayed courageous leadership, demanded accountability from senior officers, put resources into personnel and altering the opportunity structure and above all showed ruthlessness in ridding the organisation of bent cops.[170]

Such reforming leadership, which makes high demands of a police force in this change period, has been largely absent from An Garda Síochána. A great deal of the work has been delegated in a way that distances the Commissioner from it. Neither Commissioner Conroy nor Commissioner Murphy have made dramatic statements of change within the force or widely sanctioned those who may be corrupt. What can be seen instead is an effort to reinforce positive sentiments of the good within the force, perhaps out of fear, to use another orchard metaphor, of upsetting the apple cart.

Writing on the state of the reform process in March 2008, Deputy Commissioner Fitzgerald expressed the view that the Morris Tribunal has been the most important policing tribunal and has

> ... significantly influenced the character and moral fibre of the Garda organisation. It has provoked an internal debate in the organisation as to what is the purpose of policing in this State. It crystallised the understanding that the first Garda Commissioner's paradigm of 'policing's moral authority' was a fragile authority that required constant care and nurturing. It also created an awakening that the 21st century required a new paradigm for the Garda Síochána: that of policing to accountability.[171]

While this may have been stated, the reform process which emerged centred on a discourse of managerialism and performance indicators, not of moral or ethical issues, not of a return to core, fundamental policing basics. To conduct the review, with which the Deputy Commissioner had been tasked, nine areas of concern were identified out of the first report and a further five following the second report, with working groups established for each.[172] The working groups provided commentaries and recommendations where they felt necessary, and have led to reforms being implemented. In some areas, however, satisfaction with existing mechanisms has been expressed and no calls have been made for reform to the area, again ignoring the fact that they were set up on the basis of specific and detailed criticisms and recommendations from Justice Morris.

Accountability and Internal Audit
In his review of what had been achieved by March 2008, published in the Garda *Communiqué* journal, Fitzgerald pointed to the re-introduction of the officers' journal, outlined that annual policing plans were considered to be at the core of developments in this area and noted that a performance and accountability framework was being proposed. A Policy and Performance Review Section was being considered following reports from the inspectorate and the Advisory Group on Garda Leadership. He noted the overseas training which had been conducted by senior officers on leadership and the extent to which existing training and education programmes within An Garda Síochána would facilitate strong leadership in the future.

The code of ethics, the GPSU and the increased commitment to human rights were all identified as relevant to the working group on professional values and ethical standards. A Good Faith Charter was being implemented to supplement the whistleblowers system.

A separate group focused on internal audit. The context of this has changed substantially in recent years, with the emergence of a number of bodies and reports which impact on it, not only from the Garda Síochána Act 2005, which prompted Fitzgerald to respond:

> The Garda Síochána by its swift action has demonstrated maturity in the acceptance of significant external criticism and has displayed a collective, and meaningful, willingness to change. The modern management practices and organisation structures, introduced by this reform programme, has provided the solid foundations required to ensure that the organisation is change ready and dynamic; thus having the ability to meet the policing requirements of a demanding and challenging society.[173]

A civilian head has been appointed to the Internal Audit Section. Further, as required by s.44 of the 2005 Act, an Audit Committee, for financial matters, was appointed with a largely civilian staff. No specific details on the recommendations of this working group were reported, implying that these changes were perceived as sufficient to tackle the problems identified by Morris.

Discipline
The working group established to review the erosion of discipline made no recommendations, having noted the development of new disciplinary regulations. A separate working group had considered migration management and policy of tenure, as the length of time individuals spent in any one post was identified by Morris as having a deleterious impact on discipline in an area. This working group was of the view that movement within An Garda Síochána was no worse than in other public bodies. The two changes that have emerged in this area are that it is now 'accepted policy' that those seeking a promotion are informed that it *may* involve permanent relocation and a formal procedure for the transfer of responsibilities between office holders has been implemented. Given the centrality of discipline problems to all of Justice Morris's reports, this position seems untenable and indicates an unwillingness to accept the depths of criticism and to change.

In terms of disciplining those criticised in the reports, Fitzgerald reported that the advice of the AG was that the findings of the Tribunal could not be used in disciplinary proceedings against members. This would of course not prevent the force from conducting its own investigations for disciplinary action. By March 2008, four members had been dismissed, two had resigned, twelve had retired, one was on long-term sick leave, one was dismissed for an unrelated matter, one was transferred, one was issued with a letter of advice and no action was taken in two cases. Resignation and retirement prevented the proceeding of internal disciplinary action.

Recruitment
The working group on external professional assistance identified three areas in which external professional assistance could be utilised within the force: human resource management, information and communications technology and communications, media and public relations. A national analysis centre would be of use, as well as enhanced legal competence. The Garda Síochána Act Implementation Group, under Maurice Hayes, had called for the appointment of seven civilians to

senior posts in the organisation. By March 2008, a chief administration officer and a director of communications and public relations had been employed and the executive director of human resources and the director of information and communications technology posts had been advertised. A structural reorganisation had occurred, the Analysis Centre was created and a Strategic Performance and Review Section was being created. Civil servants had been appointed to the Internal Audit Section. The three-year report of 2009 noted that in this period 942 civilian support staff had been recruited, representing an 80 per cent increase in civilian staff. This represents a massive increase which will not only increase efficiency but, if properly integrated, assist in cultural reform in the force.

In terms of the recruitment of religious and ethnic minorities, as noted above, changes to the regulations have enabled recruitment, although this has had a limited impact to date. Fitzgerald stressed that 'the rushed recruitment of newly arrived immigrants was unlikely to deliver a body of professionals that understand the nuances of policing Irish society and culture.'[174] This appears to suggest that difficulties exist in recruiting the 'right' kind of people from ethnic minorities and does not extend to accepting problems of racism which may exist within the force, limiting effective integration. This is hinted at in the *Diversity Strategy* document where it states that an aim, on this particular issue, is to reduce 'stereotypes, harassment and mockery', where for all other forms of diversity it refers simply to 'stereotypes and discrimination'. The implication is that there are additional forms of abuse which need to be tackled, but at no point is this admitted.

Efforts to address this have focused on increasing diversity awareness throughout the force. Ethnic liaison officers have been trained and ethnic and cultural diversity is included as a strategic goal in the corporate strategy, and two conferences on the topic have been held. The force has produced a *Diversity Strategy* document for the years 2009–2012, establishing the framework under which diversity is to be tackled, and outlines that the approach is predicated on the concept of 'diversity beyond legalism'. The chief administrative officer of the Gardaí is to be appointed diversity champion, a Diversity Strategy Board is to be created, a Diversity Management Unit will have responsibility for internal issues arising and the (now) Garda Racial, Intercultural and Diversity Office will have responsibility for external diversity issues. The training to be provided to all Gardaí is outlined, as well as the evaluation of that training and a positive focus on issues of retention as well as recruitment. Of concern, perhaps, within this document is the presentation of work in this area as 'above all, focused on following a business case for Diversity'.[175] As with so many other documents relating to reform within An Garda Síochána, what is entirely lacking is an ethical commitment to the work, only through which, it is argued, sustainable change can be implemented. The training of all staff is presented as a minimal requirement, yet the report states that just 250 members of An Garda Síochána have, to date, undergone diversity training. This is a small proportion out of an organisation with over 14,000 members.

Management

In his discussion of the role of assistant commissioners, for which a working group was created, Fitzgerald simply reports on the already defined role of the AC, and indeed this section of his report contains no 'progress-to-date' subheading, as other areas do. In spite of Morris' criticisms, it again appears that no changes are to be made here.

The working group on management development concluded that the key 'imperatives' emerging from the reports were moral conduct, personal responsibility and transparent accountability. In a more enlightened statement than many of the other working groups, the group recognised that it was weaknesses in each of these areas which led to the conduct examined by the Tribunal. Both professional and vocational training were central to a response which could prevent Donegal from occurring again. Deputy Commissioner Fitzgerald stressed that weaknesses in training and development had been identified prior to the Tribunal reports and that action was being taken 'pre-Morris', such as a review of the student and probationer training, the sergeants' supervisory course, the inspectors' development course and enhanced forensic collision training. Added to this has been a review 'post-Morris' of superintendents' and chief superintendents' development courses, with a view to attaining third-level accreditation, the establishment of a Strategic Command course, the planning of a Garda Executive Leadership programme, advancements on the forensic collision training and the creation of a new Diploma in Policing Administration.[176]

Relationship with the Department

A working group was established to consider reporting systems, concerning systems both within An Garda Síochána and between An Garda Síochána and the Department of Justice. The group reported that these issues had largely been addressed since the introduction of PULSE in 2003.[177] With respect to communications with the Department, a review identified that the process of communication was highly problematic and the necessary changes were being made for this to be done via email in future – this requires the installation of an email service in many Garda stations. Given the fundamental flaws identified in the reports on this issue, and the descriptions provided in the Dáil of the stilted relationship between the two bodies, it seems a stretch to suggest that improved computer systems will address fundamental flaws in the relationship.

Procedure

A working group on management of informants noted how the Covert Human Intelligence System (CHIS) has been implemented and training provided to those who require it. A National Central Source Unit manages the functioning of the system and all Gardaí have received a code of practice for handling CHIS material. The working group on the role of crime and security made a range of recommendations including IT, document management, training, identification of roles, analysis training, secure communications and the need for a senior analyst within the division. By March 2008, a new IT system for handling major investigations was out for tender, a Crime and Security complex was being built and a Crime Analysis section had been developed. A Garda training working group identified specific areas deemed to require enhancement following Morris, including major crime investigation, crime scene preservation, forensic collision/road traffic investigation, initial post-mortem procedures, ethnic diversity, and re-training after long-term leave of absence. The Garda training programme was deemed in need of a review and 'revitalisation'.

The Assistant Commissioner felt that much of what was recommended by the third, fourth and fifth reports was already covered by the above reforms or the reports of the Inspectorate and just a number required further review: witness expenses, integrity checks for State witnesses, and treatment of persons in custody. He also outlined the rate of change within An Garda Síochána: there were twenty-two change projects underway in 2008 alone and a deputy commissioner for strategy and change management had been created, with responsibility for this area, on the basis of the recommendations of the Garda Act Implementation Group.

In the three-year report required under s.23 of the 2005 Act, the Commissioner spoke of ten ways in which the organisation had improved, including organisational structure, improved oversight and accountability. He also notes that over this period thirteen new Garda stations had opened, eight extensions and six refurbishments had been completed and two modular fire ranges had been built.[178] These are important for internal morale and job satisfaction. Technology has been advanced, with a number of new systems now operational.[179]

Overall much of what is reported in that three-year report involves the expansion of initiatives already begun. There is a vast number of reforms being introduced, which will undoubtedly assist in greater knowledge sharing and simpler procedures but it often resembles a pro forma, tick the box exercise laden with managerial-speak.[180] It is difficult to see how these will challenge the imbedded cultural problems which Morris encountered. One of the few instances in which this cultural aspect is even recognised is in the summary of the *Report of the Working Group on Management Development*, which appears as one of the only groups to freely admit failings within the force. From what is reported, this is the only group to specifically tackle the question of how the events in Donegal should be prevented from reoccurring.[181] Other working groups appear not to have grasped the severity of what was reported by Justice Morris to be occurring in Irish police stations or how members of the force who had been granted power over citizens of the State had been abusing both those powers and the citizens. That a working group on discipline in the force could be satisfied that the amendments to the disciplinary regulations and the new requirements of the Act would be sufficient to overcome the level of misconduct identified by Justice Morris is difficult to believe. Certainly, these are not perfectly discrete areas, and many of the other reforms will have an impact on discipline as a by-product. But a more concrete approach that both establishes that ill-discipline will not be tolerated and that seeks to understand why these problems have emerged, which was not within the terms of reference of Justice Morris, while perhaps idealised, remains nonetheless the preferred response.

No question arose as to whether there was a problem with the standard selection criteria for An Garda Síochána, which is not to say that there is, but this was an opportune moment to review this issue. The primary response to the criticisms of the relationship between Garda HQ and the Department of Justice, to move from paper responses to email when requests are made, is equally inadequate. Both Justice Morris and the Minister for Justice had previously identified much more engrained issues of trust between the two organisations and an email response will not resolve that. An equal criticism could be laid on the Minister, who through the Act has simply created reporting obligations to his own office, which itself centralises power and will do nothing on the issue of trust. Nor is the issue of human rights sufficiently present in the internal recommendations and reforms. Walsh notes that it does not receive a single mention in the working group reports.[182]

SQUARING UP TO MORRIS

A number of deficiencies are clear from these reforms introduced since the beginning of the Morris Tribunal, when compared to the recommendations of the reports. In the first report Justice Morris called for management at Garda Headquarters to develop a degree of distrust at a management level and the reforms appear to rely on the duty to account to achieve this. This will not, however, overcome the problems experienced in the reporting to HQ, but assist in the process when problems arise. Morris stated a need for truth to be the primary standard when it came to filing reports with Headquarters, but this receives no mention in recent reforms. The recommendation that postings should be on conditions of a minimum service period was not adopted by the force, despite this being a serious contributing factor in Donegal.

Efforts to recruit from ethnic minority backgrounds have not been particularly successful. Research needs to be conducted on the reasons for reticence of people in such communities to apply. Justice Morris' recommendations of the issuing of search warrants have not been acted on, despite a statement of intention from the Minister in November 2006 to replace s.29 of the Offences Against the State Act with a provision to specify the exceptional circumstances in which a Guard could issue a warrant but also raising the seniority of the issuing officer.[183]

Justice Morris called for the full implementation of the PEACE model of questioning, with all the necessary training and leadership. The force has opted not to use the PEACE model as outlined in the reports. Interrogation is likely to remain a contentious area of policing, particularly in light of the fact that, unlike in other countries, Irish detainees are not entitled to have a lawyer present during the interrogation. Morris recommended the creation of a national committee to review strategies on detention and questioning which would integrate individuals from a range of specialisations beyond An Garda Síochána. The calls for improvements in standards and external monitoring of interviews have been ignored. Nor has action been taken on the recommendation for amendments to the caution, possibly requiring legislation. His comments on the surveillance legislation have not been adhered to; 72-hour surveillance can be authorised internally. No mention has been made of amendments to the Garda codes in relation to the refuting of allegations. No statements have been published on status and training of members in charge and no indication has been given that the provisions relating to questioning after midnight are to be reviewed. The Commissioner stated in the wake of this report that revised guidelines 'on the rights and protection of persons in custody' had been issued to all members, which placed emphasis on the promotion of human rights and fundamental freedoms.[184] There are, however, regulations on the treatment of persons in custody, clearly shown by Morris to be inadequate, and this re-emphasis on rights would have been better placed in that document.

There were also reforms proposed by Justice Morris which did not relate to An Garda Síochána. He recommended changes to the process for applying for an exhumation order to prevent a repetition of events as in the Barron case. As yet, the relevant statutory instruments have not been amended. He called for amendments to how the courts system dealt with judicial review cases and for changes to the interaction between the Gardaí and Comreg, the latter of which has been reformed. He called on the Committee on Practice and Procedure of the Dáil to revisit its provisions relating to TDs approaching the Minister on a particular issue. Again, no evidence can be found on this matter. The onus was on government to respond appropriately to each, but the response has apparently been weak.

That said, a great many of the recommendations have been acted upon and it cannot, for instance, be said that the report was shelved, as has been the way in many instances around the world. Dixon discusses how the experience of commissions and inquiries in the UK is to have their recommendations ignored.[185] The Patten Commission includes a directive for government not to 'cherry-pick' from its recommendations and, seeing the broader political picture, the chair of the Runciman Commission commented that his recommendations 'will be chosen or rejected for other motives and on other grounds than those which influenced the members of the commission to make them'.[186] It was clear from the moment the Tribunal was set up that major reforms would be implemented. Specific recommendations from Justice Morris have had a bearing, but it has not been the driver of the reform process.

A discussion of the sixth, seventh and eighth reports was held in the Dáil in October 2008, in the weeks after the Tribunal had completed its work. The experiences of the detainees, as outlined in the sixth report, were described as 'mistreatment' by the Minister, a clear failure to acknowledge the long-term suffering caused by the extent of the *abuse*. Before the discussion moved in substance to consider the political aspect of the eighth report, the Minister informed the House:

> It is now an organisation that is more open to the outside. It has a new professionalism in its management development and selection systems. It is prepared as never before to perform its functions effectively, efficiently and fairly in responding to the needs of local communities. Thanks in large measure to the findings and recommendations of the Morris Tribunal, we now have a system of oversight in place to ensure, as far as humanly possible, that the abuses uncovered by the Tribunal do not recur.[187]

It will take time to assess the impact of the reforms and whether they will be accepted by serving Gardaí. Following Chan's analysis of reform processes in police organisations, discussed at the beginning of the chapter, there have been some structural changes and minor attempts, through diversity training primarily, to alter the cultural knowledge of serving officers.[188] Increased professionalism and managerialism may involve greater recognition of the police as an actor in this process. Nonetheless, more substantive reform could have been achieved in each area. As has already been outlined, numerous political parties had long been calling for the creation of a Police Authority. This was repeatedly rejected by the Minister for Justice on the grounds that 'Dáil Éireann is Ireland's police authority and accountability through the Minister and the Commissioner is the most appropriate mechanism for democratic oversight of a modern police and security service.'[189] This directly contradicts the research from Walsh on the failings of Dáil Éireann to hold the police to account, as reinforced by the work of Chapter 2. Without question, however, the legislature was not in an informed position at the time of introducing the Act to recognise fully the problems which existed, such as the nature of cultural knowledge in the Irish police or what reform was needed and would be accepted, with the result of affecting police practice. The argument for a Commission on Policing, as recommended by some political parties, will be developed in the Conclusion.

NOTES

1. P. Maas, *Serpico* (New York: Harper Publications, 1997).
2. Mollen Commission, *Report of the Commission to Investigate Allegations of Corruption and the Anti-Corruption Procedures of the Police Department* (New York, 1994).
3. M. Finnane, 'Police Corruption and Police Reform: The Fitzgerald Inquiry in Queensland, Australia', *Policing and Society*, 1, 2 (1990), pp.159–71.
4. P. Stenning and C. Shearing, 'Reforming Police: Opportunities, Drivers and Challenges', *Australian and New Zealand Journal of Criminology*, 38, 2 (2005), p.167.
5. As noted in Chapter 1.
6. See generally on this D. Walsh, *Policing and Human Rights in Ireland: Law, Policy and Practice* (Dublin: Clarus Press, 2009).
7. L. Sherman, *Scandal and Reform: Controlling Police Corruption* (Berkeley, CA: University of California Press, 1978); Punch, *Conduct Unbecoming* and Newburn, 'Understanding and Preventing Police Corruption'.
8. Sherman, *Scandal and Reform*, p.72.
9. Punch, *Conduct Unbecoming*.
10. Newburn, 'Understanding and Preventing Police Corruption', p.36.
11. This viewpoint had been expressed and heavily criticised by the Knapp Commission as mentioned in Chapter 1.
12. E. Stoddard, 'The Informal Code of Police Deviance: A Group Approach to "Blue Coat Crime"', *Journal of Criminal Law, Criminology and Police Science*, 59, 2 (1968), pp.201–13.
13. Newburn, 'Understanding and Preventing Police Corruption', p.39.
14. Knapp Commission, pp.6–7.
15. Lundman, *Police and Policing*, p.137.
16. Cited in D. Barker and D.L. Carter, *Police Deviance* (Cincinnati, OH: Anderson Publishing Company, 1986), p.10.
17. Punch, *Conduct Unbecoming*, p.200.
18. Newburn, 'Understanding and Preventing Police Corruption', p.41.
19. C. Nixon and C. Reynolds, 'Producing Change in Police Organisations: The Story of New South Wales Police Service', in D. Chappel and P. Wilson (eds), *Australian Policing: Contemporary Issues* (Sydney: Butterworths, 1996).
20. Punch, *Conduct Unbecoming*, p.200.
21. Punch, *Conduct Unbecoming*, p.220.
22. Ibid.
23. M. Punch, 'Rotten Orchards: Pestilence, Police Misconduct and System Failure, *Policing and Society*, 13, 2 (2003), p.171 (emphasis in original).
24. M. Brogden, T. Jefferson and S. Walklate, *Introducing Police Work* (Boston: Unwin Hyman, 1988).
25. Ibid., p.164.
26. T. Prenzler, 'Corruption and Reform', in T. Prenzler and J. Ransley, *Police Reform: Building Integrity* (Sydney: Hawkins Press, 2002), p.18.
27. Chan, *Changing Police Culture*, p.74. This outline is developed from Broudieur's concepts of the field and the habitus.
28. Ibid., p.237.
29. E. Byrne, TD, Dáil Éireann, 12 June 1996, vol. 466, col. 1948.
30. Dáil Éireann, 21 October 1997, vol. 481, col. 1388.
31. Mr O'Donoghue, Dáil Éireann, 10 February 1998, vol. 486, col. 1548.
32. While this commitment did not explicitly include policing, as this was a key issue for human

rights reform in Northern Ireland it could be taken as being a relevant area requiring reform in Ireland. See, further, B. Vaughan and S. Kilcommins, 'The Europeanisation of Human Rights: An Obstacle to Authoritarian Policing in Ireland?' *European Journal of Criminology*, 4, 4 (2007), pp.437–60.

33. Mr O'Donoghue, Dáil Éireann, 12 October 1999, vol. 509, col. 133.
34. Mr O'Donoghue, Dáil Éireann, 1 June 2000, vol. 520, col. 751.
35. Mr O'Donoghue, Dáil Éireann, 5 October 2000, vol. 523, col. 1142.
36. Mr O'Donoghue, Dáil Éireann, 21 May 2001, vol. 536, col. 1311.
37. Howlin, Dáil Éireann, 10 April 2001, vol. 534, col. 582.
38. For a review of the Bill see, D. Walsh, 'The Proposed Garda Complaints Procedure: A Critique', *Irish Criminal Law Journal*, 14, 4 (2004), p.2; V. Conway, 'The Garda Síochána Ombudsman Commission', *Irish Law Times*, no. 8 (2004), p.125.
39. McDowell, Dáil Éireann, 10 February 2005, vol. 597, col. 962.
40. Ibid., col. 965.
41. Ibid., col. 972.
42. Ibid., col. 994.
43. Ibid., col. 1008.
44. Ibid., col. 1021.
45. 20 April 2005, vol. 600, col. 1613.
46. 21 April 2005, vol. 601, col. C29.
47. 14 April 2005, vol. 600, col. 1035.
48. Ibid., col. 1041.
49. 20 April 2005, vol. 600, col. 1617.
50. Quinn (vol. 600, col. 1014), Sexton (vol. 600, col. 1022), Connolly (vol. 600, col. 1025), Crowe (vol. 600, col. 1997), Ferris (vol. 600, col. 1054), Broughan (vol. 600, col. 1042) included.
51. 24 March 2005, vol. 599, col. 1994.
52. Ibid., col. 1971.
53. 20 April 2005, vol. 600. col. 1630.
54. Ibid., col. 1558.
55. Garda Síochána Complaints Board, *Annual Report 2005*, p.19. The board received 1,173 complaints that year.
56. 14 April 2005, vol. 600, col. 1011.
57. 10 February 2005, vol. 597, col. 973.
58. 20 April 2005, vol. 600, col. 1562. Re-enactments of the Tribunal were aired on radio for much of the duration of the tribunal.
59. Maurice Hayes had written the report which led to the creation of the Police Ombudsman for Northern Ireland.
60. Committee 28 April 2005, vol. 48.
61. Ibid.
62. Some dispute arose over the timing of the debate. The Dáil was approaching summer recess at this point and the Minister indicated that he would try and schedule the debate for a Friday which was acceptable to the opposition, who suggested that the Dáil did not have to rise on the allotted date.
63. 17 June 2005 vol. 604, col. 518.
64. Ibid., col. 529.
65. Ibid., col. 537, such as the information about the Carty report which the Minister had revealed, the dereliction of government duty from 1997 to 2002, the failure of the Minister to provide the McBreartys with their costs while Gardaí criticised by the reports had their costs secured.
66. Ibid., col. 540. Such a suggestion does of course ignore the fact that there were another six reports to be published and that this, unknown to them, would take another three years.
67. Ibid., col. 546, such as James Sheehan, where, it is alleged, a gun was planted in his car by Gardaí. Drawing on this and the 'heavy gang' he speaks of these people 'set[ting] in stone the culture of impunity that rogue gardaí have enjoyed right up to the situation in Donegal'. He also referred to the case of Eddie Fullerton.
68. Ibid., col. 548.
69. Ibid., col. 570.

70. Ibid., col. 563.
71. Ibid., col. 566.
72. 22 June 2005, vol. 604, col. 1034.
73. Ibid., col. 1041.
74. 23 June 2005, vol. 605, col. 35.
75. Ibid., col. 38.
76. Ibid., col. 124.
77. Statement by Tánaiste on Garda accountability, 29 November 2006.
78. Report Two, para 9.43.
79. S.39(2).
80. S. 39(3), although any information so provided cannot be used in criminal proceedings against the officer in question, s 39(4).
81. These include failure to comply with the code of ethics under s.17, breaches of discipline within a force to which a member has been seconded, failure to comply with any investigations under the Act or anything contained in the existing disciplinary code, s.123 (2) (a)–(g). It then incorporates elements relating to the establishment of the Ombudsman Commission in s.123(3).
82. S.123(4) such as the power to request attendance by people, to require the production of evidence, to administer oaths, to determine the admissibility of evidence, to determine what matters the Board can make determinations in relation to and to outline an appeals system.
83. M. Hayes, *Final Report of the Advisory Group on Garda Management and Leadership* (Dublin, 2007); K. O'Toole, *Report on Senior Management Structures in the Garda Síochána* (Dublin, 2007).
84. Hayes, *Advisory Group Report*, p.7.
85. Ibid., p.8.
86. O'Toole, *Report on Senior Management Structures*, p.21.
87. S.24.
88. The Commissioner is to submit an annual report to the Minister on the activities of the unit.
89. Walsh, *Human Rights and Policing in Ireland*, p.8.
90. Ibid., p.663.
91. S.117.
92. Formerly of the Boston police and previously a member of the Patten Commission on Policing in Northern Ireland.
93. From the transparency element of accountability much has emerged in these reports which is not otherwise published. For instance, the report on barricade incidents provides a great deal of detail on the number of these incidents in Ireland annually and how these are responded to.
94. S.40.
95. Walsh, *Human Rights and Policing in Ireland*, p.371.
96. Ibid., p.369.
97. S.41 (1)(b).
98. Walsh, *Human Rights and Policing in Ireland*, p.372.
99. S.42.
100. Numerous critiques had been made of the Board. See Walsh, *The Irish Police*; The Human Rights Commission, *A Proposal for New Garda Complaints System* (Dublin, 2002).
101. Though it should be remembered that these reforms were implemented prior to that report being completed and submitted to government.
102. Appointed by the president on the nomination of the government.
103. Irish Human Rights Commission, *Observations on the Garda Síochána Bill*, 27 February 2004. This re-emerged in the appointment of Dermot Gallagher, a senior civil servant, to the Commission, following the death of its first chair, Mr Justice Kevin Haugh. See, for instance, Mark Kelly's letter to the *Irish Times*, 12 February 2009.
104. S.67(2). The objectives of the Commission are 'to ensure that its functions are performed in an efficient and effective manner and with full fairness to all persons involved in complaints and investigations' as well as 'to promote public confidence in the process for resolving those complaints'. S.67.

105. Office of the Police Ombudsman Northern Ireland, *Public Awareness of the Police Complaints System in Northern Ireland* (2009), p.3.
106. This power could, for instance, have led to a very different handling of the complaints from Donegal, as described in the seventh report of the Morris Tribunal.
107. Searches of Garda stations and the writing of protocols may only be performed by members of the Commission, not officers of the Commission.
108. More specifically it can be made to the Garda Commissioner, any Garda in any station, or someone above chief superintendent if not in a Garda station, s.83.
109. S.83. No matter who receives the complaint it must be forwarded to the Commission and the Garda Commissioner.
110. S.84. The Minister specifically rejected the suggestion to extend the time limits to match the Police Ombudsman of Northern Ireland's power to act retrospectively as had been called for by the Irish Human Rights Commission.
111. Anon, 'Lusk inquest adjourned as ombudsman intervenes', *Irish Times*, 26 September 2007.
112. Such as the full extent of harm not emerging until a later date or a fear in relation to what might happen given the circumstances of the case.
113. This being decided by whether it is made by an authorised person, concerns conduct which would be considered misbehaviour, is submitted on time and is not frivolous or vexatious as per s.87. The Commission can discontinue a complaint at any point if it later appears to have been vexatious or frivolous, it was made knowing that it was false or misleading or if the Commission considers that further investigation is unnecessary or practicable.
114. S.82, 2005 Act.
115. Walsh, 'The Garda Ombudsman Commission: A Critique', p.4.
116. Certain matters cannot be dealt with through this process and confidentiality applies, whereby nothing said can be used in civil or criminal proceedings.
117. However, the Minister can determine that a matter relates to the security of the State in which case it cannot be disclosed, unless instructed by the Minister.
118. L. Siggins, 'Watchdog recommends disciplining senior Garda', *Irish Times*, 30 October 2009.
119. S.98(1).
120. S.99.
121. Any of the matters pertaining to the security of the State will be overseen by a judge of the High Court and reported to the Taoiseach.
122. If the DPP does nothing then the Commission can conduct a s.94 (referral to Commissioner) or s.95 (conduct not involving an offence) investigation.
123. Anon, 'Garda assault case dismissed over technicality', *Irish Times*, 27 February 2009.
124. S.91.
125. The Minister may request the Commission to look into any matter if it appears a member has committed an offence or behaved in a manner meriting disciplinary proceedings.
126. Data aggregated from Annual Report 2007, Annual Report 2008 and monthly data provided on GSOC's website, http://www.gsoc.ie.
127. A large number were submitted by the Shell to Sea protestors in Rossport that month; see *Garda Síochána Ombudsman Commission Annual Report 2007* (Dublin, 2007).
128. An admissible complaint must be made by a person directly affected by behaviour which breached the disciplinary code, or constituted a criminal offence, in the preceding six months, in respect of a serving member. If the subject of the complaint is no longer a member or retires or resigns after the complaint is made then it is inadmissible. Walsh reported that resignation was being used by officers to avoid investigation. In 2008 almost two-thirds of those cases deemed inadmissible were so declared because there was no breach of discipline, 26 per cent were time barred and 4 per cent were frivolous or vexatious.
129. Indeed the new system for England and Wales has seen dramatic increases in complaint figures; the 2005/6 figures were up 44 per cent on previous years, and the 2006/7 figures represented another 28 per cent rise. See IPCC, *Police Complaints Statistics for England and Wales 2007* (London, 2007).
130. GSOC, *Garda Síochána Ombudsman Commission Annual Report 2008* (Dublin, 2008).
131. M. Maguire and C. Corbett, *A Study of the Police Complaints System* (London: HMSO, 1991), p.191.

132. GSOC, *Biannual Report on the Effectiveness of the Ombudsman Commission* (2008), Appendix 2.
133. He stated that GSOC 'are now seeking to have minor matters investigated by the Gardaí themselves – the very criticism that was levelled against the Board in the past and to which the Board itself so frequently drew attention'; *GSCB Annual Report 2007* (Dublin, 2007), p.7.
134. 'Garda Complaints Board's final Annual Report highlights flaws in Garda Ombudsman's leaseback proposals', 31 July 2008. Irish Council for Civil Liberties.
135. *Concluding Observations of the UN Human Rights Committee on Compliance with the International Covenant on Civil and Political Rights* (2008), para. 14.
136. Walsh, 'Twenty Years of Handling Police Complaints in Ireland', p.337. This issue was also pointed to by P. McVerry, *Morris Tribunal Report and Garda Síochána Bill 2004* (Dublin: Jesuit Centre for Faith and Justice, 2004).
137. S.36(2).
138. Joint Policing Committees, Guidelines 2008.
139. S.43.
140. S.44.
141. B. Vaughan, 'Reforms to Policing North and South', *Irish Criminal Law Journal*, 16, 2 (2006), p.19.
142. For a full description see Walsh, *The Irish Police*.
143. To serve on this panel an individual must be a judge of the District Court, or a practising barrister or solicitor of no less than ten years' standing.
144. Regulation 25.
145. Regulation 30.
146. Regulation 31.
147. Garda Síochána (Confidential Reporting of Corruption or Malpractice) Regulations, 2007, SI No. 168 of 2007.
148. The recipients will be a judge, former judge, barrister, solicitor or a former civil or public servant.
149. All reports of corruption must be passed in confidentiality to the Ombudsman Commission and to the Inspectorate, if they fall within their remit, for action to be taken, where appropriate.
150. Although the regulations do go on to say that the making of a false report will be dealt with 'in accordance with the law or such regulations or codes', reg. 14 (3).
151. Anon, 'Probe of serious abuse claims made by Garda whistleblowers', *Irish Times*, 2 February 2009. It is perhaps worthy of note that this also relates to actions in a border county.
152. Which appears to have involved a one-day consultation in November 2007; see statement from Department of Justice, 'Roll Out of Joint Policing Committees to 114 Authorities', announced 24 September 2008.
153. The exact numbers are determined by the size of the city or county council, Joint Policing Committees, Guidelines 2008, para. 16.
154. G. Ellison, 'Police Reform, Political Transition, and Conflict Resolution in Northern Ireland', *Police Quarterly*, no. 10 (2007), p.243.
155. Independent Commission for Policing in Northern Ireland, *A New Beginning: Policing in Northern Ireland* (The Patten Report) (Belfast: HMSO, 1998).
156. Dublin City Council, for instance, has available on its website the guidelines, committee membership details, the minutes of meetings held, an annual report, and a workshop report: http://www.dublincity.ie/YourCouncil/LocalAreaServices/CentralArea/Pages/JointPolicing-Committee.aspx.
157. Indeed phone calls and emails to access information on the Limerick system produced nothing.
158. Statement on publication of new guidelines, supra n.20.
159. Ellison, 'Police Reform, Political Transition, and Conflict Resolution in Northern Ireland'.
160. Herbert, 'Tangled up in Blue', p.500.
161. See http://www.waterfordcity.ie/documents/downloads/JPCCommunitySafetyStrategy.pdf.
162. Garda Síochána (Admissions and Appointments) (Amendment) Regulation 2005, S.I. No. 560 of 2005.
163. As Irish is, under Article 8 of the Constitution, a national language, all individuals are entitled

to have their dealings with the justice system conducted through Irish and so all officers are required to have basic proficiency in the language.

164. See http://www.independent.ie/national-news/garda-force-is-not-racist-1064513.html.
165. This will be revisited below in terms of how the force has responded to these issues internally.
166. Chan, *Changing Police Culture*.
167. SI No. 485 of 2006.
168. EU Directive 2006/24/EC.
169. Deputy Commissioner Fitzgerald had broad policing experience having joined the force in 1964, served in a variety of divisions within An Garda Síochána and internationally with the UN in numerous countries. He was appointed by the UN secretary general, Kofi Annan, to inquire into the assassination of the Prime Minister of Lebanon in 2005. He was a witness to the Morris Tribunal as he was, when it began, responsible for organisation change as well as training and human resource management.
170. Punch, *Police Corruption*, pp.192–3.
171. T.P. Fitzgerald, 'The Morris Tribunal of Inquiry and An Garda Síochána', *Communiqué*, no. 3 (2008).
172. Management development; Migration management and policy of tenure; Internal audit; Religious and ethnic minorities; The role of assistant commissioners; An accountability framework; The erosion of discipline; Issues arising involving personnel; Informant management.
173. Fitzgerald, 'The Morris Tribunal of Inquiry', editorial.
174. Fitzgerald, 'The Morris Tribunal of Inquiry', p.11.
175. Garda Síochána, *Diversity Strategy, 2009*, p.2.
176. Fitzgerald, 'The Morris Tribunal of Inquiry', p.14.
177. Though it will be remembered that issues with the reporting within PULSE (Police Using Leading Systems Effectively) became evident during the tribunal when it emerged that the Barron investigation had been downgraded on the system from a murder inquiry to a hit-and-run inquiry and the families concerned were not involved.
178. Garda Commissioner, *S.23 Garda Síochána Act Three Year Review Report* (2009), p.19.
179. These included the Garda Information Services Centre, the Automated Fingerprint Identification System, the Automatic Number Plate Recognition System, Portal, an Automated Ballistic Information System, a National Digital Radio System and further CCTV.
180. Walsh, *Human Rights and Policing in Ireland*, p.650.
181. Fitzgerald, 'The Morris Tribunal of Inquiry' p.9.
182. Walsh, *Human Rights and Policing in Ireland*, p.651.
183. Statement by Minister for Justice on the publication of the sixth Morris Report, 19 May 2006.
184. Statement by Garda Commissioner Fachtna Murphy on the sixth report of the Morris Tribunal, 7 May 2008.
185. Dixon, 'Police Governance and Official Inquiry', p.133.
186. Cited in ibid.
187. Dáil Éireann, 22 October 2008, vol. 664, col. 755.
188. It will be remembered that Chan's definition of cultural knowledge was a more encompassing notion that police culture traditionally defined, which was generally viewed as a static set of values which officers learned on induction, on the street and then passed on to others. Chan views it as a more mutable form of knowledge, into which new officers can have input and help develop.
189. Dáil Éireann, 29 November 2006, vol. 628, col. 1301.

Conclusion

This book set out to understand what the Morris Tribunal tells us about policing and police accountability in Ireland at the time of its creation, and what subsequent impact it has had. The context into which the Tribunal was set, explained in the Introduction, was one of broad policing powers available to tackle terrorist threats, recurring allegations and scandals, minimal accountability requirements which were over-reliant on internal investigation and a political class which saw more capital in supporting the force than criticising it. The reports of Justice Morris, while clearly establishing the influence of these factors on the Gardaí, sit in stark contrast to that policing discourse. With a dedication to the highest policing, legal and constitutional standards, Justice Morris conducted an in-depth review of the individual and institutional misconduct in An Garda Síochána and the way in which the accountability structures had failed to prevent and remedy these. He chronicled serious breaches of the rights of citizens and abuses of the powers afforded to the police by society. Injected into Irish policing discourse is a sharp reminder that the police can and should be held to account for the use of their powers and that the police function is to enhance the rights of a country's citizens, with any infringements of such rights legal, proportionate and justifiable. This basic principle was the opening premise of this book. It appears, however, to have been gradually swept aside in Ireland as varying criminal threats and concerns took hold, from the conflict in Northern Ireland, to the drugs crisis to gangland crime. Continued commitment to accountability and integrity is critical to the maintenance of the police claim to legitimacy and the State's claim to constitutional and democratic values.

In this concluding chapter an analysis will be conducted of the central issues which have emerged in the preceding chapters and which have a bearing on how Ireland, as a society, responds to police scandals: the politicisation of the Gardaí, the effectiveness and limitations of the Tribunal, the impact on public confidence and residual problems in the force. How effective was the Tribunal to confront the problems in holding the police to account in this instance? Have the attitudes of Irish people changed as a result of its work? Has the force been effectively reformed? The findings, the media reporting and the reform process will be interwoven in these discussions. The final part will evaluate where An Garda Síochána stands in light of the Tribunal and the completed reforms.

POLITICISING THE GARDAÍ

What has complicated the engagement with, and the response to, the Morris reports is the level of respect and support which the Gardaí receive in Irish society. To hear of such undeniable corruption, deviance and misconduct caused tensions in Ireland as it went against the proud image of the force. In this section, the way in which the Gardaí became politicised in a sustained high-profile setting will be reviewed with an assessment of the implication of this development for the absorption of the Morris reports and the reform process.

The allegations of police activity and misconduct in the Donegal division have been politicised from the first questions in the Dáil through to the statements on the final reports. This has been evident in political and media debates for the duration of that period, both detracting from the misconduct within the police but also highlighting the flawed political approach to policing. This has long been the way in Ireland. As one Minister for Justice said in 1987:

> While people in this House and people in the media may have freedom to criticise, the Government of the day should not criticise the Garda Síochána … it is obscene that the Government and the Minister responsible should be the first to lead the charge in the criticism of the Garda Síochána.[1]

Why the government should not be able to criticise the Gardaí is unclear. The government, as legislator, has given powers to the force and, where these have been abused, it should be possible to criticise them. But as Walsh's study of Dáil debates shows in detail, rather than engage in constructive debates on policing, certain politicians have vied to show greater support for the force. With the escalating crime rates of the past thirty years, this has often translated into debates over who can resource, equip and empower the Gardaí best to tackle these problems.

And when it became public knowledge that various forms of misconduct were occurring in Donegal, how the State should respond became
politicised. This was evident in the fact that an opposition motion in
November 2001 resulted in the closest vote that government had experienced. In the debates held on the Tribunal reports, discussions were
often reduced to the political matters of how the government had or
had not responded. The issue was less and less what the Gardaí had
done, but how politicians had reacted, a factor which the government
had not permitted the Tribunal to consider.

Expressions of support for the force are important given the trauma
that the Tribunal will have caused internally. Where the police are
familiar with nothing but official support, the findings, language and con-
demnation of the Tribunal will have been a shock to many. Reform
processes and change are also difficult to accept, and in the context
of a recession which is threatening the pay and pensions of officers it
appears that morale within the force is particularly low. In November
2009, retirements in the force were reported to have risen from 177
in 2007 to 708 for 2009, representing a 300 per cent increase.[2] This
number includes three assistant commissioners (just one had retired in the
previous seven years), twelve chief superintendents, twenty-eight superintendents, thirty-one inspectors and 170 sergeants, including the head
of the Limerick division just one year after he assumed the position.[3]
According to the Garda Representative Association, 43 per cent of the
force now has less than five years' experience.[4] A lack of leadership will
be highly detrimental to the reform process in the coming years and the
risk arises of a need to promote those who are not sufficiently trained or
prepared for the post. As the Tribunal came to a close, the legislature
was distracted by the political aspects of events, and the Guards were
battered from the force of the Tribunal, reforms and recession.

ASSESSING THE TRIBUNAL

It can be no exaggeration to say that these reports collectively offer
the most incisive and sustained exposé of: the nature and extent of
corruption, abuse and/or incompetence among Gardaí in junior and
managerial ranks; systemic failures in senior Garda management;
and serious deficiencies in police governance, accountability and
working practices. There is a very real sense in which the Morris
Tribunal was making up for eight decades of neglect in subjecting

these aspects of Irish policing to the sort of regular independent review necessary to keep them at the forefront of best international and human rights standards. The meticulous, incisive and frank analysis and recommendations delivered by the Tribunal paint a very stark picture ...'[5]

Walsh is correct in describing the Morris Tribunal as a key moment in Irish policing, for the simple fact that a senior member of the judiciary, after a substantive review of a succession of complaints, had produced a deeply critical report of policing in Ireland. For the first time, schemes of corruption and abuse have been exposed beyond an individual level and recognised as institutional, in as much as a district-based investigation could. The language employed by the Tribunal is unusual in its application to An Garda Síochána, which as an institution traditionally received support and praise from the legal elites of Ireland. There is also much evidence to suggest a balanced approach. So, for instance, Gardaí, politicians and victims all come in for criticism or challenge. Justice Morris was highly critical of Frank McBrearty Jnr making a false allegation of abuse against an officer, though stressed the context of this allegation. He condemned Frank McBrearty Snr for writing the anonymous letters, acknowledged the contribution of all parties in the harassment module to the escalation of the situation and criticised Deputies Howlin and Higgins for responding to them the way they did. These aspects demonstrate the level of objectivity and balance applied by Justice Morris, which, combined with his maintenance of integrity throughout, is commendable.

An important aspect faced by any thorough assessment of a tribunal is that of whether, acknowledging the seven years it spent working and the €79.5 million projected cost,[6] it was worth it. The Law Reform Commission, as considered in Chapter 2, delineated the functions of tribunals as establishing facts, learning from events, providing catharsis and reconciliation, providing reassurance to the public, establishing accountability and satisfying political needs for something to be done. These are, by that body, considered to be the functions which outweigh the resource and time implications and will guide the analysis of the Tribunal.

As regards establishing the facts, the Tribunal achieved much. While the Carty report and those of other internal inquiries have not been published, we do know that a number of officers only admitted their involvement in these events, confirming allegations made a decade previously and bringing certainty and clarity to the findings, either during interviews with tribunal staff or while giving evidence before the Tribunal itself. Examples include the eventual admission by Garda Mulligan that he had been in a pub with Garda O'Dowd when the call to attend the scene of Mr Barron's accident was made and the acceptance by some officers that the allegations of abuse in custody were accurate. The Tribunal succeeded in acquiring this information where the internal mechanisms had failed. Whether it has established what happened in a more total sense is a contentious issue.

The analysis in Chapter 2 considered how the idea that tribunals will uncover 'the truth' can be misleading as there may be no one, truthful account. Justice Morris, when faced with conflicting accounts of events, made a judgement on the basis of the evidence available to him, applying the civil standard of 'on the balance of probabilities'. There were invariably instances where Justice Morris was as stymied in his work as the other mechanisms had been by the blue wall of silence. Many of the judgements he made have not gone uncontested. All parties involved have disputed some of the findings. Numerous officers continue to deny the actions which Justice Morris found them to have participated in, including Garda McMahon and Inspector Lennon. The McBreartys and Adrienne McGlinchey are not in agreement with Justice Morris' view of their involvement. The GRA has accused the Tribunal of targeting officers, and the Commissioner has challenged the institutionalised findings. Numerous politicians have come out in disagreement of the findings regarding the politicians who spoke to the Minister about anonymous allegations they had received. Dissatisfied by the outcomes of the Tribunal, many of the victims of Garda abuse in Donegal decided to pursue civil actions, proceedings they had previously suspended in order to permit the Tribunal to commence. Through a dozen cases a total of €11 million was paid out to fifty-five victims of Garda misconduct in Donegal.[7] A number of legal challenges were taken during the course of the Tribunal, which could have stifled Justice Morris' work but did not.[8]

Of course, the fact-finding power of the Tribunal was curtailed by the exclusion of a number of important matters from its scope. The deficiencies in the terms of reference provided for the Tribunal primarily concerned the failure to include other clearly linked cases such as that of Frank Shortt and the matters investigated by the Nally report, also concerning Sergeant White, as well as the exclusion of the activities of Garda HQ, the Department of Justice and the Minister from its remit. Despite Justice Morris' broad approach to the terms of reference, our understanding of the problems in Donegal and the failings of police governance was still limited. It remains unknown who is responsible for the death of Richard Barron. His family have endured the Tribunal, media and political discussions without the question of their loss being adequately addressed. Brian Nugent has recently provided an account of over a dozen further cases from the Donegal division of persons with similar and serious complaints against the Gardaí.[9]

The terms of reference also shield us from problems in other areas and divisions. In relation to the surveillance issue in the sixth report, evidence was heard of unlawful surveillance conducted in other stations, primarily in Cork. The European Committee for the Prevention of Torture has repeatedly found support for allegations of physical abuse.[10] Countless cases were mentioned by politicians in the Dáil debates on the reports and reform. Deputy Crowe mentioned the cases of Kevin O'Reilly, who was stabbed to death and whose family have alleged that Garda informers were involved and not properly investigated. He also spoke of Stephen Hughes-Connors, killed aged twelve, whose family maintain the Gardaí involved failed to properly investigate his death. Deputy Ó Snodaigh raised the case of Róisín Miley, whose family are dissatisfied with the Garda investigation of her death. He spoke further of a Garda informer, Seán Buckley, who chased a car with a gun but remained under Garda protection in Drimnagh. Deputy O'Keeffe discussed the case of Shane Tuohey, who died in 2002 and whose father, angered by the lack of answers from the Garda investigation, tried to hire a hitman to kill the individuals he believed were responsible for his son's death. Deputy Ferris referred to the case of Kieran Boylan, a convicted drug dealer who secured an international haulage licence; the Ombudsman Commission called for a public inquiry investigation to be conducted in this case. Deputy Tuffy expressed concern at the investigation into the death of Derek O'Toole in a road traffic collision involving an off-duty Guard and regarding his family's claims that Gardaí made false allegations that he was known to them in an effort to besmirch his name. The Ombudsman Commission report, the only report of an investigation conducted by that body published to date, supported this conclusion and that the PULSE system had been checked for the criminal records of other family members. This happened in

2007, two years after the introduction of the Act and the major reforms, which warns of ongoing problems.

The scale of Garda misconduct is further revealed by reports on civil actions: in February 2004 a woman was awarded €15,000 for injuries sustained in custody over which the judge commented: 'I cannot understand how such injuries were caused through the use of reasonable force.'[11] The judge also commented on the inability of Gardaí involved to account for her injuries. In October 2003, a 15-year-old boy who was forced to strip naked in detention and remain without his clothing for nearly two hours was awarded €8,500.[12] A man who was unnecessarily batoned during an arrest in Dublin received €11,000 in July 2003.[13] In Sligo, a woman who awoke to find a Guard in her bedroom pointing a gun at her was awarded €50,000 in June 2002. Police had meant to conduct a drugs raid on a different house in the area.[14]

While there may be reasons as to why certain misconduct occurred in Donegal, such as the planting of hoax IRA bomb findings along the border, there is no reason why misconduct, abuse or corruption would be limited to that division. Members across the country receive the same training, and all move around the country, learning the culture of policing as they go. The same oversight systems apply everywhere. But Donegal was investigated, not other divisions, and efforts have been made by Gardaí and politicians alike to present it as a case of a few rotten apples.

The LRC also indicated that tribunals should assist in achieving catharsis and reconciliation for those involved. In the case of Morris, the level of dissatisfaction with the findings expressed by victims, combined with their decision to proceed with civil actions, would indicate that the Tribunal has struggled to fulfil this function. It could be argued that the depth of the investigations and the resultant delay prolonged the trauma for those who suffered from Garda abuse, although in truth the initial delay in accepting the need for a tribunal and the blue wall of silence encountered are more to blame in this regard. It was described in Chapter 2 that one of the principal benefits of a tribunal, and why it was acceptable to proceed even though sanctions would be limited, was the sense of knowing it would create. Victims want their story to be heard and the truth of what happened to be placed in the public domain. Some of the victims have not been satisfied with the outcome of the Tribunal, and indeed the McBreartys' refused to co-operate with the harassment module. The Barron family have received no satisfaction through this process. It is possible that the Tribunal has contributed to a sense of re-victimisation by the State, which was not helped by the government's refusal to allocate legal costs in advance for these families. Frank McBrearty Jnr, now a councillor for the Labour party in Donegal, stated at a 2005 rally on anti-corruption in Dublin: 'The Minister and the Morris Tribunal have used legal costs to sanction us and we now fully understand that this is the instrument by which he has tried to talk us into subdued silence.'[15]

As to accountability, Justice Morris clearly established why these events occurred, apportioning blame to named officers at all levels of the force, and indicated where factors external to the force were relevant. The Tribunal has catalogued corruption and abuse throughout Donegal and placed this information very squarely, and openly, in the public domain, which internal reports have not achieved. In this sense, it has achieved police accountability where the internal mechanisms, the Complaints Board, the Oireachtas and the media had failed. There have been limited sanctions imposed in its wake, and to the upset of many, though not wrongly, numerous officers criticised by the Tribunal have retired with full pension.[16] Again, the onus was on the Commissioner, possibly with the assistance of the government, to address this matter.

The LRC also believed that a tribunal could resolve any public confidence issues which the matter in question gave rise to. It has already been suggested in this work that the portrayal of the Tribunal's work by politicians, the media and the Gardaí may have enabled a distorted understanding of the nature of the problem in the Irish police. The findings of various empirical studies provide the basis for an analysis of public confidence in An Garda Síochána.

PUBLIC CONFIDENCE

Where crises of confidence have emerged in the UK over miscarriage of justice cases and policing of the miners' strikes or race riots,[17] in Ireland it is difficult to detect disquiet. Part of the problem is the lack of data on public attitudes towards the police – greater disquiet may exist but it has not been studied sufficiently to enable reliable conclusions to be drawn. The first study on public attitudes in Ireland was conducted by MacGréil in the early 1970s,[18] using the Bogardus Social Distance Scale.[19] This method examines how close individuals are willing to get to members of certain groups or categories, and found that 85 per cent of people would welcome a Guard into the family. This study was conducted in the same year as the killing of Garda Richard Fallon by the republican group Saor Éire and at a time when Ireland continued to have an exceptionally low crime rate, which may have impacted on the findings. Methodologically, the exclusion of individuals under the age of twenty-one, a demographic which often has high contact with the police and therefore may have a more critical viewpoint, may distort findings. Nonetheless, this study represents a resounding expression of trust and confidence in the police.

The investigation of public confidence in the police by Bohan and Yorke[20] reported that, despite a high belief that Guards used force in custody and that they would lie in court, 62 per cent of respondents had confidence in the police. This was considerably lower than MacGréil's finding, but in the context of such specific concerns and a rising crime rate[21] it does not in itself represent an expression of dissatisfaction. Further, 70 per cent believed the Gardaí did not get enough recognition for risking their lives. As Mulcahy has stated, 'this indicates that "confidence" in the police does not always equate with belief in their professionalism or propriety, and can in fact readily co-exist with bleaker assessments of police behaviour.'[22] This may be explained further by the way in which those subjected to physical or mental abuse were distinguished by society as 'other' in some way. The subjects of the 'heavy gang's abuse were republicans threatening the stability of the State. Joanne Hayes, having an affair and children with married men, threatened the social mores of Ireland in the early 1980s. Later subjects of police force or abuse can also be classified as 'other'. Dean Lyons was a drug addict. John Carthy suffered from mental ill-health. 'Ordinary', 'normal' people remained untouched by police misconduct.

In 1994, Hardiman and Whelan placed confidence in the police at 85 per cent, 20 per cent above the European average,[23] but found that unemployed people were 'substantially less likely to have confidence in the police'.[24] An Garda Síochána began conducting and commissioning studies on public confidence in the late 1990s and these have now become annual research. The central findings, set out in Table 1, show that satisfaction has continually been recorded at over 80 per cent since the commencement of the Tribunal's work in 2002.

A noticeable fact is that in the year the Morris Tribunal was set up, and also the year of the first report, the highest rates of confidence

Table 1

	Very Satisfied	Satisfied	*Positive*	Dissatisfied	Very Dissatisfied	*Negative*
2002	17	69	*86*	11	2	*13*
2003	17	64	*81*	15	4	*19*
2004	15	69	*84*	11	4	*15*
2005	16	67	*83*	14	3	*17*
2006	13	67	*80*	16	4	*20*
2007	14	67	*81*	16	3	*19*
2008	11	70	*81*	11	2	*13*

were recorded, 86 per cent and 84 per cent respectively. It may be that this is due to satisfaction with the response to the report. It may be due to a belief that the findings of the Tribunal are not representative of the force as a whole. It may be due to support for the Gardaí, fighting the 'threat' of organised and gangland crime. Or it may be due to methodological flaws in the research. A number of methodological criticisms can be levelled at the surveys, primarily the exclusion of participants under the age of eighteen. The 2008 survey acknowledged that it did not sufficiently include people from the Traveller community or non-English speaking immigrants. Either way, reviewing these figures for the duration of the Tribunal, it cannot be said that the findings and recommendations caused any substantial reduction in confidence in An Garda Síochána. This does not fit neatly with the suggested failure of scandals to penetrate public confidence due to the 'otherness' of the victims. The victims in Donegal included mothers and fathers, ordinary working members of the community.

An in-depth analysis of the 2008 survey provides a more nuanced understanding of the public's attitudes to the police. While the level of crime reporting has only fluctuated slightly from 2006 to 2008, the reasons why people have not reported crimes to the police have changed significantly. The belief that the Guards 'would not do anything about it' has dropped from 25 per cent to 18 per cent, while a 'desire to have no involvement with the Guards' has fallen from 14 per cent to 3 per cent,[25] indicating a reduction in distrust of Gardaí. That said, there were a number of statistics which should raise concerns about public interaction with the police and which might be expected to have been reflected in the confidence rating, particularly given the finding by Bradford et al. that 'personal contact and police visibility are of central importance in the formation of public confidence and police legitimacy.'[26] Some 70 per cent of individuals who reported a crime did not receive a letter from the Guards by way of follow-up. Over half of victims were never given the name of the Guard dealing with their case. Three-quarters were never informed about any significant developments. On 'Garda manner', compared to the 2004 survey, more people found their helpfulness, sensitivity, politeness and interest worse than they expected. Far fewer people found Garda manner to be better than expected (drops of, for example, 30 per cent to 19 per cent). Dissatisfaction with Garda contact increased from 17 per cent in 2002 to 21 per cent in 2008. A total of 7.7 per cent of respondents reported some form of unacceptable conduct by a Garda, reaching 14 per cent in parts of Dublin; 9 per cent of people of non-EU origin had experienced racism; 32 per cent did not agree that Gardaí are fully answerable for their conduct; 17 per cent did not believe that people in custody are treated well; and 15 per cent did not believe that the force is made up of honest people. Over half of those surveyed did not believe they had a real say in deciding policing priorities. Many of these figures, however, are not necessarily indicative of a growing distrust as they align neatly with the levels of dissatisfaction reported in the Garda Public Attitudes Survey.

There are a number of indicators which might, at first glance, suggest that satisfaction is not as high as the Garda Attitudes Survey would indicate. First is the fact that from 1997 to 2008 nearly €37 million had been awarded in civil actions against An Garda Síochána.[27] Since the Tribunal began over €4 million has been paid out for assault and over €9 million for unlawful arrest. But this is on the back of a relatively small number of cases: those figures for assault compensation relate to sixty-six cases in the last seven years, a high proportion of which related to Donegal. There has been a significant increase in the number of complaints made against the police since the introduction of the Garda Síochána Ombudsman Commission. The Commission received an average of six complaints a day in 2009, almost double the level recorded by the Complaints Board. Again though, the reasons for this, outlined in Chapter 5, are more likely the increased confidence in the system rather than increased dissatisfaction with the police. A study commissioned by the *Irish Times* in 2004, in the aftermath of a 'Prime Time' documentary in which a judge revealed that a Guard had perjured himself in his court and a leading politician alleged that a constituent had been abused in a way which was 'tantamount to torture', reported a much lower 57 per cent confidence rating; young males were the least satisfied.[28] A political breakdown of the participants explains this lower rating: among voters for the three major political parties, upwards of 67 per cent expressed confidence whereas 54 per cent of Green party voters and 63 per cent of Sinn Féin voters expressed a lack of confidence. This correlates, presumably, with clashes between environmental protestors in County Mayo and the police, an issue of particular concern for Green party voters, and the long-standing antagonism between members of republican parties and the Gardaí.

This review of public confidence surveys shows that in spite of the findings of the Morris Tribunal, and the other investigated and not-investigated cases, public confidence in the Irish police is high and stable. The reasons for this are not immediately clear, nor are they fully supported by the findings from supplementary questions in the Public Attitudes Surveys. Further understanding of these reactions is required. The current research has directed attention to the political, Garda and media discourse which has presented the Morris reports in a way which makes it feasible for the public to maintain confidence in the police. The public may have been satisfied that while the victims were not 'other', as previous victims have been, a very small number of Gardaí were responsible, the policing structures have been reformed and the misconduct was so extreme that it could possibly never happen again.

THE BLUE WALL

International research reveals that this type of corruption, deviance and misconduct is not satisfactorily explained by the rotten apples thesis. Institutional problems invariably need addressing. The Morris Tribunal may have been focused on one division, but it encountered institutional problems of which the individual actions of misconduct were symptomatic. An Garda Síochána underwent a detailed reform process but, as was argued in the previous chapter, this was largely administrative and failed to address the embedded cultural problems relating to impunity, ill-discipline and the blue wall.

The Morris Tribunal established a culture of impunity, whereby police believe they can engage in certain activity without fear of sanction, to be present in Donegal in the mid to late 1990s.[29] The accountability structures have been reformed, but the analysis in Chapter 5 suggests that this has not as yet been done sufficiently. It is of particular concern that democratic accountability of the Gardaí remains under-developed and over-politicised in Ireland. While the Ombudsman Commission has been afforded great media and public attention, this other form of accountability has not. Some parties proposed the creation of a Police Authority without sparking substantive debate at the national level.[30] A form of accountability which the Patten Commission considered to be central, and which was accepted to be necessary in the UK in the 1960s, has barely received a salutary nod in Ireland. If it were considered more seriously, Vaughan warns, 'it is likely that the community will remain the weak partner in any tri-partite structure of accountability that also involves the Gardaí and central government.'[31] In terms of the reforms that have been made, the Ombudsman Commission runs the risk of carrying the full weight of achieving the accountability of An Garda Síochána. It has been argued by Vaughan that in a holistic system the Ombudsman Commission would play a 'vital' role, but would be 'much more minor than that envisaged in the debate on police accountability hitherto'.[32] Even at this early stage it is proving an ineffective system, with substantive numbers of complaints still being investigated by Gardaí, and the grounds for admissibility are proving overly restrictive.

The culture of ill-discipline, directly linked to the culture of impunity, has been subjected to weak reforms. Amendments to the disciplinary code have been made and the procedure for investigation is now more independent. Research in other police forces has shown, however, that without a fundamental shift in attitudes, ill-discipline will, at best, disappear for a few years, before re-emerging. At worst, as Punch suggests, it will have been moved underground.[33] He demonstrates that the 'new realism' in police research has rejected the notion of 'corruption as a temporary, exceptional "problem" to be removed by "surgical" treatment, as if it was a malignant cancer, to restore an otherwise healthy agency'.[34] Newburn examines a diversity of reforms that should be introduced to prevent ill-discipline, including internal accountability, tight supervision, abolition of procedures encouraging corruption, detection from citizens, police officers and through probing police activities, and overt investigation, to be complemented by reforms to the external environment, i.e. addressing corruption in politics.[35] Policing does not, after all, occur in a vacuum. Very genuine efforts have been made to address a number of these, but gaps remain. As Newburn warns, 'reform tends not to be durable and continued vigilance and scepticism is vital.'[36] Recruitment strategies can also be important, and Karas argues that a variety of testing mechanisms can help identify candidates who may have a propensity toward misconduct.[37]

The most disconcerting finding made by Justice Morris was the extent of the unshakeable blue wall of silence. Garda Martin Leonard, in explaining his unwillingness to reveal what his colleagues had done, infamously explained to the Tribunal: 'You don't hang your own.'[38] This attitude typified the approach of all members who were involved in the Tribunal. Justice Morris stated that: 'Members of An Garda Síochána adopted a thoroughly uncooperative manner with my investigations. The Tribunal noted the same attitude in testimony.' Equally, 'The enquiries by the Tribunal have been lengthy and difficult. Let it be clearly stated that this happened because so many witnesses determined to persistently lie.'[39] Officers continued to deny involvement in the impugned actions after the Tribunal, and after the findings had been made. The blue wall is not confined to Donegal and it was present during the investigations into the 'Reclaim the Streets' riots in Dublin in 2002, where officers refused to account for their actions in the Complaints Board investigations.[40] The GSCB Annual Report for 2004 noted that 'frequently investigations were met with a wall of silence.'[41]

Justice Morris made a direct link between this wall and an 'us and them' mentality pervading the force, a cultural facet recognised in much work on police culture.[42] The legislative efforts to tackle the blue wall in the Gardaí have centred on creating a duty account, reinstating the officer's journal and introducing a whistleblowers system. Smith and Gray's research on rules within the police indicates that there is a substantial difference between presentational rules 'which are ones that exist to give an acceptable appearance to the way that police work is carried out', inhibitory rules which are not internalised by police but which 'tend to discourage them from behaving in certain ways in case they should be caught' and working rules which 'are internalised by the police to become guiding principles in their conduct'.[43] Working rules, thus, are ones which the police believe in, and will often be most effective in regulating police conduct. Implementing a rule, such as the duty to account, without any supporting structures to encourage its internalisation minimises its chances of success. The Garda management response to deny the extent of some problems, to rely on the rotten apples thesis and to reinforce the dangers experienced by members will not assist in that process. Certainly, training on professional standards and diversity has been implemented and the nature of this training is pivotal. Goldstein warned on how this training is approached: 'If recruit training is to have any impact on corruption it must explore fully and realistically all the dimensions of the problem and include specific examples of corruption known to exist or to have existed in the department.'[44] A deconstruction of Donegal and the findings of the Morris Tribunal might then be a direct way to train new recruits about police corruption.

It is a notably different attitude from that in the UK which led to the creation of a dedicated Anti-Corruption Group, whose methods included covert surveillance on suspected corrupt police officers and the use of criminal informants.[45] Moran notes that while evaluation is difficult, the fact that forty serving and fifteen former police officers were prosecuted for corruption between 1998 and 2005, as well as internal disciplinary action taken, indicates the 'strong signal [the unit] has sent out to the service about a fundamental change in attitudes to corruption'.[46] Moreover, Sherman, writing in 1977, argues that 'Prevention and detection of corruption would depend neither on line supervisors nor staff investigators, but upon the colleagues of a law-breaking officer. Pride in the organisation, belief in the rightness of its rules and *not* fear of authoritarian sanctions, would be the cement behind behavioural norms together.'[47] There is an ongoing sense that the reforms in the Gardaí have not accepted such an approach.

WHERE TO NEXT?

The Morris Tribunal, through its work, established a need for, but also provided a detailed basis for, genuine reform and a reimagining of the role and nature of policing in Ireland. A plethora of reforms have been introduced since it began issuing its reports, many of which have achieved very necessary changes to the way in which policing is conducted and overseen in Ireland. That said, due to a recurring failure to engage with the depth of criticism in the reports, as reflected in media reporting and official discourse of the Tribunal, an opportunity to address all the ills of the Irish police may have been missed. Justice Morris told Ireland what was wrong with the police force, but Ireland failed to listen. This is the real concern which now exists. In November 2006, in a statement on accountability in An Garda Síochána, the Minister for Justice stated:

> There has to be an end to wrongdoing and to any culture of cover-up and any culture of collusion which created a context for some of these activities. There has to be a different way for the Garda Síochána to carry out its functions in the future. No longer will misplaced and ill-judged loyalty to corrupt bullies be allowed to supplant the loyalty that all Gardaí and all citizens owe to the Constitution and the law, to the people and to the Garda Síochána itself.

This book has argued that the reform necessary to achieve this goal, rightly identified by the Minister, has not been implemented. This is not the fault of An Garda Síochána alone. Politicians, the media and the public have had a hand in this. It may be that the Labour party and Fine Gael are correct in arguing that a police authority would enhance democratic accountability. It is unfortunate that this has not been considered more seriously. On the other hand, it may be that a police authority would not help, for as Kempa has argued:

> Timidity has characterized the action of police authorities at nearly every turn: it is a universally held view in academia that Police Authorities have never lived up to their promise as agencies that would achieve the 'democratization' of policing.[48]

What is certain is that, as yet, there has been no systemic review of governance and police practice within An Garda Síochána. Opposition parties supported an independent commission on policing but this too was rejected, in deference to the need to push forward with reforms so as not to delay the process further. The reforms have now been introduced, but a commission could still be established and could incorporate an assessment of the 2005 Act and subsequent measures within its remit. The principal explanation as to why the Patten Commission report was so well received in Northern Ireland, and can be considered a thorough guiding template, is because of the wide review conducted and the extensive community-based consultations which enhanced the legitimacy of the process.[49] It was not reactive, as was the Morris Tribunal. It was a proactive body, one task of which was to recommend how best to achieve accountability in a Northern Irish police force. This never was the purpose of the Morris Tribunal and it should not be interpreted by government, legislators, the media, or the public thus.

There is a real need in Ireland to understand the true extent of police misconduct, mal-governance and the state of police morale. This can best be achieved by an independent commission on policing with a broad, consultative mandate. A commission will not eliminate all police misconduct, but it will provide knowledge of the current operation of policing in Ireland, as well as an understanding of what Irish society wants them to achieve and how best they can achieve it. It would provide an opportunity to explore with the communities the limitations of policing, contributing to realistic goals for the Gardaí, and a realisation of the role of others in the policing function. From here, a cultural shift in how Ireland (including the Gardaí) thinks about policing could begin and targeted reforms with a clear philosophical underpinning could be implemented.

It is possible that if Ireland does not engage in a broad consultation process of this nature then it will continue on a well-worn path of police scandal – police reform – lessening attention – police scandal. The Introduction suggested that many of the problems of police oversight in Ireland were the result of the pressures facing the police in the context of the Northern Irish conflict and the leeway they were given in dealing with the threat. A variety of bodies, including the UN Human Rights Committee,[50] have suggested that since this threat has subsided certain provisions could be withdrawn, including the Special Criminal Court. A new context is emerging in Ireland, however – gangland crime – which is now being compared in various quarters to paramilitary activity, and for which these provisions are being retained. For instance, in a 2009 debate in the Dáil, the Minister specifically stated: 'What we are trying to do is to raise the level of seriousness of organised gang crime offences to a similar level as pertained with regard to paramilitary organisations in this country.'[51] In the wake of what are perceived to be spiralling deaths and the killing of innocent people not involved in gang activities, this relatively new wave of crime in Ireland is considered to require a 'crackdown'. In particular, the killing of Roy Collins in Limerick in 2009, whose father had given evidence in the criminal trial of a leading gang member five years earlier, sparked the belief that the criminal justice system was being directly undermined. The response has been a plethora of legislative measures, with new provisions outlawing gangland activity, permitting use of the Special Criminal Court, and vastly expanding Garda powers of arrest, detention and surveillance.[52] The reforms introduced in the wake of the Morris Tribunal must be viewed in the context of those expansions of police powers. Justice Morris's proposals by and large were made prior to these reforms. The new powers given to police through these pieces of legislation will require additional safeguards, many of which Justice Morris could not have contemplated.

Media headlines, such as 'Let's hope laws end gang rule'[53] and 'A lawless ghetto?'[54] suggest that Ireland is being over-run by gang crime. The Taoiseach has spoken of the need to wage a war on gangland crime,[55] and McCullagh elucidates: 'As long as we approach criminal behaviour with a metaphor of "war" police corruption is inevitable as the space is created for normal policing standards and behaviour to be abandoned and such abandonment to be seen as culturally legitimate.'[56] The potential exists for society, out of fear, to revert to a trust in An Garda Síochána which, as Mulcahy described, does not necessarily equate with a belief in 'professionalism or propriety'. The pressure to 'defeat' gangland crime, with the new policing powers and the expansion of the Special Criminal Court, creates the potential that claims of abuse and corruption will likely emerge again. It is well documented that certain areas 'lend' themselves to police corruption.[57] Already, it has been reported that Gardaí are being investigated for assisting organised crime gangs in Dublin.[58] The lessons of the Morris Tribunal are clear: what is needed is not just a response to misconduct wherever it occurs, but an ongoing effort toward cultural and systemic reform to prevent misconduct.

NOTES

1. M. Noonan, Minister for Justice, Dáil Éireann, 10 November 1987, vol. 375, col. 227.
2. 'Fear of tax changes prompts big rise in Garda retirements', *Irish Times*, 12 November 2009.
3. Anon, 'Limerick Garda chief to retire', *Irish Times*, 6 November 2009.
4. C. Lally, 'Fear of tax changes prompts big rise in Garda retirements', *Irish Times*, 12 November 2009.
5. Walsh, 'Human Rights and Policing in Ireland', p.xi.
6. Anon, 'Morris tribunal: the costs', *Irish Times*, 12 February 2009.
7. S. Phelan, '€11m in payouts for 55 victims of Donegal Garda corruption', *Irish Independent*, 15 August 2008.
8. Early on, the McBreartys judicially reviewed Justice Morris's decisions not to seek an expansion of the terms of reference and the failure to award costs in advance: *McBrearty v. Morris* [2003] 12 May 2003. The High Court ruled that the applicants did not have *locus stani* to bring the challenge to the terms of reference, that the tribunal did not have the power to award funding and that there was no right to such funding. Sergeant White challenged the decision to proceed with the Burnfoot module while the criminal proceedings in relation to the firearm were ongoing. *White v. The Honourable Mr Justice Morris* [2005] IEHC 391. Deputy Howlin attempted, unsuccessfully, to claim privilege on the source of the anonymous allegations, the

case for which went to the Supreme Court which held that he had no right to make such a claim. *Howlin v. The Honourable Mr Justice Morris* [2005] IESC 85.

9. B. Nugent, *Orwellian Ireland* (Meath, 2005–2008), available at http://books.google.ie/books? id=rk8LhlzrJZ4C&pg=PT44&lpg=PT44&dq=brian+nugent+orwellian+ireland&source =bl&ots=x_GLyikBKf&sig=OlRNZDIBkjluxEExYhUX6KEPa4o&hl=en&ei=hyIAS-_-L5St4QbM9r34Cw&sa=X&oi=book_result&ct=result&resnum=1&ved=0CAgQ6AEwA A#v=onepage&q=&f=false.

10. European Committee for the Prevention of Torture, Report on Visit to Ireland (Strasbourg, 1993, 1998, 2002, 2007).

11. R. Managh, 'Woman hurt in Garda custody gets €15,000', *Irish Independent*, 12 February 2004.

12. R. Managh, 'Boy held naked in Garda station received €8,500', *Irish Independent*, 15 October 2003.

13. Anon, 'Man batoned by Gardaí awarded €11,000 damages', *Irish Independent*, 19 July 2003.

14. Anon, 'Woman woken by armed Garda in her bedroom is awarded €50,000', *Irish Times*, 22 June 2002.

15. 20 November 2005, cited in Nugent, *Orwellian Ireland*.

16. Justice Morris commented that just because an officer engaged in a number of unlawful acts does not mean they should lose a pension built up over thirty years of service.

17. See Hall et al., *Policing the Crisis*; J. Hawdon, J. Ryan and S. Griffin, 'Policing Tactics and Perceptions of Police Legitimacy', *Police Quarterly*, 4, 6 (2003), p.469; and J. Smyth, 'Symbolic Power and Police Legitimacy: The Royal Ulster Constabulary', *Crime, Law and Social Change*, 38, 3 (2002), p.295 for a discussion of police crises of legitimacy in the UK, and J. Habermas, *Legitimation Crisis* (Boston: Beacon Press, 1975) on crises of legitimacy more broadly.

18. Fr MacGréil, 'Confidence in the Police', *Garda Review* (1974).

19. This methodology was developed by Bogardus in 1927 to examine the attitudes of Americans towards various ethnic groupings. It is still considered a valid methodology and has been replicated on numerous occasions (see Parillo and Donoghue, 2005).

20. Bohan and Yorke, 'Law Enforcement Marketing'.

21. These findings were also set against an enormous leap in crime rates in Ireland from 30,000 a year in 1972 to 100,000 for the first time in the mid-1980s.

22. A. Mulcahy, 'Crime, Policing and Social Control', in S. O'Sullivan, *Contemporary Ireland: A Sociological Map* (Dublin: University College Dublin Press, 2007).

23. N. Hardiman and C.T. Whelan, 'Politics and Democratic Values', in C.T. Whelan, *Values and Social Change in Ireland* (Dublin: Gill & Macmillan, 1994), p.100.

24. Ibid., p.129.

25. In return, the loss being too small or there being too small a chance of recovery had risen as reasons for non-reporting.

26. B. Bradford, E. Stanko and J. Jackson, 'Using Research to Inform Policy: The Role of Public Attitudes Surveys in Understanding Public Confidence and Police Contact', *Policing*, 3, 2 (2009), p.139. See further for similar findings: M. Fitzgerald, M. Hough, I. Joseph and T. Qureshi, *Policing for London* (Devon: Willan, 2002); and B. Bradford, J. Jackson and E. Stanko, 'Contact and Confidence: Revisiting the Impact of Public Encounters with the Police', *Policing and Society*, 19, 1 (2009), p.20.

27. M. McDowell, Minister for Justice, Dáil Éireann, 27 November 2002, vol. 558, col. 509; 23 June 2005, vol. 605, col. 172; 27 April 2006, vol. 618, col. 1056; 4 April 2007, vol. 635, col. 752.

28. *Irish Times*, 10 February 2004.

29. On this topic see R. Neild, 'Confronting a Culture of Impunity: The Promise and Pitfalls of Civilian Review of Police in Latin America', in A. Goldsmith and C. Lewis (eds), *Civilian Oversight of Police: Governance, Democracy and Human Rights* (Oxford: Hart, 2000).

30. Labour, *Proposals for Legislation for a Garda Authority and a Garda Ombudsman* (Dublin, 2000); Labour and Fine Gael, *Policing Our Communities: An Agreed Agenda for Reform* (Dublin, 2006).

31. Vaughan, 'Reforms to Policing North and South', *Irish Criminal Law*, 16, 2 (2006), p.20.

32. B. Vaughan, 'A New System of Police Accountability', *Irish Criminal Law Journal*, 15, 3

(2005), p.20.

33. Punch, 'Police Corruption and its Prevention', p.316.
34. Ibid., p.317.
35. Newburn, 'Understanding and Preventing Police Corruption', pp.28–44.
36. Ibid., p.46.
37. M. Karas, 'Predicting Misconduct Before Hiring Police', in T. Prenzler and J. Ransley, *Police Reform: Building Integrity* (Sydney: Hawkins Press, 2002).
38. I/1.49.
39. I/1.08.
40. Walsh, *Human Rights and Policing in Ireland*, p.617.
41. Garda Síochána Complaints Board, *Annual Report 2004* (Dublin: Government Publications Office, 2005), p.7.
42. Reiner, *The Politics of the Police*.
43. D. Smith and J. Gray, *Police and People in London: The Report* (London: The Policy Studies Institute, 1985), p.100.
44. H. Goldstein, *Police Corruption: A Perspective on its Nature and Control* (Washington: Police Foundation, 1975), p.43.
45. J. Moran, '"Blue Walls", "Grey Areas" and "Cleanups": Issues in the Control of Police Corruption in England and Wales', *Crime, Law and Social Change*, 43, 57 (2005), p.64.
46. Ibid., p.68.
47. L. Sherman, 'Police Corruption Control: Environmental Context versus Organisational Policy', in D. Bayley (ed.), *Police and Society* (London: Sage, 1977).
48. M. Kempa, 'Tracing the Diffusion of Policing Governance Models from the British Isles and Back Again: Some Directions for Democratic Reform in Troubled Times', *Police Practice and Research*, 8, 2 (2007), p.114.
49. Ellison, 'Police Reform, Political Transition, and Conflict Resolution in Northern Ireland'.
50. Human Rights Committee, *Concluding Observations of the Human Rights Committee on Ireland*, July 2008, para. 20.
51. Dáil debates, vol. 687, no. 6 (10 July 2009), available at http://debates.oireachtas.ie/DDebate.aspx?F=DAL20090710.xml&Node=H5&Page=10.
52. See, for instance, the Criminal Assets Bureau Act 1996, the Proceeds of Crime Act 1996, the Criminal Justice (Drug Trafficking) Act 1996, the Criminal Justice Act 1999, the Criminal Justice (Theft and Fraud) Act 2001, the Criminal Justice (Terrorist Offences) Act 2005, the Criminal Justice Act 2006, the Criminal Justice Act 2007, the Criminal Justice (Forensic Evidence and Sampling) Bill 2007, the Criminal Justice (Surveillance) Act 2009, the Criminal Justice (Amendment) Act 2009, the Criminal Procedure Bill 2009 and the Criminal Justice (Miscellaneous Provisions) Bill 2009.
53. *Irish Independent*, 20 August 2009.
54. *Evening Herald*, 17 November 2008.
55. The taoiseach has stated that a war on gang crime was required and 'that war must be waged relentlessly'; cited in Hamilton, *The Presumption of Innocence*, p.102.
56. McCullagh, *From the Global to the Local: Police Corruption in Donegal*, p.10.
57. Punch, 'Police Corruption and its Prevention' identifies particular danger zones in policing which are vulnerable to corruption such as vice, drugs, undercover work and informant-handling.
58. C. Lally, 'Two Gardaí investigated for helping crime gangs', *Irish Times*, 30 October 2009.

Select Bibliography

Allen, G. *The Garda Síochána: Policing Independent Ireland 1922–82* (Dublin: Gill & Macmillan, 1999).

Barker, D. and Carter, D.L. *Police Deviance* (Cincinnati, OH: Anderson Publishing Company, 1986).

Barr, J. *The Tribunal of Inquiry into the Facts and Circumstances Surrounding the Fatal Shooting of John Carthy at Abbeylara, Co. Longford on 20 April 2000* (Dublin: The Stationery Office, 2006).

Beetham, D. *The Legitimation of Power* (London: Macmillan, 1991).

Birmingham, G. *Report of the Commission of Investigation (Dean Lyons Case)* (Dublin: The Stationery Office, 2006).

Bohan, P. and Yorke, D. 'Law Enforcement Marketing: Perceptions of a Police Force', *Irish Marketing Review*, vol. 2 (1987), pp.72–86.

Bradford, B., Jackson, J. and Stanko, E. 'Contact and Confidence: Revisiting the Impact of Public Encounters with the Police', *Policing and Society*, 19, 1 (2009), p.20.

Bradford, B., Stanko, E. and Jackson, J. 'Using Research to Inform Policy: The Role of Public Attitude Surveys in Understanding Public Confidence and Police Contact', *Policing*, 3, 2 (2009), p.139.

Brady, C. *Guardians of the Peace* (Dublin: Prendeville Publishing, 2000).

Brady, R. 'Reflections on Tribunals of Inquiry', *Bar Review*, 3, 3 (1997), p.121.

Breathnach, S. *The Irish Police: From Earliest Times to Present Day* (Dublin: Anvil Press, 1974).

Bridges, L. and McConville, M. 'Keeping Faith with their Own Convictions: The Royal Commission on Criminal Justice', *Modern Law Review*, 57, 1 (1994), p.7.

Brogden, M., Jefferson, T. and Walklate, S. *Introducing Police Work* (Boston: Unwin Hyman, 1988).

Browne, C. *Garda Public Attitudes Survey 2008* (Templemore: Garda Research Unit, 2008).

Burton, F. and Carlen, P. *Official Discourse: On Discourse Analysis, Government Publications, Ideology and the State* (London: Routledge, 1979).

Casey, J. *Constitutional Law in Ireland*, 2nd edition (London: Sweet and Maxwell, 1992).

Chan, J. 'Governing Police Practice: The Limits of the New Accountability', *British Journal of Criminology*, 50, 2 (1999), p.251.

Chin, G. and Wells, C. 'The "Blue Wall of Silence" as Evidence of Bias and Motive to Lie: A New Approach to Police Perjury', *University of Pittsburgh Law Review*, 59, 2 (1998), p.237.

Connolly, J. *Do We Need Patten Type Reforms in the South*, Presentation to James Connolly Education Trust, 2000.

Conway, V. 'The Garda Síochána Ombudsman Commission', *Irish Law Times*, vol. 22 (2004), pp.125–38.

Corcoran, M. and White, A. 'Irish Democracy and the Tribunals of Inquiry', in E. Slater and M. Peillon, *Memories of the Past: A Sociological Chronology of Ireland* (Dublin: Institute of Public Administration, 2000), p.185.

Dixon, D. 'Police Governance and Official Inquiry', in G. Gilligan and J. Pratt, *Crime, Truth and Justice* (Devon: Willan, 2004), p.115.

Dixon, D. *A Culture of Corruption* (Sydney: Hawkins, 1999).

Ellison, G. 'Police Reform, Political Transition, and Conflict Resolution in Northern Ireland', *Police Quarterly*, 10, 3 (2007), pp.243–69.

European Committee for the Prevention of Torture, *Report to the Irish Government on the Visit to Ireland*, 1993, 1998, 2003, 2007.

Farrell, M. 'Anti-terrorism and Ireland: The Experience of the Irish Republic', in T. Bunyan (ed.), *Statewatching the New Europe* (London: Statewatch, 1993), p.121.

Finnane, M. 'Police Corruption and Police Reform: The Fitzgerald Inquiry in Queensland, Australia', *Policing and Society*, 1, 2 (1990), pp.159–71.

Fitzgerald, M. Hough, M. Joseph, I. and Qureshi, T. *Policing for London* (Devon: Willan, 2002).

Fitzgerald, T.P. 'The Morris Tribunal of Inquiry and An Garda Síochána', *Communique*, no. 3 (2008), pp.1–31.

Fowler, R. *Language in the News* (London: Routledge, 1991).

Gans, H. *Deciding What's News* (Constable: London, 1980).

Garda Commissioner, *S.23 Garda Síochána Act Three Year Review Report* (Dublin, 2009).

Garda Inspectorate, *Report on Senior Management Structures in the Garda Síochána* (Dublin, 2007).

Garda Inspectorate, *Review of Practices and Procedures for Barricade Incidents* (Dublin, 2007).

Garda Research Unit, *Garda Public Attitudes Survey 2002* (Templemore: Garda Research Unit, 2002).

Garda Síochána Complaints Board, *Annual Report 2002* (Dublin, 2002).

Garda Síochána Complaints Board, *Annual Report 2005* (Dublin, 2005).

Garda Síochána Complaints Board, *Annual Report 2007* (Dublin, 2007).

Garda Síochána Ombudsman Commission, *Annual Report 2008* (Dublin, 2008).

Garda Síochána Ombudsman Commission, *Biannual Report on the Effectiveness of the Ombudsman Commission* (Dublin, 2008).

Garda Síochána, *Diversity Strategy* (Dublin, 2009), p.2.

Gatlung, J. and Ruge, M. 'Structuring and Selecting News', in S. Cohen and J. Young (eds), *The Manufacture of News: Social Problems, Deviance and the Mass Media* (London: Constable, 1973), p.284.

Goldstein, H. *Police Corruption: A Perspective on its Nature and Control* (Washington: Police Foundation, 1975).

Habermas, J. *Legitimation Crisis* (Boston: Beacon Press, 1975).

Hall, S., Critcher, C., Jefferson, T., Clarke, J. and Robert, B. *Policing the Crisis: Mugging, the State and Law and Order* (London: Palgrave Macmillan, 1978).

Hamilton, C. *The Presumption of Innocence and the Irish Criminal Law* (Dublin: Irish Academic Press, 2007).

Hardiman, N. and Whelan, C.T. 'Politics and Democratic Values', in C.T. Whelan, *Values and Social Change in Ireland* (Dublin: Gill & Macmillan, 1994), p.100.

Hartnett, H. *Inquiry Pursuant to the Dublin Police Act 1924 as Amended by the Police Force Amalgamation Act 1925* (Dublin: Government Publications Office, 2008).

Hawdon, J., Ryan, J. and Griffin, S. 'Policing Tactics and Perceptions of Police Legitimacy', *Police Quarterly*, 4, 6 (2003), p.469.

Hayes, M. *Final Report of the Advisory Group on Garda Management and Leadership* (Dublin, 2007).

Herbert, S. 'Tangled Up in Blue: Conflicting Paths to Police Legitimacy', *Theoretical Criminology*, 10, 4 (2006), p.481.

Hogan, G. and Morgan, D.G. *Administrative Law in Ireland* (Dublin: Roundhall, 1998).

Human Rights Commission, *A Proposal for a New Garda Complaints System* (Dublin, 2002).

Human Rights Committee, *Concluding Observations of the UN Human Rights Committee on Compliance with the International Covenant on Civil and Political Rights* (New York, July 2008).

Independent Commission for Policing in Northern Ireland, *A New Beginning: Policing in Northern Ireland* (The Patten Report) (Belfast: HMSO, 1998).

Independent Police Complaints Commission, *Police Complaints Statistics for England and Wales 2007* (London, 2007).

Inglis, T. *Moral Monopoly: The Rise and Fall of the Catholic Church in Modern Ireland* (Dublin: University College Dublin Press, 1998).

Inglis, T. *Truth, Power and Lies: Irish Society and the Case of the Kerry Babies* (Dublin: University College Dublin Press, 2003).

Report of Irish Council of Civil Liberties, 30 September 1997, cited by *An Phoblacht*, 'Exposed: Garda Brutality in Limerick', 2 October 1997, available at www.republican-news.org/archive/1997/October 02/02lime.html.

Irish Human Rights Commission, *Observations on the Garda Síochána Bill* (Dublin, 2004).

Johnston, L. 'Controlling Policework: Problems of Organisation Reform in Large Public Bureaucracies', *Work, Employment and Society*, 2, 1 (1988), p.51.

Jones, T., Newburn, T. and Smith, D. *Democracy and Policing* (London: Policy Studies Institute, 1990).

Karas, M. 'Predicting Misconduct Before Hiring Police', in T. Prenzler and J. Ransley, *Police Reform: Building Integrity* (Sydney: Hawkins Press, 2002), p.196.

Kempa, M. 'Tracing the Diffusion of Police Governance Models from the British Isles and Back Again: Some Directions for Democratic Reform in Troubled Times', *Police Research and Practice*, 8, 2 (2007), p.107.

Kennedy, P. and Browne, C. *Garda Public Attitudes Survey 2006* (Templemore: Garda Research Unit, 2006).

Kennedy, P. and Browne, C. *Garda Public Attitudes Survey 2007* (Templemore: Garda Research Unit, 2007).

Kerrigan, G. and Brennan, P. *This Great Little Nation: The A–Z of Irish Scandals and Controversies* (Dublin: Gill & Macmillan, 1999), p.198.

Kilcommins, S., O'Donnell, I., O'Sullivan, E. and Vaughan, B. *Crime, Punishment and the Search for Order in Ireland* (Dublin: Institute of Public Administration, 2004).

Kinsey, R., Lea, J. and Young, J. 'Discretion and Accountability: Proposals for a New Police Authority', in R. Kinsey, J. Lea and J. Young (eds), *Losing the Fight Against Crime* (London: Basil Blackwell, 1986), p.161.

Kleinig, J. 'The Blue Wall of Silence: An Ethical Analysis', Occasional Paper XIII, Centre for Research in Crime and Justice, New York University School of Law, 2000.

Kleinig, J. *The Ethics of Policing* (Cambridge: Cambridge University Press, 1996).

Klockars, C. 'The Dirty Harry Problem', in T. Newburn, *Policing: Key Readings* (Devon: Willan, 2005), p.581.

Knapp, W. *The Commission to Investigate Allegations of Police Corruption* (New York: Braziller, 1972).

Labour and Fine Gael, *Policing Our Communities: An Agreed Agenda for Reform* (Dublin, 2006).

Labour, *Proposals for Legislation for a Garda Authority and a Garda Ombudsman* (Dublin, 2000).

Law Reform Commission, *Consultation Paper on Tribunals of Inquiry* (Dublin, 2002).

Law Reform Commission, *Report on Public Inquiries Including Tribunals of Inquiry* (Dublin, 2005).

Leisman, F. and Mason, P. *Policing and the Media: Facts, Fiction and Factions* (Devon: Willan, 2003).

Leman-Langlois, S. and Shearing, C. 'Repairing the Future: The South African Truth and Reconciliation Commission at Work', in G. Gilligan, and J. Pratt (eds), *Crime, Truth and Justice: Official Inquiry, Discourse and Knowledge* (Devon: Willan, 2004), p.222.

Leyland, P. and Anthony, G. *Textbook on Administrative Law*, 3rd edition (Oxford: Oxford University Press, 2005).

Loader, I. and Mulcahy, A. *Policing and the Condition of England* (Oxford: Oxford University Press, 2003).

Lowe, W.J. 'The War Against the RIC 1919–1921', *Éire: Ireland*, 37, 3 (2002), p.79.

Lukes, L. *Power: A Radical View* (London: Macmillan, 1974).

Lundman, R. *Controlling Police and Policing: An Introduction* (London: Holt, Reinhart & Winston, 1980).

Lustgarten, L. *The Governance of the Police* (London: Sweet & Maxwell, 1986).

Lynch, K. *Report of the Tribunal of Inquiry into the 'Kerry Babies Case'* (Dublin: The Stationery Office, 1985).

Lyons, T. 'Ireland's Political Culture: Overlapping Consensus and Modus Vivendi', Paper prepared for presentation at the International Political Science Association Conference, Fukuoka, Japan, 9–13 July 2006. Available online at: www.soc.cas.cz/articles/en/5/2946/Ireland-8217-s-Political-Culture-Overlapping-Consensus-and-Modus-Vivendi.html.

Maas, P. *Serpico* (New York: Harper Publications, 1997).

MacCarthaigh, M. *Accountability in Irish Parliamentary Politics* (Dublin: Institute of Public Administration, 2005).

Maguire M. and Corbett, C. *A Study of the Police Complaints System* (London: HMSO, 1991).

Maguire, M. 'The Changing Face of Catholic Ireland: Conservatism and Liberalism in the Ann Lovett and Kerry Babies Scandals [Part 2 of 3]', *Feminist Studies*, 27, 2 (2001), p.335.

Mawby, R. *Policing Images: Policing, Communication and Legitimacy* (Devon: Willan, 2002).

McAleese, M. 'Police and People', *Dublin University Law Journal* (1987), p.45.

McCombs, M. *Setting the Agenda: The Mass Media and Public Opinion* (Cambridge: Polity Press, 2004).

McCullagh, C. 'The Global in the Local: Police Corruption in Donegal', unpublished, 2005.

McDowell, M. *Statement by Minister for Justice on the Publication of the Sixth Morris Report*, 19 May 2006 (Dublin: Department of Justice, 2006).

McDowell, M. *Statement by Tánaiste on Garda Accountability*, 29 November 2006 (Dublin: Department of Justice 2006).

McFarlane, L. *Human Rights: Realities and Possibilities* (New York: St Martin's Press, 1990).

McGarry, P. *When Justice Slept: The True Story of Nicky Kelly and the Sallins Mail Train Robbery* (Dublin: Liffey Press, 2006).

McGlinchey, K. *Charades: Adrienne McGlinchey and the Donegal Gardaí* (Dublin: Gill & Macmillan, 2005).

McGrath, E. 'Professional Ethics and Policing', in M.L. Dantzker (ed.), *Contemporary Policing: Personnel, Issues and Trends* (Oxford: Butterworth-Heineman, 1997), p.145.

McMahon, B. and Binchy, W. *Irish Law of Torts*, 3rd edition (Dublin: Butterworths, 2000).

McNiffe, L. *A History of An Garda Síochána* (Dublin: Wolfhound Press, 1997).

McVerry, P. *Morris Tribunal Report and Garda Síochána Bill 2004* (Dublin: Jesuit Centre for Faith and Justice, 2004).

Miller, J. *Police Corruption in England and Wales: An Assessment of Current Evidence* (London: HMSO, 2003).

Mollen Commission, *Report of the Commission to Investigate Allegations of Corruption and the Anti-Corruption Procedures of the Police Department* (New York, 1994).

Moran, J. '"Blue Walls", "Grey Areas" and "Cleanups": Issues in the Control of Police Corruption in England and Wales', *Crime, Law and Social Change*, 43, 1 (2005), p.57.

Morris, F. *Report of the Tribunal of Inquiry Set up Pursuant to the Tribunal of Inquiry (Evidence) Acts 1921–2003 into certain Gardaí in the Donegal Division: Term of Reference (e): Report on Explosives 'Finds' in Donegal* (Dublin: The Stationery Office, 2004).

Morris, F. *Report of the Tribunal of Inquiry Set up Pursuant to the Tribunal of Inquiry (Evidence) Acts 1921–2003 into certain Gardaí in the Donegal Division: Term of Reference (d): Report on the Circumstances Surrounding the Arrest and Detention of Mark McConnell on 1st October 1998 and Michael Peoples on 6th May 1999* (Dublin: The Stationery Office, 2006).

Morris, F. *Report of the Tribunal of Inquiry Set up Pursuant to the Tribunal of Inquiry (Evidence) Acts 1921–2003 into certain Gardaí in the Donegal Division: Terms of Reference (b), (d) and (f): Report on the Detention of 'Suspects' Following the Death of the late Richard Barron on 14th of October 1996 and Related Detentions and Issues* (Dublin: The Stationery Office, 2008).

Morris, F. *Report of the Tribunal of Inquiry Set up Pursuant to the Tribunal of Inquiry (Evidence) Acts 1921–2003 into certain Gardaí in the Donegal Division: Report on Allegations of Harassment of the McBrearty Family of Raphoe (Term of Reference (c)) and Report into the Effectiveness of the Garda Síochána Complaints Board Inquiry (Term of Reference (j)* (Dublin: The Stationery Office, 2008).

Morris, F. *Report of the Tribunal of Inquiry Set up Pursuant to the Tribunal of Inquiry (Evidence) Acts 1921–2003 into certain Gardaí in the Donegal Division: Terms of Reference (a) and (b): Report of the*

Investigation into the Death of Richard Barron and Extortion Calls to Michael and Charlotte Peoples (Dublin: The Stationery Office, 2005).

Morris, F. *Report of the Tribunal of Inquiry Set up Pursuant to the Tribunal of Inquiry (Evidence) Acts 1921–2003 into certain Gardaí in the Donegal Division: Term of Reference (i): Report on the Arrest and Detention of Seven Persons at Burnfoot, Co. Donegal on 23rd May 1998 and the Investigation Relating to Same* (Dublin: The Stationery Office, 2006).

Morris, F. *Report of the Tribunal of Inquiry Set up Pursuant to the Tribunal of Inquiry (Evidence) Acts 1921–2003 into certain Gardaí in the Donegal Division: Term of Reference (h): Report into Allegations Contained in Documents Received by Deputy Jim Higgins and Information Received by Deputy Brendan Howlin that Two Senior Members of An Garda Síochána May Have Acted with Impropriety* (Dublin: The Stationery Office, 2008).

Morris, F. *Report of the Tribunal of Inquiry Set up Pursuant to the Tribunal of Inquiry (Evidence) Acts 1921–2003 into certain Gardaí in the Donegal Division: Term of Reference (g): Report on the Garda Investigation of an Arson Attack on Property Situated on the Site of the Telecommunications Mast at Ardara, Co. Donegal in October and November of 1996* (Dublin: The Stationery Office, 2006).

Morton, J. *Bent Coppers* (London: Warner Books, 1993).

Mulcahy, A. 'The Impact of the Northern Ireland Troubles on Criminal Justice in the Irish Republic', in P. O'Mahony (ed.), *Criminal Justice in Ireland* (Dublin: Institute of Public Administration, 2000), p.275.

Murphy, F. *Statement by Garda Commissioner Fachtna Murphy on the Seventh and Eighth Reports of the Morris Tribunal*, 7 October 2008 (Dublin: Garda Press Office, 2008).

Murphy, F. *Statement by Garda Commissioner on the Sixth Report of the Morris Tribunal, 7 May 2008* (Dublin: Garda Press Office, 2008).

Neild, R. 'Confronting a Culture of Impunity: The Promise and Pitfalls of Civilian Review of Police in Latin America', in A. Goldsmith and C. Lewis (eds), *Civilian Oversight of Police: Governance, Democracy and Human Rights* (Oxford: Hart, 2000), p.223.

Newburn, T. and Jones, T. 'Police Accountability', in W. Salsbury, J. Mott and T. Newburn, *Themes in Contemporary Policing* (London: Police Studies Institute, 1996), p.120.

Newburn, T. *Understanding and Preventing Police Corruption: Lessons from the Literature*, Police Research Series Paper 110 (London: HMSO, 1999).

Neyroud, P. and Beckley, A. *Policing, Ethics and Human Rights* (Devon: Willan, 2001).

Nixon, C. and Reynolds, C. 'Producing Change in Police Organisations: The Story of New South Wales Police Service', in D. Chappel and P. Wilson (eds), *Australian Policing: Contemporary Issues*, 2nd edition (Sydney: Butterworths, 1996), p.45.

Ó Briain, B. *Report of the Committee to Recommend Certain Safeguards for Persons in Custody and for Members of An Garda Síochána* (Dublin: The Stationery Office, 1978).

O'Brien, M. 'Selling Fear? The Changing Face of Crime Reporting', in J. Horgan et al. *Mapping Irish Media: Critical Explorations* (Dublin: University College Dublin Press, 2007).

O'Dwyer, K., Kennedy, P. and Ryan, W. *Garda Public Attitudes Survey 2005* (Templemore: Garda Research Unit, 2005).

O'Halpin, E. *Defending Ireland: The Irish State and its Enemies Since 1922* (Oxford: Oxford University Press, 1999).

Office of the Police Ombudsman Northern Ireland, *Public Awareness of the Police Complaints System in Northern Ireland* (Belfast, 2009), p.3.

Ó Gráda, C. (ed.), *A Rocky Road: The Irish Economy Since the 1920s* (Manchester: Manchester University Press, 1997).

O'Mahony, P. 'The Ethics of Police Interrogation and the Garda Síochána', *Irish Criminal Law Journal*, vol. 6 (1996), pp.46–54.

Philo, G. 'Bias in the Media', in D. Coates and G. Johnston (eds), *Socialist Arguments* (Oxford: Martin Robertson, 1983), p.130.

Prenzler, T. 'Corruption and Reform', in T. Prenzler and J. Ransley, *Police Reform: Building Integrity* (Sydney: Hawkins Press, 2002), p.18.

Punch, M. 'Police Corruption and its Prevention', *European Journal on Criminal Policing and Research*, 8, 3 (2000), p.301.

Punch, M. 'Rotten Orchards: Pestilence, Police Misconduct and System Failure, *Policing and Society*, 13, 2 (2003), p.171.

Punch, M. *Conduct Unbecoming: The Social Construction of Police Deviance and Control* (London: Tavistock, 1995).

Punch, M. *Police Corruption: Deviance, Accountability and Reform in Policing* (Devon: Willan, 2009).

Reiner, R. *The Politics of the Police* (Oxford: Oxford University Press, 2000).

Reuss-Ianni, E. *Two Cultures of Policing: Street Cops and Management Cops* (New Brunswick, NJ: Transaction Publishers, 1983).

Roebuck, J. and Barker, T. 'A Typology of Police Corruption', *Social Problems*, 21, 3 (1974), pp.423–38.

Salmon, P. *Royal Commission on Tribunals of Inquiry* (London: HMSO, 1966).

Salmon, T.C. 'The Case of Ireland', in J. Roach and J. Thomaneck (eds), *Police and Public Order in Europe* (London: Croom Helm, 1985), p.73.

Sarma, K. and O'Dwyer, K. *Garda Public Attitudes Survey 2004* (Templemore: Garda Research Unit, 2004).

Sarma, K. *Garda Public Attitudes Survey 2003* (Templemore: Garda Research Unit, 2003).

Sayed, T. and Bruce, D. 'Police Corruption: Towards a Working Definition', *African Security Review*, 7, 2 (1998), p.3.

Scraton, P. 'From Deceit to Disclosure: The Politics of Official Inquiries in the United Kingdom', in G. Gilligan and J. Pratt, *Crime, Truth and Justice* (Devon: Willan, 2004), p.47.

Scraton, P. *The State of the Police: Is Law and Order Out of Control?* (London: Pluto Press, 1985).

Sherman, L. 'Police Corruption Control: Environmental Context versus Organizational Policy', in D. Bayley (ed.), *Police and Society* (Beverly Hills, CA: Sage, 1977).

Sherman, L. *Police Corruption: A Sociological Perspective* (New York: Anchor Press, 1974).

Sherman, L. *Scandal and Reform: Controlling Police Corruption* (Berkeley, CA: University of California Press, 1978).

Skolnick, J. 'Corruption and the Blue Code of Silence', *Police Practice and Research*, 3, 1 (2002), p.7.

Smith, D. and Gray, J. *Police and People in London* (London: Policy Studies Institute, 1985).

Smith, D. and Gray, J. *Police and People in London: The Report* (London: The Policy Studies Institute, 1985).

Smith, D. *New Challenges to Police Legitimacy* (Centre for Law and Society Annual Lecture, University of Edinburgh, 2006), p.9.

Smith, G. 'Rethinking Police Complaints', *British Journal of Criminology*, 44, 1 (2004), pp.15–33.

Smyth, J. 'Symbolic Power and Police Legitimacy: The Royal Ulster Constabulary', *Crime, Law and Social Change*, 38, 3 (2002), p.295.

Steering Group on the Efficiency and Effectiveness of An Garda Síochána, *Report of the Steering Group on the Efficiency and Effectiveness of An Garda Síochána* (Dublin: The Stationery Office, 1997).

Stenning, P. and Shearing, C. 'Reforming Police: Opportunities, Drivers and Challenges', *Australian and New Zealand Journal of Criminology*, 38, 2 (2005), p.167.

Stoddard, E. 'The Informal Code of Police Deviance: A Group Approach to "Blue Coat Crime"', *Journal of Criminal Law, Criminology and Police Science*, 59, 2 (1968), pp.201–13.

Tovey, H. and Share, P. *A Sociology of Ireland* (Dublin: Gill & Macmillan, 2000).

Van Maanen, J. 'Kinsmen in Response: Occupational Perspectives of Patrolmen', in P. Manning and J. Van Maanen (eds), *Policing: A View from the Street* (Santa Monica, CA: Goodyear Publishing, 1978).

Vaughan, B. and Kilcommins, S. 'The Europeanisation of Human Rights: An Obstacle to Authoritarian Policing in Ireland?' *European Journal of Criminology*, 4, 4 (2007), pp.437–60.

Vaughan, B. and Kilcommins, S. *Terrorism, Rights and the Rule of Law: Negotiating Justice in Ireland* (Devon: Willan, 2008).

Vaughan, B. 'A New System of Police Accountability: The Garda Síochána Act 2005', *Irish Criminal Law Journal*, 15, 3 (2005), p.18.

Vaughan, B. 'Accounting for Diversity of Policing in Ireland', *Irish Journal of Sociology*, 13, 1 (2004), p.51.

Vaughan, B. 'Reforms to Policing North and South', *Irish Criminal Law*, 16, 2 (2006), p.17.

Waddington, P. 'Police (Canteen) Subculture: An Appreciation', *British Journal of Criminology*, 39, 2 (1999), p.287.

Walsh, D. 'The Garda Ombudsman Commission: A Critique', *Irish Criminal Law Journal*, 14, 1 (2004), pp.2–14.

Walsh, D. 'The Proposed Garda Complaints Procedure: A Critique', *Irish Criminal Law Journal*, 14, 4 (2004), p.2.

Walsh, D. 'Twenty Years of Handling Police Complaints in Ireland: A Critical Assessment of the Supervisory Board Model', *Legal Studies*, 29, 2 (2009), p.305.

Walsh, D. *The Irish Police: A Legal and Constitutional Perspective* (Dublin: Roundhall, 1998).

Walsh, D. *Policing and Human Rights in Ireland: Law, Policy and Practice* (Dublin: Clarus Press, 2009).

Walsh, L. *The Final Beat: Gardaí Killed in the Line of Duty* (Dublin: Gill & Macmillan, 2001).

Weber, M. *Economy and Society: An Outline of Interpretive Society* (Berkley, CA: University of California Press, 1958).

Westmarland, L. 'Police Ethics and Integrity: Breaking the Blue Code of Silence', *Policing and Society*, 15, 2 (2005), p.145.

Whitaker, B. *News Limited: Why You Can't Read All About It* (London: Minority Press Group, 1981).

White, J. 'The Confessional State – Police Interrogation in the Irish Republic: Part I', *Irish Criminal Law Journal*, 10, 1 (2000), p.17.

White, J. 'The Confessional State – Police Interrogation in the Irish Republic: Part II', *Irish Criminal Law Journal*, 10, 2 (2000), p.2.

Newspaper Articles

Allen, L. 'Garda alleges police led vendetta against publican', *Irish Independent*, 25 June 2000.

Allen, L. and Mara, S. 'Clear and Present Danger', *Magill*, 29 August 2000.

Anderson, N. 'Death on a lonely road that set probe in motion', *Irish Independent*, 16 July 2004.

Anon, 'Amnesty calls for inquiry into Lusk deaths', RTÉ, 26 May 2005.

Anon, '2½ year case stopped by DPP', *Irish Times*, 22 June 2000.

Anon, 'A lawless ghetto?' *Evening Herald*, 17 November 2008.

Anon, 'A morass of corruption: Intimidation, lies, planted evidence. Indiscipline and bully-boy officers', *Daily Mail*, 18 August 2006.

Anon, 'Adverse tribunal finding on Sgt John White', RTÉ, 17 August 2006.

Anon, 'Commissioner's powers expanded to include summary dismissal', *Irish Times*, 8 August 2006.

Anon, 'Cops still doing a good job', *The Sun*, 23 August 2006.

Anon, 'Corruption, lies and wall of silence', *Irish Examiner*, 8 May 2008.

Anon, 'Coughlan denies Morris timing a stroke', *Irish Times*, 9 May 2008.

Anon, 'Coughlan denies trying to bury Morris', *Irish Independent*, 9 May 2008.

Anon, 'Dawn exhumation of Barron's body', *Donegal News*, 6 July 2001.

Anon, 'Donegal harassment case against Gardaí adjourned', *Irish Times*, 29 March 2000.

Anon, 'Donegal publican refused leave to address court though state withdraws final case', *Irish Times*, 5 September 2001.

Anon, 'Five reports and counting but the criticisms of the Gardaí are the same', *Irish Examiner*, 19 August 2006.

Anon, 'Garda assault case dismissed over technicality', *Irish Times*, 27 February 2009.

Anon, 'Garda chief: My hands were tied by courts over discipline', *Irish Independent*, 2 September 2006.

Anon, 'Garda inquiry into assault claim challenged', *Irish Times*, 21 December 1999.

Anon, 'Garda sacked over fake explosives finds', *Irish Examiner*, 6 October 2004.

Anon, 'Garda scandal set to hit big screen', *Irish Examiner*, 18 April 2009.

Anon, 'Garda sergeant remanded on arms charge', *Irish Times*, 7 December 2001.

Anon, 'Garda's finest finally get the all clear as TDs' claims blasted', *Evening Herald*, 8 October 2008.

Anon, 'Gardaí not afraid of accountability – Conroy', RTÉ, 24 June 2005.

Anon, 'Gardaí probe hit-and-run', *Irish Independent*, 15 October 1996.

Anon, 'Gardaí to get training on handling of informants', *Irish Examiner*, 23 March 2005.

Anon, 'GRA criticises treatment of White', *Irish Times*, 18 August 2006.

Anon, 'Grisly tale of crime and corruption raises haunting questions', *Irish Examiner*, 11 October 2008.

Anon, 'Howlin and Higgins criticised in report', *Irish Examiner*, 8 October 2008.

Anon, 'I'm tough and I don't give in easy', *Irish Times*, 22 June 2000.

Anon, 'Lenihan accused of burying report', *Irish Examiner*, 8 May 2008.

Anon, 'Limerick Garda chief to retire', *Irish Times*, 6 November 2009.

Anon, 'Lusk inquest adjourned as ombudsman intervenes', *Irish Times*, 26 September 2007.

Anon, 'Man (55) killed in hit and run', *Irish Times*, 15 October 1996.

Anon, 'Man batoned by Gardaí awarded €11,000 damages', *Irish Independent*, 19 July 2003.

Anon, 'McBrearty considers taking private criminal action against Gardaí', *Donegal News*, 26 January 2002.

Anon, 'McBrearty tells court three senior Gardaí conspired against him', *Irish Times*, 23 November 2001.

Anon, 'McBrearty up in court again', *Irish Times*, 23 June 2000.

Anon, 'Minister accused of burying report', *Metro*, Dublin, 8 May 2008.

Anon, 'Morris Tribunal: the costs', *Irish Times*, 12 February 2009.

Anon, 'Murder trial delay over Donegal case', *Irish Times*, 12 July 2000.

Anon, 'No decision yet on whether to hold public inquiry into Donegal Gardaí', *Irish Times*, 8 February 2001.

Anon, 'Opposition continues attack on govt over Garda reform', *Irish Examiner*, 16 June 2005.

Anon, 'Pressure grows to publish Carty Report', *Irish Examiner*, 18 June 2005.

Anon, 'Probe of serious abuse claims made by Garda whistleblowers', *Irish Times*, 2 February 2009.

Anon, 'Publican claims harassment by Gardaí after finding of body', *Irish Times*, 20 November 1999.

Anon, 'Six Gardaí face dismissal over Morris reports', *Irish Independent*, 11 May 2008.

Anon, 'Transfer of Donegal inquiry Gardaí deferred', *Irish Independent*, 10 September 2000.

Anon, 'Tribunal judge raps TDs over handling of claims', *Irish Independent*, 8 October 2008.

Anon, 'Two arrested over hit and run', *Irish Times*, 5 December 1996.

Anon, 'White calls findings perverse', *Irish Times*, 18 August 2006.

Anon, 'Woman woken by armed Garda in her bedroom is awarded €50,000', *Irish Times*, 22 June 2002.

Anon, 'Immediate reforms urged by opposition parties', *Irish Examiner*, 16 July 2004.

Anon, 'Morris: Senior Garda retires, detective faces dismissal', *Irish Examiner*, 17 July 2004.

Anon, 'Abolish Garda age limit, says TD', *Irish Examiner*, 19 July 2004.

Baker, N. and O'Brien, P. 'No date set for disciplining Donegal Gardaí', *Irish Examiner*, 6 August 2004.

Balls, R. 'Murder now suspected in road death', *Irish Times*, 18 May 1998.

Brady, T. 'Corrupt offenders face swift justice', *Irish Independent*, 16 July 2004.

Brady, T. 'DPP decision due on Garda corruption allegations', *Irish Independent*, 22 January 2001.

Brady, T. 'Hoax bomb among claims against Gardaí in probe', *Irish Independent*, 16 April 1999.

Brady, T. 'McDowell pledges action on "frightening" findings', *Irish Independent*, 16 July 2004.

Brady, T. 'Reform will mean new system of promotion', *Irish Independent*, 16 July 2004.

Breslin, J. 'I'm lucky to be alive, says whistleblower', *Irish Examiner*, 19 July 2004.

Breslin, J. 'Lawyers get €250,000 to watch tribunal', *Irish Examiner*, 1 November 2004.

Breslin, J. 'The whistleblower, the spy and the explosive tale of Garda corruption', *Irish Examiner*, 16 July 2004.

Breslin, J. 'Walter Mitty-type woman used by Gardai', *Irish Examiner*, 16 July 2004.

Breslin, J. and O'Keeffe, C. 'McBrearty scandal set to cost taxpayer over €15m', *Irish Examiner*, 9 June 2005.

Brophy, K. 'Fine Gael fears corrupt Gardaí will walk free', *Irish Examiner*, 21 March 2001.

Brophy, K. 'First Garda quizzed in probe into corruption', *Irish Examiner*, 23 March 2000.

Brophy, K. 'Gardaí face inquiry into corruption allegations', *Irish Examiner*, 2 January 2001.

Brophy, K. 'Gardaí threatened to search phone data: Howlin', *Irish Examiner*, 30 August 2000.

Brophy, K. 'Gardaí to be arrested in Donegal corruption scandal', *Irish Examiner*, 7 March 2000.

Brophy, K. 'Rough justice from the law of the land', *Irish Examiner*, 22 November 2000.

Browne, V. 'Higgins' case against the Donegal Gardaí', *Irish Times*, 5 December 2001.

Browne, V. 'The Incredibles', *Village*, 15 April 2005.

Bruce, H. 'Chastened commissioner expresses concern', *Irish Independent*, 16 July 2004.

Bruce, H. 'Shameful web of lies and deceit', *Irish Independent*, 16 July 2004.

Buckley, D. 'Key Morris Tribunal Garda to retire', *Irish Examiner*, 24 July 2007.

Buckley, D., Holohan, R. and Joyce, J. 'Beaten by six Guards', *Irish Times*, 14 February 1977.

Buckley, D., Holohan, R. and Joyce, J. 'Claustrophobia victim says Gardaí shut him in locker', *Irish Times*, 16 February 1977.

Buckley, D., Holohan, R. and Joyce, J. 'Gardaí using North-style brutality in interrogation techniques', *Irish Times*, 14 February 1977.

Buckley, D., Holohan, R. and Joyce, J. 'Heavy Gang used new act to intensify pressure on suspects', *Irish Times*, 15 February 1977.

Burnhill, E. 'Garda morale affected by recent Morris Tribunal reports', *Irish Independent*, 23 August 2006.

Bushe, A. 'Trials and tribulations as tribunal bill tops €43m', *Sunday Mirror*, 31 March 2002.

Carty, E. 'Garda tells the tribunal McBreartys were called "the Don Corleones"', *Irish Examiner*, 24 September 2004.

Carty, E. 'Morris has agenda to destroy officer', *Irish Examiner*, 15 June 2005.

Cleary, C. 'Civilian to be charged after probe of Garda misconduct', *Sunday Tribune*, 25 February 2001.

Cleary, C. 'Gardaí gave witness bogus expenses to appear in court', *Sunday Tribune*, 23 July 2000.

Cleary, C. and McGee, H. 'Donegal Gardaí allegation families to opt out of inquiry', *Sunday Tribune*, 21 April 2002.

Conlon, O. 'You are a bent cop, Sgt White', *The Sun*, 18 August 2006.

Coulter, C. 'Crude attempt to put pressure on the chief suspects' and 'Clear abuse of power of arrest', *Irish Times*, 8 May 2008.

Coulter, C. 'Gardaí abused suspect, tribunal finds', *Irish Times*, 8 May 2008.

Coulter, C. and Coughlan, D. 'Law Society stands by claim lawyers' phones were tapped', *Irish Times*, 28 August 2000.

Coulter, C., Lally, C. and Mac Cormac, R. 'Howlin and Higgins reject criticism by Morris Tribunal', *Irish Times*, 8 October 2008.

Cunningham, G. 'Tribunal chairman stands over report', *Irish Times*, 21 July 2004.

Cunningham, J. 'Garda did plant gun', *Mirror*, 18 August 2006.

Cusack, J. 'Gardaí are taking allegations seriously', *Irish Times*, 8 April 2000.

Cusack, J. 'Government considers inquiry plan on policing in Donegal', 24 January 2001.

Cusack, J. 'Statement follows 16-month internal Garda inquiry', *Irish Times*, 27 July 2000.

Cusack, J. 'Suspect Garda recorded conversation – report', *Irish Times*, 25 July 2000.

De Bréadún, D. and Lally, C. 'Senior Garda officers "would welcome any outside expertise"', *Irish Times*, 21 August 2006.

Donaghy, K. 'Call for Garda pensions review', *Irish Independent*, 19 July 2004.

Donaghy, K. 'Pressure mounts for inquiry into "Garda corruption"', *Irish Independent*, 2 November 2001.

Doyle, D. and Andrews, R. 'Forced to account', *Sunday Tribune*, 17 September 2000.

Drapier, 'Flaky week for coalition in face of united opposition', *Irish Times*, 24 November 2001.

Editorial, 'Dangerous political games', *Irish Times*, 23 November 2001.

Editorial, 'Inquiring into the Garda', *Irish Times*, 13 February 2002.

Editorial, 'Investigating the Garda', *Irish Times*, 14 November 2001.

Fay, L. 'Morris Tribunal blows whistle in wrong direction', *Sunday Times*, 12 October 2008.

Guerin, J. 'Family seek new Barron death probe', *Irish Independent*, 17 February 2002.

Guerin, J. 'More cases to follow on from Barron death probe', *Irish Independent*, 20 January 2002.

Guidera, A. 'Garda probe leads to exhumation', *Irish Independent*, 06 July 2001.

Guidera, A. 'White's pension terms revealed', *Irish Independent*, 21 August 2006.

Hannon, K. 'Full inquiry into Garda corruption now likely', *Irish Examiner*, 10 July 2000.

Hennessy, M. 'Senior Garda to retire after tribunal findings', *Irish Times*, 17 July 2004.

Hennessy, M. 'Tribunal finds two Gardaí offered a "tissue of lies"', *Irish Times*, 16 July 2004.

Hogan, L. 'Gardaí sacked in wake of corruption probe revelations', *Irish Examiner*, 8 December 2004.

Hogan, S. 'Morris reports are damaging to Gardaí', *Irish News*, 23 August 2006.

J. Cusack, 'Government considers inquiry plan on policing in Donegal', *Irish Times*, 24 January 2001.

Judge, T. 'Gardaí receive Barron autopsy report', *Irish Times*, 12 October 2001.

Judge, T. 'Barron case Gardaí to investigate locals over hit-and-run', *Irish Times*, 2 November 2001.

Keane, E. 'Mum and Garda the true heroines of Morris inquiry', *Irish Independent*, 11 May 2008.

Lally, C. 'Fear of tax changes prompts big rise in Garda retirements', *Irish Times*, 12 November 2009.

Lally, C. 'Garda O'Dowd knowingly took false statement, tribunal concluded', *Irish Times*, 8 May 2008.

Lally, C. 'Gross abuses of power "unacceptable"', *Irish Times*, 18 August 2006.

Lally, C. 'Insubordination not widespread, says Garda chief', *Irish Times*, 2 September 2006.

Lally, C. 'Two Gardaí investigated for helping crime gangs', *Irish Times*, 30 October 2009.

Lally, C. and Clancy, P. 'Det Sgt White set to keep Garda pension', *Irish Times*, 21 August 2006.

Leahy, P. and O'Kelly, B. '€101m payout for tribunal lawyers', *Sunday Business Post*, 29 February 2004.

Mac Carthaigh, S. 'Trouble ahead for McDowell over McBrearty legal costs decision', *Sunday Business Post*, 24 October 2004.

Mac Cormaic, R. 'Without our intervention abuses would still be going on, say politicians', *Irish Times*, 8 October 2008.

Managh, R. 'Boy held naked in Garda station received €8,500', *Irish Independent*, 15 October 2003.

Managh, R. 'Woman hurt in Garda custody gets €15,000', *Irish Independent*, 12 February 2004.

Mara, S. 'New suspect revealed in Barron killing', *Sunday Tribune*, 28 January 2001.

McDaid, B. 'Actions of some Garda officers a "dark period"', *Belfast Telegraph*, 8 October 2008.

McGee, H. 'Government criticised over timing of report', *Irish Times*, 8 May 2008.

McGee, H. 'McDowell defends record on Garda affair', *Irish Examiner*, 9 June 2005.

McGee, H. 'Morris fallout sparks overhaul', *Irish Examiner*, 22 June 2005.

McGee, H. and McEnroe, J. 'Gardaí set to blow the whistle on malpractice', *Irish Examiner*, 14 April 2004.

McGreevy, R. 'McBrearty criticises report and denies he exaggerated abuse', *Irish Times*, 8 May 2008.

McKenna, G. 'Pay McBrearty legal bill, says FG', *Irish Independent*, 16 July 2004.

McKenna, G. 'Reform of the force more crucial than ever, says opposition', *Irish Independent*, 16 July 2004.

McMorrow C. and Burke, J. 'Once, twice, three times a tribunal Garda', *Sunday Tribune*, 23 July 2006.

McMorrow, C. 'Victims slam Morris report as a "fudge"', *Sunday Tribune*, 20 August 2006.

Melia, P. 'Suspended officer claims he's the subject of a vendetta', *Irish Independent*, 18 August 2006.

Moloney, S. 'Major reforms ordered after Tribunal lifts lid on widespread misconduct in force', *Belfast Telegraph*, 18 August 2006.

Moloney, S. 'Parties hit out at Morris report's criticism of TDs', *Irish Independent*, 9 October 2008.

Molony, S. 'Blackest day for disgraced Garda', *Belfast Telegraph*, 18 August 2006.

Mooney, J. 'His own worst enemy', *Sunday Times*, 11 May 2008.

Murphy, C. 'Inquiry seeking to make sense of a web of claims', *Irish Times*, 22 June 2000.

Murphy, C. 'Inquiry on Donegal Gardaí widening', *Irish Times*, 8 July 2000.

Murray, M. 'Garda corruption a national blight', *Sunday Business Post*, 2 December 2001.

O'Brien, C. 'Government slammed over McBrearty probe', *Irish Examiner*, 6 May 2002.

O'Brien, P. 'More Gardaí to leave, says Ahern', *Irish Examiner*, 1 July 2005.

O'Brien, S. 'Rainbow to shake up Garda body', *Sunday Times*, 3 September 2006.

O'Doherty, C. 'Morris Tribunal Garda may take legal action over sacking', *Irish Examiner*, 7 October 2004.

O'Farrell, M. 'Ward's family and friends jubilant after Guerin murder rap quashed', *Irish Examiner*, 23 March 2002.

O'Keeffe, C. 'Force promises to act on tribunal findings', *Irish Examiner*, 16 July 2004.

O'Keeffe, C. 'Garda changes aim to prevent abuse', *Irish Examiner*, 3 March 2006.

O'Keeffe, C. 'Gardaí who misled Morris Tribunal still serving in the force', *Irish Examiner*, 18 April 2005.

O'Keeffe, C. 'Morris Gardaí still not moved from Donegal', *Irish Examiner*, 15 September 2005.

O'Keeffe, C. 'Patten, Hayes should review Garda Síochána, says Labour', *Irish Examiner*, 21 July 2004.

O'Keeffe, C. and McGee, H. 'Comreg set for talks over Morris recommendations', *Irish Examiner*, 14 June 2005.

O'Keeffe, C. and O'Brien, P. 'Barron death probe a cock-up, says Garda chief', *Irish Examiner*, 18 June 2005.

O'Kelly, B. 'Murder, mystery and mayhem in Donegal', *Sunday Business Post*, 17 November 2002.

O'Kelly, B. 'Revealed: why Donegal Gardaí won't be prosecuted', *Sunday Business Post*, 18 July 2004.

O'Kelly, B. 'The Murder that Never Was', *Sunday Business Post*, 4 October 2005.

O'Regan, M. 'Gilmore defends two TDs criticised by Morris Tribunal', *Irish Times*, 9 October 2008.

Phelan, S. '€11m in payouts for 55 victims of Donegal Garda corruption', *Irish Independent*, 15 August 2008.

Sheehan, F. 'Arms, bullets and bombs: a "litany of lies"', *Irish Examiner*, 16 July 2004.

Sheehan, F. 'Corruption claims spark new inquiry into Gardaí', *Irish Examiner*, 6 February 2002.

Sheehan, M. 'An arch-manipulator tripped up on his own tangled web of lies', *Irish Independent*, 20 August 2006.

Sheehan, M. and Mooney, J. 'Fitted up', *Sunday Times*, 25 June 2000.

Siggins, L. 'Watchdog recommends disciplining senior Garda', *Irish Times*, 30 October 2009.

Smyth, S. 'Donegal scandal will damage the Garda Síochána', *Sunday Tribune*, 9 July 2000.

Stack, S. 'The disgraced detective', *Irish News*, 8 October 2008.

Stone, P.J. 'Rank and file Gardaí feel maligned by Morris findings', *Irish Times*, 25 August 2006.

Walsh, J. 'Concern over tribunal criticisms', *Irish Times*, 9 October 2008.

Ward, V. and O'Doherty, C. 'Disgraced detective set to leave Donegal Garda', *Irish Independent*, 19 August 2006.

Dáil Debates

16 October 1984, vol. 352, cols 2399–2402: Questions re Kerry Babies Case.

23 October 1984, vol. 353, cols 34–50: Call for Inquiry over death of Peter Matthews.

Noonan, M. 29 January 1985, vol. 355, col. 861: Ban-Gharda Recruitment.

Noonan, M. 10 November 1987, vol. 375, col. 227: O'Grady Kidnap.

McCartan, 24 October 1989, vol. 392, col. 190: Deaths in Custody.

Byrne, E. 12 June 1996, vol. 466, cols 1944–1996: Garda Síochána Bill 1996.

Howlin, B. 21 October 1997, vol. 481, col. 1388: Independent Garda Authority.

Mr O'Donoghue, 10 February 1998, vol. 486, col. 1548: Complaints against Gardaí.

Higgins, 5 May 1999, vol. 504, col. 156: Questions re Donegal.

Higgins, 12 October 1999, vol. 509, col. 24: Investigations in Donegal.

O'Shea, 12 October 1999, vol. 509, col. 153: Investigations in Donegal.

Stagg, 23 November 1999, vol. 511, col. 579: Investigations in Donegal.

Higgins, 16 December 1999, vol. 512, col. 1973: Investigations in Donegal.

Higgins, 7 March 2000, vol. 515, col. 1326: Investigations in Donegal.

O'Donoghue, J. 1 June 2000, vol. 520, col. 751: Garda Complaints Board.

Higgins, 21 June 2000, vol. 521, col. 1278: Investigations in Donegal.

O'Donoghue, J. 5 October 2000, vol. 523, col. 1127: Investigations in Donegal.

Howlin, Dáil Éireann, 10 April 2001, vol. 534, col. 582: Private Member's Bill for Garda Reform.

O'Donoghue, J. 22 May 2001, vol. 536, col. 1311: Garda Reform.

Shatter, A. 23 May 2001, vol. 536, col. 1414: Investigations in Donegal.

Shatter and Howlin, 13 November 2001, vol. 543, col. 1299: Inquiry for Donegal.

Shatter, 20 November 2001, vol. 544, col. 581: Motion to Establish Tribunal.

21 November 2001, vol. 544, col. 1015: Motion to Establish Tribunal Resumed.

O'Donoghue, J. 20 March 2002, vol. 550, col. 1373: Garda Investigations.

O'Donoghue, J. 22 March 2002, vol. 551, col. 3: Tribunals of Inquiry Bill.

O'Donoghue, J. 28 March 2002, vol. 551, col. 926: Tribunals of Inquiry Motion.

Costello, 26 November 2002, vol. 558, col. 85: Private Member's Motion on Tribunal of Inquiry.

McDowell, M. 27 November 2002, vol. 558, col. 509: Private Member's Motion Resumed.

McDowell, M. 10 February 2005, vol. 597, col. 953: Garda Síochána Bill.

McGrath, F. 24 March 2005, vol. 599, col. 1957: Garda Síochána Bill Resumed.

O'Shea, 20 April 2005, vol. 600, col. 1554: Garda Síochána Bill Resumed.

Rabbitte, P. 21 April 2005, vol. 601, col. 13: Garda Síochána Bill Resumed.

McDowell, M. 17 June 2005, vol. 604, col. 517: Morris Tribunal Statements.

Costello, 22 June 2005, vol. 604, col. 1076: Garda Síochána Bill Resumed.

Crowe, 23 June 2005, vol. 605, col. 34: Garda Síochána Bill Resumed.

McDowell, M. 27 April 2006, vol. 618, col. 1056: Claims against An Garda Síochána.

McDowell, M. 29 November 2006, vol. 628, col. 1301: Garda Reform Statements.

McDowell, M. 4 April 2007, vol. 635, col. 752: Claims against An Garda Síochána.

Ahern, D. 22 October 2008, vol. 664, col. 755: Morris Tribunal Statements.

Index

Youth Justice in Ireland
Tough Lives, Rough Justice

Ursula Kilkelly

Foreword by Fr Peter McVerry S.J.

Juvenile justice in Ireland is in crisis. Kilkelly draws a picture of the juvenile offender in Ireland, aiming to: highlight the circumstances of offending children and their families, show the type and number of offences committed, identify and explore trends in juvenile offending, and consider the complexity of problems that such children face. The book sets out a comprehensive and critical analysis of the legislative and policy framework currently governing the operation of the juvenile justice system. This includes evaluating the continued use of the Children Act, 1908 and examining the extent to which the Children Act, 2001 has been implemented. It critically evaluates the response of the legal system to juvenile offending in the light of the modern legislative framework and international best practice. In this context, the book adopts a critical approach to the operation of the juvenile justice system looking at the following elements: the Garda Diversion Scheme; the operation of the Children Court; custodial and non-custodial sanctions imposed on children, and the detention of children. In addition, the book considers the complex problems that such children present to the legal system. It compares cases of offending and non-offending children and examines the overlap between, and different approaches of the care and justice systems in this area. In this regard, it considers the approach taken by many children who have been forced to take High Court proceedings to have their needs met, and it contrasts this with the route most children take through the (criminal) Children Court. Throughout, the approach is one which challenges certain perceptions about juvenile offending and crime in Ireland, and the justice system's response to it.

September 2006   304 pages
978 0 7165 2836 3   cloth   €55.00/£37.50/$65.00
978 0 7165 3348 0   paper €27.50/£20.00/$30.00

The Presumption of Innocence and Irish Criminal Law
Whittling the 'Golden Thread'

Claire Hamilton

Foreword by Hon. Justice Adrian Hardiman

The right to be presumed innocent until proven guilty has been described as the 'golden thread' running through the web of "fundamental postulate" of Irish criminal law which enjoys constitutional protection. Reflecting on the bail laws in the O'Callaghan case, Walsh J. described the presumption as a 'very real thing and not simply a procedural rule taking effect only at the trial'. The purpose of this book is to consider whether the reality matches the rhetoric surrounding this central precept of our criminal law and to consider its efficacy in the light of recent or proposed legislative innovations. Considerable space is devoted to the anti-crime package introduced by the government in the period of heightened concern about crime which followed the murder of journalist Veronica Guerin. Described by the Bar Council as "the most radical single package of alterations to Irish criminal law and procedure ever put together", the effect of the package was an amendment of the bail laws and the introduction of preventative detention; a curtailment of the right to silence for those charged with serious drugs offences and the introduction of a novel civil forfeiture process to facilitate the seizure of the proceeds of crime, a development which arguably circumvents the presumption. Given these developments, the question posed in the book is whether we can lay claim to a presumption that is more than merely theoretical or illusory.

February 2007   256 pages   illus

978 0 7165 3407 5   cloth   €55.00/£37.50/$65.00

978 0 7165 3408 2   paper   €27.50/£20.00/$30.00

Ireland's 'Moral Hospital'

The Irish Borstal System 1906–1956

Conor Reidy

Clonmel borstal in county Tipperary was the first and only such institution in Ireland and opened in 1906 for the purpose of reforming male offenders aged between sixteen and twenty-one years. The book also provides comparisons between the administration of the system by the British government prior to Independence and the Irish state after 1921. Two key periods, from 1922–24 and from 1940–46, when the borstal was removed from Clonmel for military purposes, are examined.

The book explores the renewed government interest and investment in the borstal in the aftermath of the *'Father Flanagan controversy'*, following its return to Clonmel in 1946. With signs that the system might finally be on course to fulfill its potential, a number of factors ensured that this optimism was to be short-lived and in 1956 Clonmel borstal ceased operations and the institution was transferred to Dublin. Reidy utilises primarily unpublished official sources to analyse the daily operation of Clonmel borstal.

September 2009   272 pages
978 0 7165 2980 4 cloth   €60.00/£45.00/$69.95
978 0 7165 2981 1 paper €24.95 (Ireland only)

Inspector Mallon

Buying Irish Patriotism for a Five-Pound Note

Donal P. McCracken

He was a farm boy from republican south Armagh who rose to become Ireland's most famous detective and most feared secret policeman, the first catholic to rise as high as assistant commissioner of the Dublin Metropolitan Police.

For decades Inspector Mallon and the detective G men at Dublin Castle hounded the Irish Fenian revolutionaries. Walking daily through the cobbled streets of Dublin; chatting with the gentry or greengrocers; holing up in seedy smoky bars in the Liberties and Temple Bar; or leading his men on night raids, this bear of a man came to know Victorian Dubliners as few others did. Always courteous and never violent in his own methods, his policing philosophy was one of deterrent and intimidation rather than entrapment. Generally contemptuous of his enemy, Mallon maintained an extensive network of poorly paid informers. He is notorious for having said, 'A good deal of that kind of patriotism can be bought for a five pound note in this poor country'.

Often described as catlike for his cunning, and backed by only 30 G men, for a generation Inspector Mallon kept a lid on the Irish revolution in Dublin, gaining the respect of moderate nationalists and unionist alike, but also the fear of most republicans. It is not surprising that he was the subject of numerous assassination plots. He is most noted for bringing to the gallows the Invincibles, the members of the 'murder society' who carried out the Phoenix Park assassinations.

Lord Lieutenant Spencer, the head of the British government in Ireland, once commented, 'Without Mallon we have no one worth a row of pins'.

June 2009   256 pages illus
978 07165 299 34 cloth €60.00/£45.00/$69.95
978 07165 299 41 paper €19.95/£19.95

The Corporate take over of Ireland
Kieran Allen

Fifty one of the hundred largest global entities are now corporations rather than nation states and this has led to a profound transformation. The public sphere, which is subject to democratic decision-making is diminishing and the for-profit motive dominates in areas previously regarded as public services. Written in a highly accessible style, this book looks at the changes this process has brought in Ireland in the last ten years, covering health, education, the environment, electricity, transport and telecommunications. The book is based on interviews with key participants and is supplemented with documentary information. New material challenges arguments for privatisation/de-regulation in Ireland; suggests that public resources are being squandered on 'corporate welfare'; and questions the notion that the consumer has gained from the changes.

May 2007 288 pages
978 0 7165 3411 2 cloth €65.00/£45.00/$75.00
978 0 7165 3412 9 paper €19.95/£18.00/$29.95

Irish Academic Press is a long established Dublin-based publisher of high quality books of Irish interest. Our publishing programme includes Irish History, Contemporary Irish History, Military and Political History, Literature, Arts and the Media, Social History, Women's Studies and Genealogy. We hope that among our past and present titles you will find titles of interest.

Our new and forthcoming publications include several important and eagerly awaited titles.

Visit our website

www.iap.ie

to read blurbs, see jackets and more.

Irish Academic Press